For Whom There Is No Room

Scenes from the Refugee World

EILEEN EGAN

Eileen Egan (signature)

PAULIST PRESS

New York • Mahwah, NJ

ACKNOWLEDGEMENTS

My thanks are due to many persons whose help was pivotal in the publication of this book, in particular to Ms. Jean Gartlan of Catholic Relief Services and Donald F. Brophy of Paulist Press. I dedicate the book to the memory of Edward E. Swanstrom, man of compassion, bishop, and for thirty ground-breaking years, Executive Director of Catholic Relief Services.

Book design by Theresa M. Sparacio

Library of Congress Cataloging-in-Publication Data

Egan, Eileen.
    For whom there is no room : scenes from the refugee world / by Eileen Egan.
      p. cm.
    ISBN 0-8091-0473-3 (hdbk.)
    1. Refugees—Services for. 2. Church work with refugees. 3. Refugees—International cooperation. 4. Catholic Relief Services. I. Title.
HV640.E35   1995
362.87—dc20
                                        94-38521
                                           CIP

Published by Paulist Press
997 Macarthur Boulevard
Mahwah, NJ 07430

Printed and bound in the
United States of America

CONTENTS

THREE: DISPLACED PERSONS
AND THE RIGHT OF ASYLUM

FOUR: PAPER WAR FOR THE D.P.'S

FIVE: BORDERCROSSERS UNLIMITED

SIX: UPROOTING IN THE INDIAN SUB-CONTINENT

SEVEN: GENGHIS KHAN AND THE
MULTI-BILLION DOLLAR MOUNTAIN

EIGHT: NATIONAL GOLGOTHA—VIETNAM

Into this world, this demented inn, in which there is absolutely no room for Him at all, Christ has come uninvited. But because He cannot be at home in it, because He is out of place in it, His place is with those others for whom there is no room. His place is with those who do not belong, who are rejected by power because they are regarded as weak, those who are discredited, who are denied the status of persons, who are tortured, bombed and exterminated. With those for whom there is no room, Christ is present in the world. He is mysteriously present in those for whom there seems to be nothing but the world at its worst. . . . It is in these that He hides himself, **for whom there is no room**.

THOMAS MERTON
Raids on the Unspeakable

INTRODUCTION

In 1943, amidst the chaos and human suffering of a world at war, Catholic Relief Services (CRS) was founded by the bishops of the United States as a vehicle to help alleviate that suffering. Then known as War Relief Services, its first programs were directed to the needs of refugees and displaced persons.

Each decade since has seen new waves of refugees in every corner of the world. CRS has always been present with emergency relief and long-term rehabilitation programs for those forced from their homes by natural and man-made disasters.

As she describes in this book Eileen Egan participated in CRS's first project, that of serving and resettling Polish refugees in Mexico. From then on she was a major participant in our operations around the world. A gifted writer, she always kept careful notes. This book is a result.

One of the great strengths of CRS, I believe, is the talent and dedication of our staff, often at personal sacrifice, in the service of the poorest of the poor around the world. As one of the first professional lay people to join the staff, Eileen Egan is an outstanding example of a person using her talents on behalf of those CRS serves.

An important aspect of her work was the preparation of the materials used in the annual "Bishops' Fund" appeal and collection conducted in parishes throughout the country which provides basic support for CRS. Information gathered on her field visits supplied background for the appeal materials—and for this book.

One of her most innovative and productive contributions was establishing, at the beginning of our work, a link with the

National Council of Catholic Women (NCCW). In 1946 the council through its affiliates throughout the United States collected children's clothing for distribution in war-torn Europe. This was the start of our fruitful collaboration. Through its Works of Peace program the NCCW continues to this day to respond generously to needs identified by CRS, particularly those of women and children.

In the course of an assignment as India desk officer she helped to establish a lasting CRS collaboration with Mother Teresa and the work of her sisters among the poorest of the poor. The collaboration today with the Missionaries of Charity extends far beyond India.

Refugees and displaced persons are, indeed, a sign of our times, victims and symbols of a harsh reality. Their numbers are staggering—at the end of 1993, 18.2 million refugees and at least 24 million additional people displaced within their own countries. The causes of this monumental displacement and suffering are complex and varied. And, tragically, we can expect that the numbers of refugees and displaced will not lessen and may even increase as we approach the third millennium.

It is the role of a humanitarian agency such as CRS to meet the emergency needs of refugees, and, equally important, to assist in their rehabilitation toward self-sufficient, productive lives of human dignity. Resettlement outside their country of origin has been a traditional solution but new solutions now need to be explored. Also, most urgently, the world community needs to address the reasons people are forced to flee their homelands in search of just solutions.

In this narrative Eileen Egan touches on past injustices and their human consequences. She brought to her work at CRS the added dimension of her lifelong concerns of justice, peace and non-violence. The gospel mandates of justice and charity are at the core of her writing and work.

The same motivation of those who serve through CRS was cited by CRS President and Chairman of the Board, Bishop James A. Griffin of Columbus, Ohio, on the occasion of CRS's fiftieth anniversary. On November 15, 1993, at a liturgy concelebrated by the full body of American bishops at the National

Shrine of the Immaculate Conception in Washington, D.C., he said in his homily:

"How is it that when natural ties of nationhood, of language, and history fail to hold people together, when politics poisons friendships and even marriages, men and women nonetheless are willing to make unbelievable sacrifices—sacrifice their lives, if necessary—for the sake of strangers in need?

"For ourselves as people of faith, our works of solidarity are reflections of the all-embracing love of God 'whose sun rises on the bad and the good and who rains on the just and the unjust.'

"It is from that sense of the love of God for suffering humanity that fifty years ago Catholic Relief Services was born.

"Beginning in 1943 with its services to the refugees of World War II and continuing today through its support for refugees in Bosnia and Sudan, CRS has extended the charity of the U.S. church in imitation of the God whose love knows no bounds."

As CRS reaffirms its commitment to assisting refugees and the displaced in the years ahead, we also strengthen our commitment to supporting self-help programs which involve people and communities in their own development, helping them to restore and preserve their dignity and realize their potential. In the broadest sense CRS is an agency in solidarity with all "for whom there is no room."

Kenneth Hackett
Executive Director
Catholic Relief Services

FOREWORD

On a hazy Saturday morning, July 28, 1945, a B-45 bomber crashed into the 79th floor of the Empire State Building in New York City. The bomber then exploded with such force that the walls of the steel-skeletoned building trembled. The crew of three men perished in the flaming wreckage.

The floors above and below the 79th floor were empty of occupants. A staff of sixteen men and women were at work in an office on the 79th floor. The high octane fuel in the plane's tank exploded inside the office, sending brilliant orange flames and plumes of black smoke high into the air. Nine people met instant death at their desks. Their charred remains were a reminder of the fate of people surprised at their desks in the bombarded cities of the Second World War. The office was the headquarters of Catholic Relief Services.

Six people found refuge in a large corner office and escaped being engulfed by the rolling orange fireball. A seventh, Joseph Fountain, emerged from the flames to join them.

"He was on fire, "recalled Thérèse Fortier, a young staff member who survived. "His hair was burnt off and blisters covered his face and skull. He must have been in agony, but he was the one who told us to close the door."

"When the building shook and the fire surrounded us, I was sure I was going to die," she told me. "Flames began shooting under the door and the smoke was choking us."

Thérèse related that she took off her high school ring and the ruby friendship ring she wore for the young soldier she was going to marry. She threw them out of the window.

"I thought it would be a shame to let them burn up. Someone ought to have them."

Joseph Fountain, though almost mortally burned, led his co-workers in prayer.

"We recited an act of contrition together," recalled Thérèse. "We asked God to forgive us for all our sins. At last, the firemen appeared. I was not going to die after all. Everyone in that office was rescued."

Joseph Fountain died three days later, bringing to ten the number of Catholic Relief Services staff members to die. The corner office was the only intact section of the offices of an agency founded to serve as a channel of mercy from the American Catholic community to a world being ravaged by war. The agency had been brought into being early in 1943, and its first project was put into operation almost exactly two years before the accident. In one tragedy ten core staff members crucial to the continuance of the work were gone. Only illness prevented my being at my desk on that tragic morning.

A journalist pointed out that Catholic Relief Services had been "touched by the cross." In some small measure, the agency shared the fate of those it served, human beings stretched out on the cross of agony by the mercilessness of war's violence.

The files of the agency were saved from the flames, but consultation of them always evoked the tragedy that struck that office in New York City and none other. Letters and reports, though protected by metal file cabinets, were irrevocably marked, their edges brittle and singed by fire.

*   *   *

The American bishops, in forming Catholic Relief Services (first entitled War Relief Services), determined that its aim would be to bring help to the war-afflicted on the basis of need alone, without reference to creed, race or nationality. The heart-stopping news of the destruction of cities along with their inhabitants, and of the deaths of combatants in war fronts in Europe, Asia and on the seas, indicated that the tasks facing an aid agency would be immense. The challenge to the American

Catholic community would be to focus far beyond its own concerns to the needs of men, women and children who "knew the world at its worst." Some of these were already within reach, refugees who had escaped into Spain and Portugal from the conflagration of Europe. Another group were European deportees into Siberia, and who had emerged from Stalin's great prison empire known as the Gulag. They had been scattered like loose grains of sand over the face of the earth. They went from Persia to India to the Middle East, to eastern, northern, and southern Africa, and, at the very doorstep of the United States, Mexico.

They were Poles.

They stood for the millions who never emerged alive from the Gulag.

Over the years, CRS was called the "best-kept secret" of the American Catholic Church. This was in many respects a statement of fact, since its workers were too occupied with human need to write of their work for publication.*

On occasion it was necessary for a voluntary agency to keep its most dramatic accomplishments from public notice. This happened when Catholic Relief Services helped prevent a whole generation of Eastern Europeans, most of them former slave laborers in the German war machine, from being forced back into homelands that had entered the Soviet orbit—homelands where their human rights would be in jeopardy.

Bishop Edward E. Swanstrom, for nearly three decades the director of Catholic Relief Services, had asked the writer to gather the early ground-breaking history of the refugee communities, east and west, helped by CRS. This history was to be written to present the human dimension of the refugee story, in particular for the people who made the refugee program possible.

It is written from the point of view of a participant-observer. The author takes responsibility for views asserted and conclusions drawn. Its publication has been helped by the generosity of a man and wife, who as children suffered deportation and

---

* Except for "Catholic Relief Services, the Beginning Years," by Eileen Egan, published in 1988.

privation. They "knew the world at its worst," yet preserved their faith in God and their fellow human beings.

For Whom There Is No Room presents the reality of mercy, as love responding to need, in this case the need of the human being who is the most threatened, the most humiliated, the most scourged—the refugee.

Chapter One

CLOUD OF WITNESSES

1. Siberia to Mexico

Before the Second World War had finished its raging course over the globe, I stood in a peaceful railroad station in a town in north central Mexico. It was toward noon on a November day in León, in the province of Guanajuato, and the midday sun beat down on a long train as it wound its way past us and came to a standstill. The sun seemed to set fire to the fair hair of hundreds of people with weary, grey faces who awkwardly and dazedly climbed out of the steaming train.

Only little children stepped out of one section. With their light coloring, the boys and girls presented a strange contrast to the dark-haired black-eyed Mexican children gathered on the platform to see the newcomers. There were nearly three hundred of these children, all unaccompanied, because of the loss of one or both parents, and mostly under fourteen years of age. These were the children who had been uprooted from the towns and remotest villages of eastern Poland in 1940 and 1941. Along with more than a million and a half Polish citizens they had been loaded into cattle cars, in a massive, anonymous deportation, and then scattered to the far wastes of Siberia and Central Asia.

Each child held a bundle tied with a string, or a cardboard valise. All that the child owned in the world was contained in one pitiful piece of baggage.

American, Polish and Mexican citizens, representing official and private agencies, had mobilized to meet what had been called the "Transport" of seven hundred and twenty-six Polish refugees. They moved into action to shepherd them to a haven, a camp site offered as a temporary home by the Mexican government until peace should return to Poland.

I helped lead forty little orphaned boys to a bus which would carry them to a strange D.P. camp. It was known as Santa Rosa

11

and had been the center of an extensive hacienda of the old style
with its own granary, warehouses, and living quarters for hundreds of families. During the trip I studied their faces, the faces
of children who had gazed on the great nameless wastes of
Siberia, of Asiatic Russia. They had been deported with their parents into a vast empty land. They had seen them break virgin
earth—earth that had not been opened to the plow since time
began. And they had looked down on the agonizing and dead
bodies of their parents. These little faces showed no curiosity
about the new surroundings. There was no visible reaction at all
to the grotesque dead trees that curled and writhed over the
swampland through which we rode, to the brilliant flowers that
caught the sunlight, or to the pale green cactus that grew in
clumps at the approach to the camp. They were reserved and still,
these faces, and they wore the expression of old men. It was with
old men's eyes that they looked out on this strange new country,
on the fourth continent they had touched in their journey.

Some had shiny, closely-shaven skulls, like soldiers in a small,
unwilling army. I could not help noticing a boy I came to know
as Kaziu, a diminutive, I learned, for Casimir. He was about
nine, and, like an old campaigner, had already lost an eye. He
was wearing a grotesquely outsized grey glass eye that clashed
with the bright blue remaining right eye. I supposed that in
some remote hospital in one of the four continents on his journey, he had been fitted with an adult eye. The stillness in the
bus was for me a remarkable experience. The attention of each
child was riveted on the package or valise held close with a
fierce sense of possession.

From the time when they had been herded in cattle cars in
the lonely villages and isolated farms of Poland, and in the border towns and cities, until they had reached Mexico by a route
that included Siberia, Central Asia, Iran, India, Australia, New
Zealand and a Pacific Ocean crossing, these children had been
spared nothing. These were children who had started out with
their whole families, mothers and fathers, brothers and sisters,
even grandmothers and grandfathers. Most of them had seen
their brothers and sisters die on the trek through Russia, or
near the border of Iran.

Some had helped to bury their own parents in far-off places. They knew it all: uprooting, the agony of repeated separation, death and hurried burials, wanderings over ice, taiga, and trackless sands, confusion of tongues, homelessness in continent after continent. Such was the knowledge locked behind incommunicative eyes. Their little burdens of possessions they hugged close to their stunted bodies; but still closer they held the burden that the world had laid on their spirits.

This pitiful band had been rescued from the wastes of Siberia and the steppes of central Asia, and here, in an old Mexican hacienda they alighted, woodenly and fearfully. They did not respond to the cheers of the hundreds of Polish exiles who had arrived on an earlier "Transport." I went with them to their dormitory, a long, cavernous hall of heavy grey stone, formerly a granary, and we showed them that above each bed a little shrine had been set up by the camp residents. It consisted of a familiar holy card of the ancient, dark-visaged image of the Virgin of Czestochowa surrounded by happily garish flowers plucked from nearby fields. It was too soon for these children to shake off the habit of fear and the garment of weariness that shrouded them. Their natural caution told us that they had so often met and surmounted agony that they were poised to meet it again. The bundles and valises were carefully deposited on the beds, and the little boys stood at attention beside their beds as though awaiting the next order. A Polish anthem was sung, and what I began to call Polish tears—the special tears of those who belong to a martyred people—flowed down the constricted faces of the adults and older children, as they watched the stiff little figures. Then Polish conversation filled the air, and the little boys began to talk and move about.

It became clear that the Polish deportees in Siberia, central and Asiatic Russia were no more than the tip of the iceberg with relation to the millions of others still held in slave labor. The Poles described in "Cloud of Witnesses" were among the first, and certainly the largest group up to that time, to reveal the dimensions of the Soviet penal network.

A survivor had called the closed area of Siberia and Soviet Asia the "dark side of the moon," and for decades it remained so. In the immense expanse of Kazakhstan, the third largest of the Soviet republics, were tracts of virgin land that had never known the plow. Some of the Polish deportees were thrust into these areas to "break" the soil for cultivation. Many of these never escaped, tied to a land they never chose. The Poles described here escaped at a time when western nations found it inconvenient to heed their message.

2. D.P. Camp in the New World

It was the first displaced persons camp of the western hemisphere. In fact, it was the first of World War II's D.P. camps. Of all the camps sheltering eastern European refugees it was, owing to its bizarre location, the least known. Hidden away in north central Mexico, it was the eventual home for close to fifteen hundred homeless Poles.

In order to know how people from eastern Poland, many of them simple peasant farmers, had reached a sequestered haven in Mexico, you would have to take out a map of the world. Your finger would tire tracing the route that took them to Arkhangelsk in the Soviet Arctic, to Novosibirsk in Siberia, to Bokhara and Samarkand in Turkestan, central Asia, to Iran, India, New Zealand, Australia, the United States, and finally to a tiny dot near the town of León in the province of Guanajuato, Mexico. The camp was called Santa Rosa because it was located on an old hacienda named for Saint Rose of Lima.

When I first saw Colonia Santa Rosa on a day in late August, a soft cloud of orange hazy dust lay before and over it. Inside the camp people were moving about and children were calling to each other as they ran about in an open dirt space inside the main gate. I saw the inhabitants as forming a "cloud of witnesses" to an excruciating fact of the time. All of them, from the aged grandmother to the smallest orphan, bore witness in body and spirit to the great system of Stalinist tyranny.

It had been possible to read the stories of individual survivors who had escaped one by one to tell what befell them after deportation to the slave labor regions of the Soviet Union. Here for the first time was a cross-section of European society which, after being transported into the farthest zones of silence, had come out to tell the world about the types of slavery to which

15

they had been subjected. In my first intensive work with refugees, those at the displaced persons camp of Santa Rosa, I spent part of my working hours and most of my spare hours for six months listening to the testimony of those witnesses. It was here that a long involvement with refugees—the ultimate victims of all the evils of twentieth century history—really took shape.

The confrontation with refugees had begun for me two years earlier in Europe's doorstep, Lisbon. In that city to write a series of news articles, I discovered that I was in the midst of a refugee community that swarmed from consulate to consulate. Desperate people were attempting to pick up any visa that would allow them to step off the continental doorstep for any part of the Americas—in fact, for any destination that would separate them from Europe.

Some of the best stories I could not make public. One such was the secretive work of rescue of Catholics of Jewish origin who had managed to escape from Mittel-Europa. As long as they could reach Portugal, they could qualify for a visa to Brazil. Adalbert Turowski, a Polish priest from the Silesian region, who conducted the program, told me that Brazil had offered three thousand visas for this purpose. No strict count was kept on the total number of visas issued. The figure was considered a compassionate rather than a mathematical one—elastic enough to meet the number of refugees who presented themselves. Turowski's rescue work was conducted from the sequestered little office of the St. Raphael Society, a European Catholic aid association.

In a city of asylum one was thrown into the life and problems of exiles. I was asked to edit the English version of a memorandum prepared by the Polish refugee committee of Lisbon. It was dated July 20, 1941, and grew out of the June 22 Nazi attack on the Soviet Union. The Poles had been driven into a frenzy of emotion when the Polish government-in-exile in London was expected by Britain to end its state of war with the Soviet Union without conditions. The Soviet occupiers of large areas of eastern Poland were suspected of planning to incorporate that area permanently into the Soviet Empire. The memorandum grew into an eight-page document which we called our "Pro-Memoria." Its main burden was that ending the state of war with the Soviet

Union should be based on recognition of Poland's eastern boundary. It cited the Riga Act of 1921 as legally defining Poland's eastern border. It made the point that the Soviet invasion of eastern Poland in 1939 had "raised the problem of the eastern boundaries in the eyes of the Polish nation to the level of a dogma." It ended by asserting that the fact that Polish soldiers were fighting and dying by the side of British soldiers "spells to them the defense of their own country and their own territory."

The fears of the Poles were grounded not only in their history but in the reports that were reaching Lisbon. One day, Princess Sapieha of an old Cracow family told us, "Our people, whole families together, are being sent from Polesie, from Wilno and Lwow, to the Caucasus, Central Asia and Siberia. We have received letters and messages from those who are left. Probably they will be the next to be deported. Whole areas of eastern Poland are being combed by the Red Army and the NKVD."

Much that I heard I failed to understand at that time. What I failed to understand I stored in notes and in my mind until my notebooks as well as my mind became stuffed with unfinished, mysterious and often cryptic items. The reported mass deportation was one such item, since little or nothing of this had been documented in the press of the world. I came to know not only the refugees but the American services set up to help them. The Quakers, the Unitarian Service Committee, the Polish Aid Committee, and, above all, the American Jewish Joint Distribution Committee had staff and funds in Lisbon. Through the latter, variously referred to as "AJDC" or "The Joint," an estimated thirty thousand Jewish refugees escaped through Lisbon.

What I could not put into news articles, I put into reports which were lodged with American Catholic authorities. These reports may or may not have had the effect of speeding up Catholic activity for refugees, but they certainly had the effect of plunging me into refugee work in Mexico in 1943 and in Spain the following year.

* * *

Lisbon led directly to my walking the Mexican dirt road into Colonia Santa Rosa from the town of León. There was other transportation—a single trolley car that was pulled along rusty tracks by a heavy white work horse—but one could walk as fast.

Until the fertile wheat and corn land had been divided up among smaller cultivators, called "ejidatarios," the Santa Rosa hacienda had played a commanding role in the agricultural economy of the area. Now, more than seven hundred Polish refugees, fresh from exile in Siberia and Asiatic Russia, were clustered within its confines.

This first displaced persons camp in the western hemisphere served as a forerunner of the network of D.P. camps that marked Europe after World War II, the home places of the war-born nation, of nationless displaced persons.

A more improbable D.P. camp could hardly have been dreamed up. On the sun-baked plain stood a complex of buildings, most of them the same beige-orange color as the parched earth on which they stood. A four-story building of impressive proportions, with rows of gaping glassless window-openings and a sharply sloping roof, dominated the other structures. This was the Molino, formerly the mill and granary. Squatting around the Molino were monolithic adobe buildings with flat unbroken surfaces that seemed to grow out of the earth. These had served as storehouses for the various products of the hacienda. A series of long, low buildings, arranged in squares around open patios, were the former homes of the hacienda workers. Each one-room dwelling, about twelve feet square, had its own entrance on the patio.

With the arrival of the second transport of refugees, the population of the exile colony rose to 1,472. I have described the arrival of the long slow train carrying the second group of exiles into León's railroad station, situated on the main rail line between El Paso, Texas, and Mexico City. The crowded train, speeding through landscapes totally strange to them and passing the homes of people with whom they could have no contact, was a symbolic thing to the Poles old enough to remember the start of their wanderings. For it was into long, dark green trains that most of them were herded, with less care than would be expended on cattle for the market, for their journey to the unknown reaches of a darkly mysterious land mass.

As a sealed train had been the beginning of the trek of agony that carried simple people across three, four and, in the end, all five continents, of the world, so also the train that brought them into León and Colonia Santa Rosa was, in effect, also a sealed train. No stops had been allowed at any point in the United States after the Poles had been carefully shepherded from dockside at San Pedro, California to the railroad station. A specially reserved train had been prepared in advance. At the border crossing between the United States and Mexico, soldiers with bayonets had been placed on guard duty so that the refugees could not leave the carriages to mingle with American citizens.

In that period, the United States and Russia were allies in a war, and any broadcasting of the experiences of these people during their Russian captivity could hardly contribute to the closeness of the alliance. Truth, as someone has remarked, is always the first casualty of war. The truths about the Stalinist system that these victims could relate had to be buried, at least for the duration of the war effort.

Immediately on being installed at Colonia Santa Rosa, the family groups were given the one-room dwellings formerly occupied by hacienda laborers. It was discovered that only a quarter of the camp population consisted of family groups, and that in these groups only one family had remained intact throughout the period of deportation. With that exception, every family had lost one or more members after the initial uprooting, leaving the dead bodies on deportation trains, on remote station platforms, in the depths of Siberia or the Soviet Asian republics, or in Iran after the worst of the trek had been endured. The members lost by a single family varied between one and eleven persons. Of the 1,472 persons numbered in the camp population in November 1943, more than half were children under eighteen: 521 were women, and there were 200 men, mainly too old or otherwise unfit for military service.

Among my first memories of Santa Rosa are those of the camp chapel, and of the patios whose arching palms and flowering bushes gave an exotic quality to the crowded living quarters. The stone chapel, dedicated to Saint Rosa of Lima, was scrubbed inch by inch by squads of women on their arrival. Its

altars were never without fresh plants and flowers picked in
neighboring fields. A few kneeling figures were crouched there
at any hour of the day.

After Sunday masses, the refugees filled the Mexican countryside with the special patriotic anthem reserved for church,
"Boże Coś Polske," "May God Protect Poland." It was untrained
singing of natural voices, remarkable for its depth and unison.
They sang as they sang at home in Polesie, the area of the isolated marshes, of long twilights. The melancholy sound evoking
their homeland, and their bereavement at its loss, stole through
an open door of the chapel and traveled through the sunshine
of the Mexican morning like an unhappy wanderer forced to
loiter in a golden kingdom.

At first, there was a sort of happy chaos in the patios, with
mothers shouting in Polish, and children running wildly from
dwelling to dwelling. But soon came remarkable control and stillness when, for want of other quarters, the first elementary school
classes were held in the open squares. In the shining heat of the
morning and midday the great palm fronds cast shadows on the
grateful earth and on the faces of the children squatting on the
ground or on bare wooden benches. The children absorbed in
their lessons, laboriously writing Polish grammatical forms on
individual slates, were often the focus of attention for silent
watchers. The onlookers were chiefly the older men and women
of the Colonia. Some of the old square-faced women wore, even
on the hottest days, grey babushka headpieces, and their faces
seemed as ashen as the woolen head-wrappings. From the weath-
erbeaten faces of the old men sprouted the luxuriant handlebar
moustaches of the old country. Their sapphire-bright eyes
seemed to have a bemused look as they took in the scene.

These were of peasant stock, people who in their normal living might never have had occasion to make the journey to the
nearest big town of their province, not to speak of a capital city
like Warsaw. They were border people, with a few simple deep
loyalties. When asked what citizenship or nationality they
claimed, their mode of reply had long been, "I am from here."
Despite any partition or change of political overlordship, there
was no wavering in their sense of rootedness to their own soil.

Sometimes, even to the query about their nationality, they would give the answer, "I am a Catholic," or "We belong to the Ruthenian rite," testifying by such replies to the invisible religious and cultural frontiers that characterize a border region.

Over their stolid old figures the tropical fronds hovered incongruously, and the bushes with their overblown flame-colored flowers, seemed part of an exaggerated stage setting for some incredible peasant tragedy. It was hard to tell what they made of their traversings over seas and continents, of the races and tongues of Siberia, Central Asia, Iran, India, Australia, New Zealand, Mexico, of cruelty and uprooting from some foreigners, and loving care from others, of the proscription of religion in one place and freedom in another. What kind of synthesis of all this—and of the great mystery of human suffering—were they making in this time of rest and stillness? One really aged babka, who prayed much, seemed to have found the synthesis of all this in those prayers. Her deportation had begun in company with eleven other members of her family— including married sons and daughters and grandchildren. She was utterly alone in the Colonia. She had seen most of her relatives die in Siberia, and she had received word that the remainder had perished in other places of exile.

To a visitor from Chicago, who had made her a present of a rosary, she showed a strange object consisting of discolored strands of wool with small shapeless lumps attached at regular intervals.

"Where God took my family, there was no church to pray in, Reverend Father. I had to keep on praying, so I pulled this wool from my sweater, and then I put little pieces of black bread on it for the "Hail Marys" and "Our Fathers." The bread got hard like rosary beads. It had no cross on it because I couldn't make one. I never stopped saying the prayers on it. It was the rosary of bread that kept me from going mad, Reverend Father."

When the priest asked her for the rosary fashioned out of the bitter bread of exile, and handled it like a blessed object, the old babka seemed surprised. Her new rosary had a beautifully fashioned crucifix. On it she continued to recite her "Hail Marys" and "Our Fathers," elaborating her own personal medi-

tations on those "mysteries of the rosary" that could illumine
the great mystery of innocent human suffering, the agony of
Christ in the garden, and the crucifixion.

We had, in Colonia Santa Rosa, chiefly the remnants of those
who had been deported as families—simple people like tenant
farmers, small cultivators and foresters. They had been committed to "free exile," a term used to distinguish the compulsory
labor on state farms (*sovkhoz*) and collective farms (*kolkhoz*), from
sentences to regular prisons or to lagiers commanded by the
secret police system then called the NKVD. For the majority their
exile had been spent in one of the most remote parts of the
whole globe—as far as Americans or Europeans are concerned.

It was—and still is—often referred to by the generic term of
Turkestan. Starting roughly at the present borders of Iran and
the southeastern borders of the Caspian Sea, it sweeps across the
Kara Kum steppe, across the Amu-Daria and Syr-Daria rivers to
the borders of Siberia. South and southeast lies Afghanistan with
its mountains forming part of the roof of the world. Over
Turkestan as a whole have swept the greatest conquerors the
world has ever known—including two men who probably
changed secular history more than any other individuals. From
the west, out of Macedonia, came Alexander who led his hosts
through the iron gates of Derbent on the Caspian Sea, took
Samarkand and moved down from Afghanistan into Hindustan.
Against the ancient cities of Turkestan, Samarkand and Bokhara,
Genghis Khan flung his Mongol armies on their rough-haired
horses and the whole region became fief to his hordes.

From earliest times, Turkestan was the nexus of the eastern
and western worlds, and the route of the caravans of merchants
bringing to the winding, covered bazaars masterpieces of patient
handiwork—the luxurious silks, carved ivories and carpets in jew-
eled colors. Here Europe, Persia, China and India met. When the
tread of conquerors faded away, the slow steady plodding of the
merchants to the caravanseries and bazaars continued through
the millennia.

The groups of Polish deportees, who found themselves plodding the golden road to Samarkand and the great silk route to
Tashkent, were perhaps the strangest, and certainly the most trag-

ic of all the caravans through Turkestan. People from a far-off land, denuded of possessions, the fleeing Poles had nothing to exchange, no money to put up at the caravanseries for a night's rest. Racked with every disease, they staggered forward over desert stretches, determined to share with the free world their only burden—a mighty and incredible burden of anguish and fearsome truth.

In the nineteenth century, Russia, pressing inexorably southward in military campaigns against the Khanates and Emirates, annexed Turkestan. The very same process by which the Russia of the czars secured its southern border—annexation—was in store for Poland's eastern provinces. Ironically, in the interim before Soviet Russia's western border could be secured by the annexation of eastern Poland, deported Poles would work along with Uzbeks, Kazakhs, Tadjiks and other peoples to fulfill the plans and work norms formulated by Russia's leaders. More than ten percent of the population of eastern Poland was deported between the late fall of 1939 and June of 1941—the people scattered over the tundra and taiga of Siberia and into Kazakstan, Uzbekistan, Tadjikistan and Kirgizistan.

Watching the people who had been caught and twirled like scraps of paper in the great currents of history, one's mind becomes paralyzed with the wild incongruities of their lot.

3. Frozen Children Thaw Out

Colonia Santa Rosa, adjoining the town of León, was, for the time being, the end of the line for the caravans of Poles driven over the oldest and newest roads of the world. León, in the province of Guanajuato, where they came to rest, was a town rich with the relics of its nearly four hundred years of history. Once the second city of Mexico, it was now a town of faded stateliness, with a vaulted cathedral, flanked by a chapel in gold mosaic dedicated to Christ the King. The "Aristocrático Hotel Méjico," located on the Paseo de las Delicias, where I lived, was only a square away from the cathedral. The Hotel Méjico was near enough to vibrate from its foundations every weekday morning when the great bell clanged in the cathedral belfry, the "alarm clock" donated by the leather workers and shoemakers.

León had its classic touches, like the smiling old leper who daily sat on the cathedral steps, holding out his bulbous, useless hands for alms, and offering thanks in pious Castilian phrases. "May God repay you, my daughter. Go with God," he would say, and after we became friends, he wanted me to tell him about all my trips to Mexico City so that he would not worry about my absences.

In one item León departed from tradition. It had two plazas, or main squares, located diagonally with respect to each other, in the center of town. This made it almost as unique as the town of Zaragoza in Spain, with its two cathedrals. On Saturday and Sunday evenings, the people of León walked in ritual-like procession around the larger of the two squares. First we looked on, as foreigners watching an archaic folk dance. It was not long before we joined in and the procession in the plaza seemed to me and my co-workers a normal way to pass an evening. A small group of American and European residents at the Aristocrático

24

Hotel Méjico merged with the outer ring. There were generally four of us, the camp doctor, the delegate of the Polish Ministry of Education, the American social worker and myself. As there was no single language we all could share, we added to the sibilant Mexican Spanish our own Castilian-type Spanish, as well as Polish, English and French.

While we who served the refugees became acclimatized to León, the refugees settled into the life of the Colonia. The old people were a special study to us. They seemed content to see the young people being taught and cared for. While watching the swirls of orange dust on sunny days and the swampy pools during the rainy season, they seemed to be ruminating on the things the world had done to them, and the landscapes of the world on which they had gazed. They now had time to miss their own lost country, and sometimes, when asked how they liked the Mexican camp, they would, after thanking God for the good things, add such a phrase as "We are not from here." Sometimes an old man would shake his head in a kind of numb regret when he mentioned the name of his home village. Their feeling for their home places in a border region was probably closest to the deep visceral regret that the poet Mickiewicz felt when he said "Our homeland is like good health. It is only when we have lost it that we miss it." It was of such as these enforced world wanderers and pilgrims that Adam Mickiewicz composed the "Litany of the Pilgrims." "By the wounds, tears and sufferings of all the Polish captives and exiles, deliver us, O Lord."

One wondered why Mexico became the country of temporary refuge and how such a site as Colonia Santa Rosa had come to be chosen by a commission composed of representatives of the American, British, Mexican, and Polish exiled governments. The remote camp was backed by two bilateral pacts, a Mexican-Polish agreement to receive the refugees, and a U.S.-Polish agreement to cover the financing from American funds. Hardly any other country could offer the same advantages as the Mexican countryside—namely, secure and humane living conditions, and a continued entombment of the truth about slave labor in the Soviet Union.

One of the most forcible things that struck one about the

administration of Colonia Santa Rosa was that by order of some government department, the hospitality of Mexico faltered in one respect. The Poles of the colony could not leave the camp without a special pass, and could not travel to nearby towns and villages. It was an understandable ruling since the Polish exiles were only temporary visitors, without claim to citizen or residence rights.

The effect of this ruling was so intense as to cause a new psychic wound. The residents felt that they were still the defenseless playthings of alien governments, still not free after all the agonies, the wanderings. The placement of armed Mexican police at the entrance to Colonia Santa Rosa was a sore point. There was no explaining them away to the Poles. They did, however, set up their own police force inside the Colonia grounds, a police force which made its rounds sporting a semblance of uniforms and real nightsticks.

One of the chief aims of my agency's program, I decided, would be to restore, insofar as was possible, the climate of freedom for these people in the new world. I discovered that the Mexican authorities would grant blanket permits for guided trips to almost anywhere in Mexico. With funds from Catholic Relief Services, a bus was chartered to take the young people to various spots of interest in the countryside.

I accompanied the first outing for the orphan group. It was the month of December, and I could not help reliving the November bus ride to the camp with the forty boys immediately after their arrival in León. There were about forty boys and girls with us this time. They were again carrying little bundles, but, this time, of newly acquired possessions, a bathing suit, and towel. Somehow I had become accustomed to their quiet orderliness as they filed in to take their seats. I even had ceased to marvel at the withdrawn expression of their eyes, belying all childish emotion. There was no spontaneity in their movements, and they seemed to have a suspicion of me as one of those threatening outsiders who could not speak to them in their own language. They would fasten on my eyes clouded with a dull suspicion, and when I countered with a smile and a few words of foreign-accented Polish, the cloud would begin to fall away. Then they would look away and smile at each other in a secretive way. When they stole new glances at me, the dull cloud would have taken over again. I did not force matters, but continued to throw out my childish Polish and a general smile.

We had chosen as our destination the village of Comanjilla, the site of some curative hot springs. There was not the terrible stillness of my first bus ride. There was excited talk, but it was low and guarded. It seemed to be centered about the bathing suits. I hardly looked at the rolling countryside in my concentration on the children. I had come to accept the reserved manner of these boys and girls, but I could not learn to accept the grey-pinched faces slashed by the scars of scurvy. The strange grey-green color of a few little faces was the legacy of anti-malaria treatments. The skulls of little boys were still shaven. Their stunted, bony little bodies and sallow, even wizened, faces were heart-stopping spectacles. It was not surprising that when they lined up before an American woman visitor from Chicago, she fainted dead away before them.

At Comanjilla, they marched out with their little bundles and settled themselves in orderly groups for a picnic under a gentle sun. Then came the time to scurry behind hillocks and trees to try on their bathing suits. A large swimming tank had been constructed to hold the waters gushing from the hot springs. One by one the boys and girls edged into the water. There were yells of surprise, "Goraco, jest goraco." "Hot, it's hot."

In a mad rush the rest jumped in. The shouts of joy were so delirious and prolonged that I began to be a little concerned. They screamed on and on, jumping up and down, dipping their heads in the water, and rubbing each other's backs. After an hour, I suggested that they get out and dry themselves, but they were still luxuriating in a wild way. The contrast with the restrained, almost suspicious behavior to which I had become accustomed was enormous. I began to talk to the teachers and some of the older children. "You know we have no hot water for bathing at Colonia Santa Rosa," someone explained. "Do you realize that most of these youngsters have not had a real hot bath in all their years of wandering?" The realization stunned me. It was a minor footnote that illuminated a whole page of deprivation.

Something had been released in the children and they gamboled about incessantly like a school of porpoises which had suddenly found itself in a sunlit bay where the supply of small fish was inexhaustible.

No sooner had the children darted out of the vehicle at Colonia Santa Rosa than I heard them shouting "Basen, basen goracy, basen." It took less than an hour for the whole camp to know about a swimming pool, or "basen do plywania," where one could swim, take a hot bath, and get stronger—all at the same time.

A meeting of the Santa Rosa Committee of Counselors took place on future plans for Comanjilla Hot Springs. As the springs were reputed to be especially helpful to those suffering from rheumatic disorders, the medical member of the committee, Dr. Samuel Chrabolowski, suggested that the first excursions be planned for those afflicted with the disease.

A notice was affixed to the door of the camp dispensary announcing that bus trips would for a certain time be limited to those suffering from some form of rheumatism. A wave of pandemonium hit the camp. The doctor was so besieged that it was evident that no one in the Colonia was free from some form of rheumatism. In fact, every pain became a rheumatic one entitling a person to be added to the trip list.

I decided that it would be less expensive, and better programming, to acquire a bus and a chauffeur. A cable to New York elicited an affirmative response to my query regarding such a large outlay and I negotiated the purchase of a forty-two passenger vehicle. It was then planned that, beginning with the smallest unaccompanied children, the trips would include everyone. The trips to the springs started in earnest, four times every week. The lingering signs of scurvy began to disappear from the faces of the children. The Mexican sun took away the ghastly grey and greenish pallor and gave a golden tan.

In general, the group of unaccompanied children were kept apart from the other camp residents. After the style of European child care institutions, their life was quite severely regimented. Boys and girls would march in regular files like little wooden soldiers for each meal. At first, the children looked neither to the right or left, and it would not have occurred to them to break ranks, or to wave or smile at other children in the Colonia. Old and despirited before their time, the children needed a different regime—one that would bring them backward in time from their premature adulthood into a state nearer that of childhood. The general role of my agency was to supply supplementary welfare and vocational services, since basic support came from U.S. government funds, while clothing, medical aid and schooling was paid for by a voluntary organization of Polish-Americans, Polish War Relief.

I was not alone in thinking that the heavily routinized life of the two hundred and sixty-four institutionalized children should be varied with play activities in the camp as well as the excursions beyond its confines. Plans were made for scout troops, folk dancing, picnics, short plays and operettas. The new director of the Colonia, an imaginative and vivid personality, backed every initiative, and as funds and willing volunteers were available, the programs for the children took shape immediately. In a few months' time, the children were obviously shedding the false garment of age. They were still disciplined, and it seemed helpful to have them walk in line to the meals and classes, but they would smile and wave enroute, and a few would call out to me from the line, "Moja Pani, moja Pani," "My Lady, my Lady." At other times they would sidle up to me, watching my expression. If I kept on smiling, they would tug at my skirt and finally throw their arms around me.

The director of the camp, from November 1941 onward, was a delegate of the Polish Ministry of Labor and Social Affairs, Bohdan Szmejko. Under his sponsorship, a committee of camp personnel, called the counselors, met regularly to discuss problems and to make decisions on many matters, including program plans of my agency. Members of the committee were the representatives of the Office of Foreign Relief and Rehabilitation Operations (OFRRO); a skilled social worker from New York City, Miss Irene Dalgiewicz; the delegate of the Polish Ministry of Education, Feliks Sobota; the Rev. Leonard Kaszynski, a priest of Polish origin from the United States; a young priest of the Byzantine-Slavonic Rite who had accompanied the orphan group, the Rev. Leon Porendowski; the medical director, Dr. Samuel Chrabolowski, a Pole who had found asylum in Mexico after serving as an officer in the Spanish Civil War; and myself, as representative of Catholic Relief Services. To this committee of seven were later added seven refugees concerned with a similar number of branches of camp activity.

Towering over everyone in Santa Rosa was a priest and former missioner to Japan, Fr. Jozef Jarzebowski. He was at least six and a half feet tall and could have been a forbidding figure except for the gentleness of his demeanor and the compassion of his manner. His congregation the Marian Fathers, had lent him to the refugee community for the duration. For the older people, his presence was a benediction. Sometimes all they needed was a word of consolation or reassurance and Fr. Jozef never failed them. His chief ministry, however, was to the youngsters of Santa Rosa. Deprived of religious training and church attendance during their years of wandering, they were ready for the teaching and witness of a deeply spiritual man. While the Felician Sisters focused on the religious training of the younger children as part of the grammar school program, Fr. Jozef paid particular attention to the needs of the older boys and girls. They were of an age to question the meaning of what had befallen them and they looked to Fr. Jozef to relate their lived experience to the teaching of Jesus, and above all, to the cross he bore. He encouraged the scouting program, emphasizing its spiritual base and its character-building aspect.

4. Annals of Child Refugees

Any tendency on our part to let our energies flag was quickly overcome by the sight of the child refugees, and, in particular, the orphans. Day by day we came to know them better, and we came to know the details of their travail. The one orphan I knew best was Weronika Jankowska. The reason was simple. She could communicate with me in stiff but very clear English.

She had been on the road of exile since her early teens. As she was now seventeen years of age, she had been assigned to mass living quarters with the adult women. Her one surviving brother was then serving with the Royal Air Force in Britain. She was slight in figure, and her movements were deliberate and almost painfully controlled. Her face was slight and her nose fine. Her nondescript off-blond hair was parted in the center and brushed severely back from her forehead. What one remembered about her were deep-set eyes of an intense violet-blue.

At various times after a busy day at the camp, Weronika and I would sit quietly under the shade of a tree or in a corner of the Colonia while she would recount to me the events which brought her across the world to a corner of the province of Guanajuato, Mexico. "I speak English because my mother came of English origin," she explained. "But my father was a Pole, and we lived in the city of Wilno. In 1939 my father was killed. He was a soldier, and many other Polish people died at the same time in the attack on Poland. We were four children, two boys and two girls, but when the NKVD (which she called "En Kah Voo Day") came to search our home, only my mother and my sister and I myself were there. It was on the first day of November 1939."

It was known later that in preparation for the mass deportation of Poles that started in February 1940, many homes were subjected to preliminary searches by agents of the NKVD.

31

People who were considered dangerous to the Soviet occupation of eastern Poland were arrested individually and imprisoned before the mass round-ups of ordinary Polish citizens. These individual searches took place after the September 28 protocol of the Nazi-Soviet pact. "Both parties," stated the protocol, "will tolerate in their territories no Polish agitation which affects the territory of the other party. They will suppress in their territories all the beginnings of such agitation and inform each other concerning suitable measures for this purpose."

It was long after the end of World War II that the secrets of that Nazi-Soviet pact were verified. In what was termed the "deadly embrace," Hitler and Stalin agreed to divide Poland. Stalin obtained, through the pact with his ally of choice, thirteen million people as new Soviet citizens. This pact became, tragically, one of the basic pillars of the peace that ended the Second World War.

The early raid on Weronika Jankowska's home was probably occasioned by the fact that her mother was of foreign origin.

"I was fourteen at that time. My mother did not say anything to the men. And my sister was quiet, but I followed the two men and I saw that they were writing down everything that we had in the house. They put all our furniture on the list, and I said to them, 'This house is our house and this is our furniture. You should not come into a private home.'"

They thrust her away and went on to finish the task, but the child continued to argue with them. When their inspection of the premises was complete, they came back, arrested the girl, and took her then and there from her mother.

As she spoke, her blue eyes maintained their remoteness, and she seemed to be recounting a story that had happened to someone else in some era far removed from the present.

"There was no process (trial) in a courtroom. They thought I was a spy because I resisted the searches of the Soviet officials. And also my mother is English. I was in prison for four months in Wilejka, and nineteen women were in the same room. But in February, they moved me to the prison in Orsza. They placed me in a small cell with six young girls and also three old women.

"Orsza, I think, was a convent for nuns in the old times. It was dark inside, and always damp and sad. We had the same food each day. It was half a kilo of dark bread, and water only to drink. But sometimes they would bring us a piece of fish.

"At first we counted the days, and we know how many days we were in prison. The seven girls practiced to sing together many Polish hymns and songs. We sang in the afternoons and other people in the prison listened to the Polish music. Sometimes we would finish the concert with 'Boże Coś Polske,' but it made us cry so and we were often swallowing our tears. But the time became long. I think we were in that dark room about half a year. In the middle of the room was one slop pail and we all had to use it. We could not go anywhere even to take a walk. One of the girls was permitted to take the slop pail to the latrine to empty it. This is what we all wanted to do, because we could leave the filthy room. The latrine was full with a terrible stink, but I or my friends would wait after we threw out the slops. Someone would come in with another slop pail and we would whisper the news and then we would have something to talk about.

"The little walk to the latrine down the long stone corridor like a cave—that was like being free for five or ten minutes. We could not wait for our turn to carry the pail. I would be so excited. I would forget about the lice in my head and all over me. New people came to the prison and they told about the big deportation from Poland. But we did not know where everybody was sent—maybe to other filthy prisons."

From her description, it was clear that little or no provision was made for the bodily needs of the women, and their clothing and aspect became so filthy that they felt utterly degraded. Nights and days merged finally into an unending struggle with nausea and with the ever-crawling lice whose numbers they could not control.

"Sometimes we still sang, but not often. One or two of us were always sick from the food that was unclean. But even if we were very sick, we still wanted to carry the pail because we could take so many steps to the end of the hall."

Suddenly, about September of 1940, the girls were told that they were going to be freed from the prison. Some were given sentences in a so-called *kolonja*, a corrective work settlement for

youthful offenders. Others were to be sent to "free exile."
Weronika was marked for the latter. Under convoy, she and a
small group walked a few miles to a railway station, and were
ordered aboard a train. It was a long journey under guard, ending at a fishing port on the Caspian Sea—the ancient city of
Derbent. All that fall, she worked with other Poles on a *kolkhoz*,
or collective farm, in the hinterland of Derbent. She worked like
all the other deportees at least twelve hours a day.

"Almost all the workers were Polish, like me—many boys and
girls, young like me. I asked everybody the same question—if
they knew anything about my mother and family. We were
always asking the same questions when we met a Pole for the
first time. I met a woman from Wilno. She said, 'Your mother
and sisters went with the big deportations from Wilno in
February of 1940. Most of these are around Petropavlovsk. If
you could get there, you would probably find her!' I kept thinking of Petropavlovsk. It was in Kazakhstan. But Poles could not
leave the kolkhoz.

"But just before Christmas, all the Polish workers could be
free again. The amnesty was for all Polish workers and prisoners in the Soviet Union."

In point of fact, the so-called "Amnesty" was an addendum to
the Polish-Soviet Pact signed in London on July 30, 1941. The
addendum stated:

> The government of the Union of Socialist Soviet Republics
> will grant amnesty to all Polish citizens at present deprived
> of their liberty within the territory of the Union of Socialist
> Soviet Republics.

An amnesty is a grace or pardon granted to prisoners serving sentence for a crime after due process of law—and therefore
was not strictly applicable to innocent civilians snatched from
their homes and deported into slave labor by the officialdom of
an aggressive power. To the Polish deportees, however, the word
"amnesty" was a word with magic power, like "Open Sesame" in
the ancient tale. The literal meaning was as insignificant as the
fact that sesame was only a herb. It meant freedom to leave

their places of detention, and possibly an exit from the Soviet Union. They seized the word without question, and blazoned it, like an imperial seal, at any *kolkhoz* official or lagier-commander who tried to prevent the Polish exodus. Many of them who were formally released were presented with a document, with space for filling in name, birthplace and choice of residence, certifying to the fact that he or she

> as a Polish citizen, has been included in the amnesty declared in the decree of the Council of Peoples' Commissars sitting on the 12th of August 1941, and is entitled in consequence to take up residence anywhere within the territory of the Soviet Union, with the exception of the frontier and regime towns of the first and second categories.

To Weronika, and to the Poles around her, there was no waiting for a formal release. They simply used their freedom to leave the collective farms and take to the road that led to the nearest town or rail junction. Families tried to get word of missing members, separated haphazardly during the deportation. Mothers and fathers searched for lost children, and, as in the case of Weronika, children wandered around Asia in search of parents.

She made her way back to Derbent. From this city, founded by the Persians in the sixth century A.D., she began her journey. Weronika entered the still mysterious region of central Asia, a lonely child on a lonely search. It was in the Christmas season of 1941. Somehow, a poem of the war years by Sister Madeleva entitled "Christmas 1940," seems to catch best the spirit of her wanderings: "There is a night too circumspect for stars/ a night too circumspect for song./ Kings do not walk abroad, nor shepherds watch,/ none save a child is strong./ . . . Voices are crying through the wilderness/ and children wander in a nameless land."

She met other Poles who had wandered through the lands that were nameless to them. They had marched over the naked steppe that was lashed in winter by winds screaming by at sixty miles an hour. One city seemed to be the goal of all—Tashkent, the Polish Army center. Weronika could not reach Kazakhstan alone, so she soon joined the general trek. Through marches and train trips carrying her over Kara Kum, the windswept desert of black sands, and past Bokhara, she arrived in Tashkent. There the location of her mother, on a *kolkhoz* seven miles outside of the town of Petropavlovsk in Kazakhstan, was confirmed. Armed with a train ticket, she went on this part of her search utterly alone. For six days and nights, in primitive trains, she saw the landscape of Uzbekistan and Kazakhstan swim by, the stretches of open steppe undulating like the ocean. Occasionally there were clusters of buildings where the formerly nomad Turkomens, Uzbeks and Kazakhs had been forced to settle down to the monotonous routine of the collective or the state farms, the *kolkhozy* or *sovkhozy*. Finally, ill and exhausted, she came to her destination, a junction of the Trans-Siberian railroads.

"I could not eat on this journey. I could have had fruit and other foods. But I could only drink water at each station. It was easy to find the *kolkhoz* where all the Polish people had been working.

"I told my name and my mother's name to the man in charge but they did not say anything to me. Then someone brought me a package. It had my mother's name on it, and my sister's name. There were only pieces of clothing inside—just rags, and some of our families' photos. They had both died there. I kept asking where they were buried. I wanted to kneel and say prayers as we do in our country. Many people had died in the *kolkhoz*. Some had died out in the fields like dogs. There was no priest. They were buried quickly and nobody put any sign over the graves."

There was no emotion in her voice—just the same carefully enunciated English. The fine little face, with its large almost violet eyes did not change expression. Then I realized why Weronika, whose features were as exquisite as those of the violet-eyed girls in the Salvation Army posters, never struck anyone as being beautiful. Her face had a quality of age, of deadness about it. Her frozen eyes never even shone with a tear as she spoke to me. It was as though a single tear would have unlocked the frozen barrier to let loose a tide of misery that would have overwhelmed her—or perhaps that she was encased in a great tear that had congealed around her.

I read of another girl who showed how cruelty and loss had made her old at seventeen. Of Russian nationality, she was in a *kolonja* for youthful offenders along with young deported Poles. She conducted herself more or less like other teenagers, but her dark pigtails seemed to hang down her back as from a grey cap. Her hair was already turning grey. Perhaps physical deprivation had been the cause. African children become fair-haired when they develop kwashiorkor, the disease of protein starvation. But her emotional deprivation was enough to drain the youth from her body. Her father had been executed in a purge, her mother condemned to a long sentence, the greying child banished to a work colony.

"I took the package and I went back to Tashkent. The town was filled with Polish people. They asked me if I would work in the kitchen for the Polish soldiers who were ill. So I worked for the Fifth Division of the Polish Army. Many had typhus and dysentery—and they were exhausted because they had walked many miles to come to Tashkent. Everyday I asked the men if they had any news of my two brothers. Some of the men could not remember to say anything. They were weak and dying. Some days thirty men died and some days even more. We were too busy to think about it because we were trying to keep the others alive.

"One day I met someone who had seen one of my brothers— he told me that he had been in the deportation to Arkhangelsk. My brother had died near Arkhangelsk. Only one brother I had now, and I did not know where he could be."

This was the period when it was thought possible that a Polish Army could be formed on Soviet territory. General Wladyslaw Anders and other leaders were freed from prison in Moscow, and Soviet printing presses were set to work to print Roman Catholic prayer books for the men so long deprived of religious practice. But a Polish Army could not materialize on Russian soil and the move to the nearest frontier was on.

On March 28, 1942, Weronika accompanied the trek of Poles across the southwestern frontier of the Soviet Union into Iran.

Men, women and children, already spectre-like from imprisonment, hunger and the inhuman work conditions of the camps
of slow death, made their way by boat across the Caspian Sea to
get to the far side of the Soviet boundary. Arriving in Iran,
many of them died before friendly hands could save them. I was
shown a photograph taken in those days of a field near Pahlevi,
in Iran. It depicted a series of small mounds of earth, and
though Iran is a Moslem land, there was a makeshift cross
above each mound. It was a cemetery where hundreds of Polish
children were buried. They had come out of Russia in groups,
having lost their parents, shepherded by any deportee able to
assume the task, and they had perished in sight of rescue.

Weronika had enough strength to reach Teheran and then
collapsed utterly. "I was put in a hospital of the British. They
were so good with me and I got better. So they decided I could
go with the transport of young Polish to Karachi. I was nearly
ready to leave when someone came to ask about me. He was my
brother! This was my only family left! We sat outside the hospital and told each other the things that had happened to our
family. After that, we did not talk very much. We sat quietly. We
did not know if we could see each other once more in life. He
had to leave for England to train with the army and I had to go
with the Children's Transport to Ahwaz.

"On June 21, 1942, I left Teheran for Ahwaz. From there we
were taken by buses to India, to the port of Karachi. They were
good and kind to us there."

The hot winds from the desert of Sind blew across the Polish
settlement in British India, now Pakistan, but the months there
were a time of peace and healing for the Poles. Chiefly women,
children and old men, they were stranded until definite offers
of refuge were made on their behalf to General Wladyslaw
Sikorski, premier of Poland's government in exile. Then they
learned that a haven had been given in the new world. An
American troopship, bringing back American casualties from
the Middle Eastern war theater, picked up the Polish exiles.
Before crossing the Pacific Ocean, the ship put in at New
Zealand and Australia, thus giving the deportees a new continent to include as part of their enforced trajectory.

During the voyage, the troops learned of the experiences of their shipboard companions, and before long they were giving concerts for the children, plying them with gifts of army clothes, T-shirts, toothpaste and any possessions they could spare. Before the ship docked at San Pedro, the American soldiers took up a collection so that the children would have pocket money on their arrival in the United States.

In the train trip to Mexico Weronika was to see once more the great expanse of desert landscape swim by her, not the fearsome steppe of Central Asia, but the free open deserts of America's southwest. In a sense, the American deserts and the remote Asian steppes had become linked through the fact of a war alliance. Weronika's inability to make a more prolonged visit to the United States, even on a visitor's visa, reflected the accommodation made with Stalin in order to put down Hitler.

In Mexico, Weronika preserved for a time the still tautness of body, the remote and impersonal gaze. As the seventeen-year old girl talked to me, a lone little creature prematurely aged from a life that had spared her nothing, my deepest immediate concern was that this reed should not break. At the same time, my mind darted to the moral dilemma incarnated in the helpless, victimized little figure—the dilemma of the alliances of modern global warfare.

* * *

Helenka was an active child of ten with grey-green eyes and curly brown hair. She had the look of a well-cared for child who might have grown up in a settled community in an American suburb. I could see why she had been protected, even during a cruel deportation, when I made the acquaintance of her mother—a broad-faced, able-bodied peasant woman. She had been the one to barter for a suckling pig and butcher and roast it for her family in the Soviet Arctic. She was a survivor, like her neighbors in Colonia Santa Rosa who found themselves and their families starving near Tashkent. Stealing a small donkey, one held it down while the other slit its throat. Roasted donkey flesh gave them strength for many days.

Through a translator, I encouraged Helenka to talk. Her

memories were the vivid pictures of a child's world; her tale was punctured from time to time by plain facts from the mother. Helenka was seven when the family was swept out of Novogrodek, near Wilno.

"I remember it was dark when the soldiers came to our house. We knew that they would be taking us away, so we put on all the clothing we could. We made bundles of everything we could carry. It was so cold. It was before the sun came up. They took us all together, our mother and father and three brothers, Marek, Rafal and Witold.

"They told us to get into two big sleighs. We didn't know where we were supposed to go."

"But *they* knew," said the mother. "They had horses and sleighs for our people. Sometimes we had to change the horses at camps. Finally when we came to Posiolek, they said, 'Here you will stay.'"

"Posiolek is near Arkhangelsk," said Helenka.

Helenka recalled that her father used to cut down trees in Posiolek. The hinterland of the port city was rich in timberland. His place of work was a day's journey on foot from where the rest of the family lived. They hardly ever saw him. "Our father was a carpenter, and when we went to see him, he was often making coffins for Polish people who died. We had our own cemetery, and the Ukrainians had a big cemetery."

Her mother explained that the camp had been full of Ukrainians who had been there many years. They told the incoming Poles that three quarters of their people had died in the country around Arkhangelsk.

"I remember Mamusia pushing the big logs into the river at Arkhangelsk. And then, after the 'amnesty,' Mamusia roasted a pig for us—a whole baby pig."

The mother interposed that she had sold some clothes for two suckling pigs to give her reunited family of eight a good meal. But someone had stolen one of the pigs.

To show me that she could still picture the trains in which they had eventually traveled to Tashkent—the great trajectory after being freed from the logging camps around Arkhangelsk—she drew diagrams of the inside and outside of the cattle cars.

She drew the two shelf-like wooden layers on which people lived and slept en route.

"It took us two months to reach Tashkent. You know we had to stop and change trains and sometimes sleep in stations. When we arrived in Uzbekistan, it was very hot—and we all slept the first nights in the open fields.

"Then later we went to the railroad station again, and the train took us to Krasnovodsk. All the trains stopped there. They put hundreds of us in an open field near the sea. The sun was roasting us. My father got very sick and he was thirsty all the time. He was calling 'Woda, woda,' and there was only dirty, salty water. My mother still had a lace tablecloth. It was a hand-made one. She gave it away for a bottle of fresh water for my father. That was the last day we spent in Russia. I always think of that terrible open field with all the thirsty people. In the evening they took us to a ship. All night we were on the water. That was the Caspian Sea. The next morning we got off in Pahlevi. My father died there." Her mother said nothing. Her lips were tightly closed and her grey eyes seemed to recede. They had a dead look.

"I was put in the *ochronka*—that means protection. It was for the children whose parents were sick or something. My two big brothers, Marek and Rafal, said goodbye to us. They were old enough to be soldiers in the Polish Army.

"Then they told us that the whole *ochronka* was supposed to leave for Africa. We all stood in line and the *nauczycielka* (teacher) made us put the prints of our fingers on a paper. This was like a passport.

"I found out that my mother was in Polish Camp Three near Teheran. I would not go without her. But they wanted to separate us and then all the children could stay together. I raised my two fingers. That means to go to the toilet. The teacher said 'Yes, but come right back.' I went to the toilet and stood and stood. The toilet in the camp at Pahlevi had only walls and a door, but no roof. The sun was shining down on my head. It was hard to breathe, but I did not move all day. I was thinking of Mamusia. When I could not hear the children, I knew I could come out.

"The *nauczycielka* saw me and she was very angry. 'Where were you all day, Helenka?' she asked.

"'I got sick,' I told her. 'I was sick. My face was swollen, and it was like I was walking in a fog.'"

"'Now you have to go to your mother.'" Both smiled proudly at the courage of a small girl.

"I fell down and they put me in bed. That is how I came to Colonia Santa Rosa. Otherwise I would have been in Africa, far from my family.

"In Karachi, we lived in tents. In the night the *szakale* cried and screamed. I was nine years old and I used to be frightened. We have no *szakale* here."

We checked the word. *Szakale* were jackals. "Did you ever see them?" I asked.

"Oh yes. We would peep out and see shining things moving. They were like flashlights. They were the eyes of the *szakale*. But not close.

"And I remember a funny thing. On the Hermitage ship— that was the ship that brought us to California—I used to lie on my hammock and look up at the hammock over me. It had writing on it—Polish writing. 'Tu spala Hela Zak,' it said. 'Here slept Hela Zak.' I got a crayon and I wrote next to it. 'Tu spala Helenka.' When I came to Colonia Santa Rosa, I met Hela Zak and she was my friend. She belonged in the First Transport."

Long sleigh rides to slave labor camp, coffins for the victims of the Arctic tundra, cattle trains, exiles dying of thirst in an unprotected field on Russia's Caspian coast, the day-long hideout to avoid a further separation from her mother, jackals howling around a Polish tent colony in Pakistan, the memorial words of a Polish girl on the hammock of a troop transport—all accepted as part of a Polish childhood.

I asked her mother why she thought the deportation had occurred. Her usually impassive expression gave way to a look of concern, and she shook her head, back and forth, back and forth.

"That is what I kept asking myself in Arkhangelsk," she finally replied. "And I shall keep asking myself. Why did they do this to us just when we had made our lives so good. We had so many acres that at harvest time we brought in workers from the whole countryside to help us. I got angry one day in Arkhangelsk and I said to the Russian: 'Why did you do this to us? Why did you take everything away from us and bring us here. Panie Kommandant, tell me why Russia had to do this to us?' But he answered me nothing.

"Then I said to him, 'Will we ever get back to our own house in Poland?' and he only answered with an old saying, 'You'll get back to Poland when you can see your ear with your own eye.'"

Helenka said, "Mamusia, we escaped from him. We will all go back to Poland."

5. So That the Bruised Reeds Should Not Break

We could only deal with the concrete at Colonia Santa Rosa in those days—and we worked so that bruised reeds like Weronika should not be broken. The things we did and the programs we worked out were simple, but we could see the results even on Weronika. During the months of my stay, she reached out to take part in the recreation, school courses, and work projects of the camp. Her cheeks took on a pink glow; her eyes began to thaw out, to smile, and to light up with the eager interests of a young girl.

The purchase of a bus for the exclusive use of the people of the Colonia opened windows on the surrounding countryside. The excursions to the hot springs of Comanjilla became a part of the rhythm of Colonia life. Cultural excursions and special projects were planned for the units of Polish boy and girl scouts. There was a hunger among the people to visit the religious shrines of Mexico. The older people especially wanted to take part in pilgrimages to a shrine of a Virgin Morena, a black-visaged image of the Mother of Jesus. It seemed to have reminders for them of the ancient images of the Black Virgin of Czestochowa and of Ostra-Brama in their own land.

As their knowledge of the Spanish language grew, the Poles, young and old, began to seek for participation in the rituals of Mexican life, not so very different from their own in respect to the celebration of patronal feasts of saints, and in religious holidays. The bus permitted them to be in the town of San Francisco del Rincón for the feast of St. Francis, and to attend the bullfight traditional for that day. The bus became the link with the events of the countryside in the provinces of Guanajuato and with the outside world. We helped make the presence of the Polish guests known to the Mexican people. It was not long before invitations started to come in and Polish scouts were joining in meetings with Mexican scouting groups. Polish delegations marched in the Mexican Independence Day parades of September 16. A great red and white allegorical float bearing the banner POLONIA was the unique international feature of the parade to commemorate the 370th anniversary of the founding of the city of León, Guanajuato.

When the Mexican government officials came from the capital for a function in the jewel-like Teatro Juàrez of Guanajuato, the provincial capital, Polish exiles were given honored places in the ornately antique boxes. The winding cobblestoned streets of the capital, wedged snugly into the Canadà del Marfil, the Ivory Ravine, had a European air. Guanajuato was nearly four hundred years old. The colonial Cathedral of Santa Fé de Guanajuato, with its pillars of sea-green marble, entranced the Polish visitors. But some of them stood uncomprehending before other sights of Guanajuato—the cemetery of mummies, and the great monument commemorating the siege of a public granary at the outset of the struggle against Spain.

The former president, then defense minister of Mexico, Lázaro Cárdenas, paid an unannounced visit to the Colonia in its early days. He interested himself in having the road connecting the Colonia with the city of León improved so that it became passable even in the rainy season. It was not long before the president of Mexico, then in office, Miguel Alemán, inspected the Colonia Santa Rosa.

The guards were removed from the main entrance, and the camp ceased to be a place of enforced residence. Polish refugees could accept jobs outside the Colonia. The feeling of being guarded, of still not being free, left the Poles, and Mexico became a country very dear to them.

Besides the unfettered travel to various parts of the Mexican countryside, it was decided that my agency would supply welfare services unmet from other sources, namely a recreation and meeting center designed for adults, the support and provisioning of the Polish scouting groups, pre-vocational and vocational training, and as much camp recreational activity as possible, including the exhibiting of films.

As soon as the ground floor of the main building, called the Molino, was assigned for the recreation center, I arranged with workmen, Mexican and Polish, to lay a new floor, and equip various areas for meetings, for listening to the radio, and for just relaxing or reading Polish newspapers. Most of the living quarters were without chairs and had only room for sleeping cots. This was the first *Swietlica NCWC*, NCWC Recreation Center, for homeless Poles. It was the first of scores that later grew up in the agency's program for Polish refugees and military in North Africa and the Holy Land. The refugees could meet in the Swietlica in a climate of freedom and just chat or discuss what their problems were. At one time, the chain of Swietlica numbered two hundred and forty-two. The network was inaugurated by the Rev. Aloysius Wycislo, later bishop of Green Bay, Wisconsin. NCWC referred to the first title of our agency, Catholic Relief Services, National Catholic Welfare Conference.

The support and promotion of the girl and boy scout movement was also a concern of my agency. The direction of the scout movement came from the Rev. Josef Jarzebowski and from scout leaders in the Colonia, but help was needed in the supplying of uniforms, in the necessities for field trips, in early contacts with Mexican scout and youth groups. In a few short weeks, the bedraggled scout brigades were supplied with the official scout uniform, complete in every detail, even to the tie in the red and white national colors of Poland.

Fr. Jarzebowski was proud of the scouting program, and was soon accepting invitations for his well-drilled troops to participate in festive events of the Mexican community. The Colonia was given an atmosphere of formality by the incessant formations and spare-time marching in the new uniforms. On the arrival of any important visitor in the Colonia, the scouts would squirm into the new grey uniforms, and, excused from classes, would frantically present themselves in parade-ground order in front of the granary. Scouts often staged plays and entertainments for visitors and for festivals in the Colonia.

For the very young orphaned and unaccompanied children, there were soon regular dance rehearsals in polkas, mazurkas and krakowiaks. With materials supplied by my agency, needlewomen in the camp made colorful national costumes. Everything had to be perfect, even to the colors of the ribbon streamers and the embroidered designs on the jackets of the little boys. The sight of the streaming red, white and yellow ribbons flying in the abandon of their dance was unforgettable, as was the pleasure the little ones took in public appearances. Each month showed differences in their health and in the resilience of their bodies and spirits. Each time the children danced, or put on a little play, the camp went wild with applause. The aplomb of the children on the stage was impressive. They announced their own numbers and seemed to run their own performances. Though I was gaining a little in catching the drift of Polish sentences, I missed the point of a dedication one evening, and clapped enthusiastically and long, after a child had made what I later discovered was a flowery dedication to me and the work of the agency.

For the frailest of the orphans, Wladka, aged eight, we could do nothing but bring dolls to her cot. Tuberculosis of the bone was so far advanced that she was moved to a little room of her own. Her room had no window, but through the open door the sun shone on her ashen, wizened little face. The three months in which the other children were busily moving backward to regain their childhood, Wladka spent in slow dying. Hers was the first death during my stay at the Colonia.

A great need among the exiles was for vocational and pre-vocational training. Using talents in the Colonia and the skills and resources of the Mexican community, courses were given in tailoring, dressmaking, and mechanical dentistry. The latter course was under the direction of Canon Leonard Kaszynski. As Mexican silver was plentiful and amazingly cheap, an unusual course of training in silver work under a gifted Mexican craftsmen was offered to the enthusiastic Poles.

After I had left the Colonia, the two Polish-speaking social workers who carried out the program for Catholic Relief Services—NCWC enlarged the vocational training to include courses in printing and beauty culture in enterprises of the town of León. Many of the graduates of these practical courses found employment in their fields in Mexico and later in the United States.

As it was almost impossible for the older members of the Colonia to see the films playing in León, I recommended that a dark warehouse building be converted into a theater. While this plan was being put into effect, I flew to Mexico City and contracted to purchase a used film projector.

Great interest developed in sports of all types, and before the Colonia Santa Rosa ceased to exist as a camp, it counted a cemented swimming hole among its attractions. The two social workers of my agency identified themselves with the Colonia and stayed to the bitter end of the camp's existence. As the numbers thinned out and the need for programming became less, they concentrated more on the problems of processing individuals and families for migration to the United States.

The heaviest burdens of the emerging camp organization fell in the first eight months on the young woman who represented the organization which, on the American side, formed the seed for UNRRA. She was Irene Dalgiewicz who was on loan from the Catholic Charities organization in New York to OFRRO, the Office for Foreign Relief and Rehabilitation Operations. Besides meeting the problems of general camp organization that came up every day, she made it a policy to pay individual attention to everyone who approached her. Hers was the ear that everyone wanted to monopolize, the shoulder that everyone wanted to weep on. At times she served as the focus for the resentment that had to be camouflaged during the days of deportation in the Soviet Union. But whether the subject was of warm attention, or of curses whose edges were sharpened in Russia, Miss Dalgiewicz was always the unhurried counselor.

"Listening is a therapy to them," she would say, "I cannot give them any of the things they want, but hearing them out is sometimes the only therapy I can make available to them. I see it as a corrective for the impersonal cruelty they have known in the past years. They have been part of an anonymous mass in the Soviet Union, thrust about and never listened to, much less consulted. That is over."

As she walked across a patio, she would be besieged by one after another of the residents for a conversation that was hard to break off. "Panna Dalgiewiczowna" was the call from every patio doorway and from behind every post and bush when they wanted to waylay her. She often took an hour to go from her office to the Molino where we had lunch. When she emerged from the building, there were always a few persons standing in wait to ask for advice, for more clothing, for better living quarters, for help in domestic problems, or possibly just to make their presence known to her. Very shortly, Miss Dalgiewicz knew the individual residents of the Colonia in depth. She bore their burdens with them, and showed by inexhaustible patience and attention that each individual being was important to her, and to the scheme of things in general. She was knowledgeable and realistic about the Polish character, because she had worked as a social worker in the Warsaw slums for three years after finishing her training in the United States. When the camp drunk, a red-faced lady of unutterable blowsy dignity, whom we called Madame K., would bring her a bouquet of lovely cultivated flowers, she would remark: "I wonder how much this will cost me. Madame K. has been raiding someone's garden." When the owner of the garden would present himself at the camp office to make a formal complaint, she would be ready with mollifying words and market prices.

One day she had to deal with urgent labor problems. That was the day the kitchen and general camp workers ran up the flag of a general strike. They tried to get all the workers in the camp to join because their wages were so out of line with what they had been told were American pay scales. In the Soviet Union they had been used on the collective farms as cheap labor, and they feared to be exploited again. The letters of American relatives told them what American workers were getting paid during World War II. The Poles were drawing only a pittance from American funds to cook, to clean, to tend the hospital in the camp; was it not the exploitation of cheap labor to allow them almost nothing for a full day's work? The strike was called off after a general meeting with much oratory all around.

In the evenings, we would sit in the Hotel Mexico, or walk

around the plaza of the town of León, and we would talk over the problems of our Colonia people. Irene Dalgiewicz would interpret to me many things that were strange and far from my experience.

As I learned a few Polish phrases, and came to know the people in the Colonia, I would greet them with "Dobry wieczor, Pani (or Panu) jak sie Pani czuje?" "Good evening, how are you?" For a few phrases after that I could carry on—but almost inevitably, I would be pigeonholed to hear a story that would start in Wilno and end in Mexico. At various times I would try to interrupt with a simple "Ja nie rozumie"—"I don't understand." Sometimes it wasn't possible to halt the flood of words until it was over, and I did not have the heart to mouth the anticlimactical remark—one could only say "Tak, tak, bardzo dziekuje," and add "Panna Dalgiewiczowna is doing everything possible." A suggestion that covered the situation was for me to say right off "Dobry wieczor, Pani, jak sie Pani miewa, ja nic nie rozumie"—"Good day and how are you. I don't understand anything at all."

There was one man who refused work of any kind because of his "important writing." The literary output of this disturbed person consisted of letters, generally of horrendous and precisely detailed complaints to every official U.S. address he could find. When asked to join in some work project in camp, he would shake his head, point to the papers he always carried, and intone "Moje Pisma." Naturally he was christened "Pizarz" by the camp residents. During his creative career, he caused Camp Director Szmejko and other camp counselors many difficult hours of explanation and refutation.

*   *   *

One day, two heavy-set women from Chicago registered at the "Aristocrático Hotel Méjico." One was past middle age, the other in her forties. Their faces were smooth, with clear baby-like skin, bare of any trace of make-up. They were dressed exactly alike in black crepe dresses of uncertain style, identical ropes of cheap pearls, and black reefered sport coats. Black shiny straw hats stood on their tightly curled hair like helmets. Their movements were circumspect, and they looked to neither right nor left as they made their way through the hotel lobby to their rooms.

They were nuns, who in order to visit Colonia Santa Rosa bowed to Mexican regulations that no religious garb was to be worn in public in the republic of Mexico. "The conversion of manners" that nuns used to assume along with their religious habits set a seal, a definite mark, on the two women. Their careful gaze, mindful of the custody of the eyes, the way they sat and rose and arranged their garments, seemed to surround them with a palpable aura, an aura that was a substitute for the enveloping veils they had laid aside.

One of the women, we learned, was the mother superior of a large Chicago convent of the Felician Sisters, an order of nuns founded in Poland, and devoted to teaching. Mother Jolanta's visit to Mexico marked the first time in thirty years that she had put aside the veil. She had received a request from Camp Director Szmejko for a corps of teaching nuns and wished to survey the educational needs of the children of the Colonia. She saw the children concentrating on their teachers' every word, and absorbing knowledge without textbooks, notebooks, desks or classrooms. In the open patios, they continued to write laboriously on slates while squatting on the ground, so lost in the luxury of being school children again that the songs of birds or the stares of visitors did not reach them. Nuns were requested, not only as teachers, but as directors for the institution for orphans and unaccompanied children. Mother Jolanta studied the plight of these nearly four hundred children. The statistics told her the monstrous tale; eighty-seven of them were orphaned during the deportation; one-hundred and thirty of them had suffered the loss of a father, and one-hundred and sixty-two of a mother, in flight. Of the remainder, eighty-nine of them knew that their mothers were still in exile within the Soviet Union and twenty-six of them knew then that their fathers were still alive but still detained. A few had fathers serving in the Polish Army.

Though the living accommodations for the nuns would be minimal, and though they would have to abide by Mexican law in the matter or religious habits, Mother Jolanta decided to send seven of her young nuns to Colonia Santa Rosa.

The energetic young nuns arrived, looking like tintypes of the grade school teacher of the 1920s in neat dark dresses with old-fashioned white collars and cuffs. As Americans of Polish descent, they were fluent in the Polish language and started their teaching and child-care tasks immediately. They concentrated unwavering attention on the unaccompanied children, and superintended the move from the large warehouse to dormitories when a special children's home was constructed on the Colonia grounds.

The institution, named for General Wladyslaw Sikorski, was built around four interior patios after the Mexican style. The militaristic discipline over the children fell away after the arrival of the sisters. These patios gave a sense of rootedness to children whose roots had been torn away. The all-embracing love and care of the sisters from Chicago gave a firm and sheltering sky to children whose skies had become a meaningless kaleidoscope of dread.

The sisters' contribution was crucial in the general scheme of Colonia Santa Rosa. Overall plans were worked out under the direction of the delegate of the ministry of education of the Polish government-in-exile, Professor Feliks Sobota. A full high school course, as well as the grammar school was inaugurated. The sisters donated their educational experience to all levels of the educational establishment of Colonia Santa Rosa.

6. The Chill Wind of Katyn

Among the stream of visitors to Colonia Santa Rosa was one whose conversation brought a chill wind, a dread reminder of the Soviet power of life and death, into the mild air of the Colonia. The visitor was Emmanuel Freyd, a special delegate of the Polish government-in-exile in London. He had been the counselor of the Polish embassy that was opened in the Soviet Union in August 1941. He had served in that capacity through 1942 and part of 1943 when, due to Nazi advances, the government offices of the Soviet Union had been removed from Moscow to the city of Samara, renamed Kuibyshev.

Freyd was a dark vigorous man, a vivid raconteur in a small group, and an arresting speaker before the Colonia residents. By conviction he belonged to the humanistic socialist tradition of Europe's intellectuals. Freyd had suffered through that grim period when the embassy's efforts were turned to the locating of Polish deportees and prisoners of war within Russia so that they could take advantage of the amnesty appended to the Polish-Soviet agreement of July 1941. During late 1941 and 1942 the Polish ambassador and his staff had engaged in endlessly repeated conferences with Russian officials concerning the location of the deported and prisoner groups. Steps were then taken so that the groups could be notified of their new status and of the possibilities of rejoining their compatriots.

As part of the gigantic effort to locate, advise, and help the deportees in their far-flung places of exile, the Polish embassy set up close to eight hundred contact centers. Manned often by the least exhausted of the deportees, the centers turned to whatever task was most needed—care for orphans and children separated from their parents, temporary clinics for the diseased and dying, feeding stations for the famished. In the first months

after the invasion of Soviet territory, the Poles received help in
tracing their co-nationals from the "People's Commissariat of
Internal Affairs," the notorious NKVD. Only through the great
intricate network of the NKVD, charged with deploying the
"enemies of the Soviet State" in slave labor camps, could the
Polish embassy and military officials reach the scattered groups
of Poles and help them into their restored freedom. Despite the
turmoil of a Russia at war, thousands of tons of clothing, foods
and medical supplies were given out through the hastily assembled network of information and emergency aid centers.

One group of Poles became of particular concern to the staff
of the Polish embassy because every time it was raised in conference, a wall of silence was erected by the Soviets. The group
being sought comprised about fifteen thousand Polish intellectuals and officers, nearly five thousand of them senior military
officers. They had been taken prisoner by the Red Army after
its invasion of eastern Poland, following the Nazi invasion from
the west. More and more groups of Poles were being located,
and arrangements were being discussed for the formation of a
Polish Army on Russian soil. It was the moment to bring the
army officers into the plans, Freyd explained. How could an
army be put in the field without senior officers, as well as
reserve officers, lawyers, judges, and all manner of professional
men who had assumed officer and non-commissioned officer
status in the military call-up before the 1939 invasion?

Among the mission group were the flower of the intellectual
life of Poland, Freyd pointed out. A number of them were
Polish officers of Jewish origin.

So ominous and total was the silence regarding the Polish
officers in Soviet custody that Freyd and the Polish embassy
staff began to concentrate on that issue. Freyd recalled that he
made it his business to pay a daily call on the Soviet Ministry to
ask for news of the Polish officer prisoners. News was coming
through on the release of large numbers of captured Polish soldiers. At one time, the Soviets had claimed the capture of more
than one hundred thousand Polish troops and over ten thousand officers and non-commissioned officers.

Facts were being gathered on the men in slave labor camps

(lagiers) in prisons, or in "free exile" from the Arctic taiga to the Republic of Uzbekistan, from Arkhangelsk to Alma Ata. As Hitler's forces were penetrating deep into the soil of Russia, the additional battalions of Poles would be important in defense. Polish officers would be able to weld the available Polish manpower into a disciplined corps. Word had darted like the unquenchable "spark among the reeds" that Polish volunteers could join Polish divisions to face the common enemy. Men almost blinded from close confinement, bloated from weakness and hunger, exhausted by disease, gathered at recruiting centers to form into fighting groups.

Nowhere among them, however, appeared any of the missing officers. Soviet authorities kept insisting that all Polish war prisoners had been released.

Wild theories and rumors grew up regarding them, Freyd told us, the least alarming of which was that the men, potential resisters to Soviet ideology by reason of intellectual attainments, had been shipped to remote camps in Siberia. On one of his daily calls, Freyd recounted, the conversation with Soviet officialdom struck a land mine. A Soviet spokesman, having heard the Polish request on the missing officers countless times, blurted out, "A mistake was made in that matter."

As though an explosion had rent the air, he looked aghast, and then lapsed into his usual glacial silence. There was no elaboration, and no one in Soviet officialdom ever repeated the word "mistake."

That one word, inadvertently dropped, was all that Emmanuel Freyd received for all his probing. He told us, as we drank tequilas together in the warm Mexican evening, that he feared the worst, that they were no longer in the land of the living. We shivered as he talked. He had left the Colonia when the bodies of Polish Army officers and reserve officers were produced and the extent of the Soviet "mistake" was made known to the world. German armies, sweeping in a wave of death over the countryside of eastern Europe, uncovered mass graves of Polish officers, still in their uniforms, in the lonely Katyn forest.

Amid Soviet denials of guilt and counter-charges that the Germans themselves had perpetrated the massacre, German science came forward to prove that the "mistake" had been committed during the Soviet occupation of eastern Poland.

A book of horror was published by a Nazi information service containing hundreds of photographs of the Poles as they were exhumed from the soil of the forest. Because of my contacts with Polish refugees, a copy fell into my hands of the almost unbearably gruesome record. I forced myself to study the tragic reality of those moldering bodies. The skeletonized hands of each man were tied by ropes behind his back. Each man had been executed by a shot through the back of the head. The shoulders of the officers' overcoats, which were their shrouds, bore the epaulettes and marks of their ranks.

Through a neutral capital, the expensively printed and documented annals of death reached members of the Polish government-in-exile. They in turn saw to it that the witness of the Soviet Union's lethal intentions toward Poles and Poland was shared with the western allies. In particular, a piece of scientific evidence was stressed. Alongside the photographs of corpses, there were a large number of photographs of saplings and trees. The growth rings gave proof that they had grown in the undisturbed forest soil since the spring of 1940, the spring of the Soviet occupation. The date of the liquidation was proved beyond any doubt.

* * *

After January 16, 1943, the August 1941 "amnesty" of the Peoples' Commissars of the Soviet Union, which allowed Polish citizens freedom of movement, including departure from the Soviet Union, was revoked by a dread decree. From that date forward, all persons were to be considered citizens of the Soviet Union if they had been residing within the borders of the Soviet Union as of November 1, 1939. The borders of the Soviet Union were to be considered co-terminous with the eastern Polish provinces occupied in the Nazi-Soviet pact. The deported Poles were now doubly bereft. They were not only exiles from their home places and deprived of their own citizenship, but their home places were to become Soviet territory. The Allies, involved in the prosecution of the war were unable to obtain clarification of such issues.

In the meantime, the Polish Army recruiting headquarters had been moved to Tashkent. The lack of a sufficient officer corps, and the formidable and seemingly senseless roadblocks erected by the Soviet leaders to the formation of any Polish fighting force, counseled a wholesale evacuation of Soviet territory. Insufficient rations were allotted by Soviet order to the emaciated bands of men ready to defend not only Poland but the country that reduced them to physical ruin. In the end, the camps were broken up, and during the spring of 1942 transports crossed the Caspian Sea and disgorged at Pahlevi, in Iran. The tattered, typhus-ridden battalions conserved only one thing—the spirit to continue the struggle. While the British military establishment absorbed the men, and also the active women and even young boys, into various army units, the aged, the incapacitated, the women with young children and the orphans and unaccompanied children had to be sheltered in any available corner of the world. And so they went to the Middle East, India, Africa, New Zealand, even as far away as Mexico, spreading out as a "cloud of witnesses" to the truth regarding conditions within the Soviet Union. As the members of the first mass exodus from the Soviet Union—an exodus that represented an entire cross-section of the society of an ancient European nation—they spoke not only for themselves but for the fifteen million or more human beings still held in free exile, lagiers, or prisons. They received scant hearing. But no one could accuse them of not trying to tell the world some unpleasant truths before it was too late.

Even while engaged in the fighting that took them yard by yard up the Italian peninsula, Polish Army members compiled listings of the location of Soviet slave labor camps and numbers of inmates.

The Polish Army Corps, all victims of Soviet deportation, felt great impulsion to tell the world their unique aspect of political truth while the atmosphere was still molten with raging battles, and before anything should begin to harden into a peacetime mold. Their impulsion was also based on the very real possibility of their suddenly being silenced forever, in fact of their not surviving the Italian campaign. And so it was from among these men—each represented by a small cross—that the great cruciform memorial cemetery grew on the hill facing the destroyed Abbey of Monte Casino.

It was not only blood that the Poles had given to the Allied cause. The survivors of the Polish Army Corps, who had become exiles all over the world, learned of another crucial Polish donation to the Allied struggle in the Second World War. Nearly three decades after the end of the war, they and their children, in Scotland, Australia, Canada, Latin America and the United States, became aware that it was the genius of Polish mathematicians, working secretly in the forest of Pyry outside Warsaw, which achieved the breakthrough to the code and code signaling system of the German general staff and diplomatic corps. An accepted version of a complicated story tells how mathematicians of the Polish Cipher Bureau were aided by a rough model of "Enigma," the cipher signaling machine. There was also a contribution by French intelligence. Less than six weeks before September 3, 1939, the outbreak of World War II, the Polish mathematicians presented a gift of immeasurable value to the British and French. To each it was a working model of "Enigma."

In possession of the code and the mechanical cipher signaling machine, the British, for example, could receive and decode battle orders and flight plans during the Battle of Britain. The prior knowledge of German bombing targets allowed the Royal Air Force to blunt the attacks and prevent the expected German invasion.

The possession of "Enigma" and the German code, referred to as "Ultra" in intelligence circles, was only revealed in books published in the 1970s. The Polish contribution remained unknown to the masses of Poles and to the world until then. Yet the breakthrough by the Poles was termed "one of the great cipher solutions of history" by David Kahn, the author of *The Code-Breakers*. Kahn called it "the greatest secret of World War II after the atom bomb." The Poles could feel the satisfaction of having saved others. Themselves they could not save.

7. Types of Exile

Certain faces rose up for us from the picture of mass exile that was before our eyes every day.

One of the warmest and most brilliant personalities among the deportees was a former professor who had experienced all three types of punitive exile in the Soviet Union, "free exile" on a collective farm, servitude in a penal colony, and actual incarceration behind prison walls. Mrs. Czeslawa Prywer, former professor of psychology and researcher in cytology at the University of Warsaw, was a heavy-set woman with short-cropped, greying hair. No matter what injustice or anguish she was recounting, she never displayed any rancor. A gentleness of manner and a certain compassion in her deep brown eyes were constant. The roots of this outlook grew from deep convictions of ethical humanism and a profound tolerance of human shortcomings.

We often had lunch together in the Molino as she recounted her story. "I was taken into custody by the NKVD in February 1940," she told me in fluent English. "I considered it to be a mistake because I had always been a person of what we call 'advanced social views.' In fact, I would have been classed as a 'leftist' if I had taken any part in politics. I had never spoken against the Soviet Union. I was too conscious of the shortcomings of Poland's social system."

"On what charge were you picked up?" I wanted to know.

"As a counter-revolutionary, just in general terms. There were no specific charges against me. I was thunderstruck. When I was arrested I had been homeless for five months. My apartment had been destroyed in the bombing of Warsaw in September 1939, and I had been living with friends."

It later developed that leftist Poles, especially socialists, had been marked for incarceration by the NKVD or secret police.

From February to the following October, Mrs. Prywer was held
with hundreds of other women in the prison of Oszmiana. "We
were nearly five hundred Polish women in a fetid hall. Our daily
bread was literally a pound of bread, plus some barley or oats
and a small amount of rancid fat. The cold food was handed to
us twice a day. Only in the morning did we get anything that
was not cold—warm tea with a little sugar in it. How we looked
forward to that! In all that time, I never got a message to any of
my family or friends, and heard nothing from anyone. In
October I became an inmate of a monastery thirty miles within
the Russian border. It was the Polock Monastery Prison. After a
few weeks I was again shipped out as a prisoner, first to Moscow
and then from Moscow to Kuibyshev. Up to Kuibyshev, the trip
had been by train, but now I was transferred to a prison truck
without windows.

"I didn't know where or why I was driven in this wagon
across the country. First the most terrible thoughts go through
your mind, and then you become numb. You know you are not
guilty of anything, yet you feel guilty and degraded—you could
let people dispose of you almost as they wish.

"Finally the prison truck stopped and I found out that I was
in the rail junction of Syzran. Then I knew why they had
brought me and the other women. A train filled with Polish
deportees was at the junction and we were thrust inside. You
know how those trains were—the ones that took masses of people to Siberia. They had doors that opened only in the center,
like cattle cars. It was in those that we traveled across Europe
and Asia, beyond the Ural Mountains to Novosibirsk."

From dozens of people I had learned of those classic journeys
to Siberia or Asiatic Russia, in the wooden boxcars that were like
great rattling coffins for the people locked inside them. As far
as any contact with the world through which they passed, the
Poles might as well have been already dead. Journeys lasted from
several days to two and even three weeks. Always at journey's
end, corpses as well as living deportees were carried from the
trains. At station stops en route, Red Army men delivered gruel
or bread, and buckets of water or soup, car by car. Consumed by
thirst between station stops, the deportees tried to act like

human beings, struggling against the urge to drink their urine like the chimpanzees at the zoo. They fought against the growing urge to edge the older and weaker people away from the air space high in the car, and to relieve their bodily needs where they happened to be rather than push their way to the toilet-hole set into the floor. In the end, nearly all feeling and inhibition fell away except that of keeping in life that which was not already dead. As day followed day, and sometimes stretched into weeks, the pressure of stenchful bodies, the retching and delirium of the sick pushed even human grief and terror into the background of the mind. The terror of what awaited them at the end of the line was lost in the frenzied desire to reach some destination. Mrs. Prywer's destination was western Siberia.

"At Novosibirsk, we were sorted out and deployed like battalions of serfs. I was transferred to a place sixty miles from Novosibirsk. The whole area around was occupied by lagiers, real penal colonies. It was very well organized, with the smaller Kolonja directed by the central lagier. We would see formations of men led to the mines. At night the lines of men would crawl back through the snow like armies of tired caterpillars. After a while I noticed that in these squads of miners were large numbers of men from Kazakhstan and Uzbekistan.

"I did not have contact with them, but they seemed to suffer very much from the climate. Later on, when my exile took me to those places, I knew why they did not survive long around Novosibirsk.

"But then I got the surprise of my life, next to being arrested in the first place. I was assigned to a scientific laboratory and I found myself participating in a real intellectual life. My companions were doctors, writers and scientists. They were political prisoners. You know, those scientists were still producing papers in their fields. From time to time, these papers were being published, but of course there was no mention that the authors were in a lagier. One man there was known for his cellular research. His work was already known to me in Warsaw, but I had never suspected that he was not a free man."

When, at a later date, I read that the Soviet delegation to the Ninth International Botanical Congress reported that tropical plants had been successfully grown in Siberia, I thought of Mrs. Prywer. The announcement was greeted by the other scientists gathered at Montreal, Canada, with considerable surprise. It was pointed out that such a successful experiment could "pave the way for extensive colonization of the Canadian sub-arctic areas." No one mentioned the manner in which the scientists had been transported to the sub-arctic regions of the Soviet Union. And no one inquired whether the experiments had been performed by enslaved or free persons.

Mrs. Prywer gave me some details.

"Living and working in the laboratory in Siberia was like being hidden from the world in a cave. One of my real friends in those strange days was a Soviet woman writer. She was of Jewish origin, as I am, and her freedom had been taken away for writing one article which displeased the authorities. At the same time, her husband was ordered to join a scientific expedition bound for Sakhalin. They had one daughter, a seventeen year old, and she was left completely alone.

"Yes, we had good meals, even meat. And we were warm, but all of us were eaten away inside, like this mother pulled away from her daughter. She was thinking all the time about her and about her husband. We all knew what was behind our eyes. I shall never forget how good the Russian prisoners were to me, a Pole. They knew that besides suffering for the few members of my family that were left, I felt a load of guilt. I knew what was happening to the other Poles, to the children.

"There were many writers in our lagier—really a concentration camp for intellectuals. Quite a few were not Russian at all. A German Jewish columnist who had expected to find refuge in the Soviet Union was sent to this remote camp. It was so strange to feel that as human beings we were prisoners, but that our work, after it was screened, could be free. It could go out into circulation through being published. We felt very close and united, like a team against the world."

Czeslawa Prywer's incredible revelations about the islands of creative work in the heart of the slave labor empire received dramatic confirmation thirty years later with the publication of *The Gulag Archipelago*. Alexandr Solzhenitsyn also landed in one of these islands. It happened because he was thought to be a scientist. It was 1946 and Soviet concern with the atom bomb was overriding. On his Gulag registration card he had written after *Trade or Profession* the words "Nuclear Physicist." He was not a physicist at all, and he had inserted these words in the belief that it would not matter what he put down since no one would look at the card. Those two words meant his survival.

About these islands, Solzhenitsyn wrote, "There was a vague unverified legend, unconfirmed by anybody, that you might nevertheless hear in camps: that somewhere in this archipelago were tiny *paradise islands*. No one had seen them. No one had been there. Whoever had, kept silent about them and never let on. On these islands, they said, flowed rivers of milk and honey, and eggs and sour cream were the least they fed you; things were neat and clean, they said, and it was always warm, and the only work was mental work—and all of it was supersecret.

"And so it was that I got to those paradise islands myself (in convict lingo they are called 'sharashkas') and spent half my sentence in them."

Solzhenitsyn's experience in the paradise islands formed the factual basis for his fictional account entitled *The First Circle*. The title was an echo of Dante's first circle of hell. There the inmates, the wise men of ancient times, had a sort of paradisiac existence, but they were definitely enclosed within the gates of hell. The author also used the details of ordinary camp life for the novel *A Day in the Life of Ivan Denisovich*.

Czeslawa Prywer's life in the hidden laboratory of paradise island was interrupted suddenly.

"One day," she related, "I was called by the camp director and he told me that I was a free woman. A hundred rubles and a third-class railway ticket were waiting for me. I said goodbye to my friends and took on the life of the Russian railways. Maybe I should call it the life of the railway stations.

"The 'amnesty,' as we called it, was obeyed to the letter in some camps, but in others not at all. The Poles who were freed started a great trek and I was part of it.

"The Russian railway stations—they were our inns, our information centers, our hospitals. We gathered and asked for the latest word about the Polish Army and about our families and friends. We exchanged pieces of clothing with each other. Sometimes we stayed over a couple of days until we gathered enough strength to go further. Sleeping on benches or on the floor did not seem strange to us. We left notes attached to the walls in case anyone we knew should be coming through. We picked up children who had lost their parents.

"By the time I was free, the trek was on to Tashkent, to draw near the Polish Army. Many of us would never have reached there except for the kindness of the Russian civilians. We had become used to the NKVD and to the Red Army on our first journey. Then we had been placed under officials in the lagiers. These were all part of a brutal system, and they were cold and brutal with us. We were not people to them, I think—just anonymous items they had to dispose of in their duty. But the Russian civilians! We will never forget them. They were poor, but they shared their food with me and with others in these third class carriages. A train came into a station all filled up. A Russian woman got off and gave me her place. She knew I was a Pole, and that I could leave Russia. As I climbed in she leaned over and whispered, 'I wish I could go out, too. God be with you.'

"Finally I arrived in the Uzbek SSR. I had thought I was to be free, but I had to go through another experience of deported Poles. Now it was free exile on a *kolkhoz* near Nukus, the capital of the oblast Karakalpak. One day, an order came that all Poles must assemble in Nukus. We were used to obeying orders now, and we all walked several miles through the mud to reach the town. It was November 1941, and it was cold and windy.

"Nukus is on the Amu Darya River. I never thought I would even see this river, but now I had to travel on it. Four large motor barges were waiting for the Poles, and about three hundred of us were crowded into each one. The only place for us to live and sleep was on the open deck. We sat and lay close to each other, sharing our lice for seven days and nights. It began to rain and we could hardly move at all because we were afraid of sliding off the slimy deck. But it got colder and we just huddled together, waiting for the Russian crew to give us the bread and boiled potatoes that had been loaded below deck.

"There was hope among the simple people. They thought we were leaving Russia. They had heard of Iran and were longing to get there. Oxus was the old name of the river. I knew that the Amu Darya did not go near Iran. I did not tear down the little hope they had.

"'Do Persii,' 'To Iran,' was the cry of these Poles."

We were sitting in the main building of the camp, the Molino, where teachers ate their lunch. I looked out of the paneless window space and saw some old men and kerchiefed women walk by, carrying the midday meal to their billets in white enamel dishes. They walked silently. Perhaps a few of these had clung to the open deck on the voyage along the Amu Darya, the river crossed by the conquerors going east and west—Alexander pushing to the east, Genghis Khan riding triumphantly westward. Under the name of the Oxus, it had given its name to the whole region of Transoxania, the region rich in such centers of culture as Samarkand and Bokhara. I pictured them huddled on the river barges, adding their hoarse old voices to the Polish folk songs and Christmas carols that rose like dirges from the unsheltered decks—bringing the sounds of their homeland to the land of the Uzbeks and Turkmen that stretched along the banks.

As I gazed on the heavy, stolid backs disappearing beyond the palms, I thought of the general longing for Iran that marked their days of Soviet exile. Iran became a name that signified the promised land, the place of deliverance from the house of bondage. Bokhara and Samarkand were to them only cities of death. They might have echoed, if they had ever heard, the famous words of the poet Hafiz, who sang of Shiraz, the old south Iranian capital, "Oh Shiraz, my Beloved, I lay my heart in thy hand/And at thy dear feet I fling Bokhara and Samarkand."

Mrs. Prywer pursued the narrative. "Then came the first deaths, and the barge stopped so that we could quickly cover the bodies with earth a few feet from the banks. The next day there were even more deaths, but the barge would not stop anymore. The bodies were lowered into the icy water, and we went on. Instead of singing together, we wept together."

The barges put in at a town where there was a railway junction. They were taken by train to a large collective farm in the vicinity of Bokhara. After a few weeks, Mrs. Prywer was able to leave the *kolkhoz* to work as a cleaner in a nearby hospital center. An attack of typhus nearly took her life but she recovered and became one of the workers in the Polish children's center at Kagan. Kagan was the new town built a few miles from Old Bokhara, sometimes known as New Bokhara. Here was located the railroad station to serve the old town left to dream in its moldering walls, and molder in its dreams.

"Everything that went before was nothing compared with this," she related, her brown eyes burning with misery. "It was in the early days of 1942, and the wind that came across the steppe was a wind of death. In December, before I arrived, hundreds of children had died and their little graves were all around us. We dragged ourselves from one child to the next, trying to tend the spark of life that was left.

"They had been living on refuse. They had survived the long train journeys and the barge trips, but lice-borne typhus spread from child to child. Their bodies could not fight it. Two, three, or more died every day. The smell of death was around us. There were no coffins for them, just the bare earth.

"The ones who did survive only did so because by that time food and medicines reached Kagan from British stocks in India, and even from Australia. At last, I was given charge of one hundred of the surviving children, and I led them into Iran and from Iran into India where I could turn them over to the director of the Polish Red Cross. And from India, you know our story."

Sitting with us that day at lunch was a teacher, always silent about her own experiences. Mrs. Zofia Orlowska was still a young woman, with features of cleanly sculptured loveliness. Her brown hair was pulled back in a classic knot. Her mouth was drawn in a tight line of sorrow, and her grey eyes were alert with a terrible watchfulness. Her engineer husband and her little girl, the younger of two children, had died during the deportation. She once showed me a tiny religious medal of gold—the only possession she had saved of her lost child. Now before her eyes, the only living member of her family, her ten-year-old son, Witek, was wasting away. No medical aid or medicines seemed to help. His thin face, yellow, and drawn from continual quinine dosage, became more and more mask-like. The anguished concern for Witek that showed in her glance proved to be tragically justified. A few months afterward, Witek died, victim of a slight wound from which a stronger child would have recovered.

Mrs. Prywer, in addition to her teaching schedule at the Colonia high school, made contacts with scientific activities in Mexico. We visited together a hybrid corn experimental center not far from the town of León. She did not join the migration to the United States when the Colonia high school was disbanded. The Mexican government offered her a post as professor and research worker in an institute of agronomy, and she decided to settle in Mexico where she could be free both as a person and as a scientist. Her witness to three different types of punitive exile made her unusual even in the society of Colonia Santa Rosa.

That Czeslawa Prywer, of Polish-Jewish origin, did not exaggerate the repression of intellectuals and the dread crimes of the Stalinist period was confirmed when the victimized Russians themselves were able to make known their experiences to the world. Not only Solzhenitsyn, whose strong and seemingly rigid opinions irritated many, but objective scientists like André Sakharov, who helped develop the nuclear bomb for Russia, joined in condemning Stalin and his heirs for their war on intellectual freedom and human rights. Roy A. Medvedev's *Let History Judge*, an intellectual's chronicle of the evils of Stalinism and the system that followed it, was probably the account most widely accepted by his fellow intellectuals overseas.

After reading Medvedev's sustained indictment, Harrison E. Salisbury, who had written extensively on the Soviet Union, commented:

> I put down Roy A. Medvedev's book with the same feeling of glazed horror that comes when reading of a tidal wave in West Bengal, an earthquake in Turkey or a cholera epidemic in pre-Communist China. Stalin's terrible impact on the world, specifically the world of Russia but spreading far beyond its borders to touch almost every human being in one way or another, is so monumental, so epic in its evil that even now, nearly two decades after his melodramatic

death, we find ourselves like archeologists on site still trying to trace out its colossal dimensions.

The experiences recounted by Czeslawa Prywer and the other victims in Colonia Santa Rosa were among the first on-site tracings of the dimensions of this evil to be contributed to public knowledge.

8. Death in Central Asia

"Social origin" was an important factor in the deportation schemes engineered under the Stalinist regime. Though whole villages of foresters and peasants of eastern Poland were thrust into deportation trains, there was a more individualized round-up of the capitalist and land-owning groups.

One of the residents of the Colonia Santa Rosa was a countess, a descendent of the noble Polish families that included Zamoyskis, Lubeckis and other names going back over a thousand years. Teresa has been part of the great deportation of June 1941 from Wilno along with her husband, the count, and their four children. She still had the gray squirrel fur coat she had snatched before boarding the deportation train in Poland. She had managed to keep it through forced labor in Uzbekistan, the march to the safety of Iran and the long bus journey from Iran to Karachi.

It was often the few possessions caught up frantically in the hour before boarding the truck or train for deportation that saved lives later on. Each deportee was allowed a package of personal possessions. Parents thrust on their children such items as medicines, cooking pots, family papers and photographs, pillows, cushions, shoes, every conceivable garment. Some of the families in Colonia Santa Rosa displayed to me small filthied cushions that they had taken from their home the night they were ordered into exile.

The Wilno family of mother and four children each carried a package, as well as all the layers of warm garments that could be wrapped around their bodies. Though it was early June, the family was ready for the wastes of Siberia. The father of the family, because of his social origin, had been arrested a few months before, but instead of being imprisoned, had been assigned to making bricks. The youngest of the boys, whose ages ranged

69

from twelve to three, thereafter answered any questions relating to "social origin" by stating literally, "Our father is a bricklayer." As the mother and children climbed into the boxcar, they saw the father being led into another car of the same dark green prison train. The rattling cattle cars, instead of taking them to the taiga of Siberia where so many deportees were employed in felling part of the great forests, deposited them in the steppes of central Asia. Others who were taken over this route told me how, as the weather got warmer and the air more fetid, the toilet-hole of the car became the spot that people fought to sleep near at night. Their noses might rub in the filth, but at least they were able to catch some of the air that came up from the dusty roadbed. The walls and roof of the car shed waves of heat over the stifling deportees. Their feet and hands swelled up and their eyes became burning holes in their heads.

It was only at the last stop, when the tide of human misery spewed forth from the prison on wheels, that families were reunited to crawl into waiting trucks for transport to the factories or collective farms for slave labor in so-called "free exile." The terrible irony of the fate of the lost battalion of deportees was that by the time they had been assigned to their slave labor tasks, the Soviet Union had been attacked by Hitler's forces and moves were afoot to make Poland and Russia allies. They were in Uzbekistan, one of the five Socialist Soviet Republics carved by Moscow out of central Asian khanates, emirates and ancient kingdoms. The largest, the Kazakh SSR, or Kazakhstan, bordered on China, and had as its capital Alma-Ata, the fabled "Mother of Apples" of remotest Asia. The town of Karaganda became famous for the number of Europeans who worked at slave labor as part of mine-, road-, and railroad-building gangs. The Uzbek SSR, though its herdsmen and landowners in mud- and dung-covered huts seemed unutterably primitive to the Polish exiles, was in fact one of the oldest civilized regions of the earth. In the fourth century B.C., as the Persian province of Sogdiana, it was conquered by Alexander the Great. Known also as Transoxania because of its location beyond the Oxus River it alternately bowed to and spawned conquerors.

The proud semi-nomadic herdsmen were compelled to give

up their ancestral grazing and water rights and merge into the set pattern of *kolkhoz* life. The Uzbeks, a remnant of the fabulous golden horde of the Mongols, consider themselves the purest descendants of Genghis Khan. They took their tribal name from Uzbeg, Khan of the Golden Horde at the time of its greatest splendor during the fourteenth century. To Uzbek at Sarai on the Volga, the princes of Russia paid fief. The khan's sister became princess of Moscow through marriage to Yuri, grand prince of Muscovy. According to one account, it was on Uzbeg's conversion to Islam that his horde became followers of Mohammed. Though they now acted in dumb obedience to plans and goals formulated in Moscow, the Uzbeks had not only influenced Russian history from Sarai, but had played a fateful role in world history. It was when they swept back from the Volga into Transoxania in the early years of the sixteenth century, that they forced the ruler Babur to flee. Babur led his troops in the capture of Kabul, Afghanistan, and later of Delhi, India and thus became the founder of the Moghul empire.

Side by side with the Muslim Uzbeks worked the Polish family, the mother milking goats, the father making dung bricks for fuel. The few items sold by Teresa, a scarf, a blouse, a cooking pot, a handful of tea, bought precious butter and flour that helped to allay the appetites of the always-hungry children, and helped the father survive the fourteen- to sixteen-hour work day. It was through parting with a few garments that the family was able to rent, or buy—the family was never sure—a passable hut, by local standards. It was the usual twig and mud construction, smoothed over with dung—a general type encountered with slight variation in villages in many parts of Asia. At first cruelly hostile, and anxious to divest the Poles of all their possessions, the Uzbeks began to show a fraternal feeling for the strangers. This happened when they were convinced that the Poles were not spies or minions of Moscow, but rather fellow victims. They would show their seething resentment after any great Russian presented himself by shouting wild curses and by spitting in contempt.

Day by day, the father of the family grew weaker, though he forced himself to work. For the second time, a terrible irony of timing seized the tale of this family. On December 20, 1941, just when the news of the "amnesty" was reaching out to their place of exile, the father died. Again and again in stories told to me at first hand, or related to me by witnesses, it was the bread-winners of the deported families who died first. In this case, the dawn-to-dark working day imposed on a man unused to physical labor, and the usual sacrifice of nourishment to keep hungry children alive, had reduced him to a skeleton even before he collapsed in death.

The eldest boy, then fourteen years old, trundled the body to the edge of the *kolkhoz* where the steppe began, and hollowed out a grave. In it he laid the uncoffined shroudless body of his father. As the boy covered the pitiful frame with icy handfuls of earth, his mother formed the words of a prayer for the dead.

In a few days, the family was free to leave the *kolkhoz*. Getting ready to leave for Tashkent, the goal of all the Poles in the area, Teresa sold a few remaining possessions for food to sustain her four boys on the journey. Suddenly she missed the eldest boy. The wind from the steppe drove before it a sleety rain, and she feared that the boy had become lost, or had fallen ill somewhere. When he reappeared, he did not want to talk about his absence, but finally admitted that he had stolen away to the mound under which his father lay. He wanted to fix the spot in his memory so that after his return to Poland, he would know where to recover the corpse and take it to Poland for Christian burial.

At Tashkent, there was the blessed comfort of contact with the welfare centers of the Polish embassy—but then the trek was on again. The caravan route through Samarkand and Bokhara to Iran was a journey of nearly eight hundred miles. The mother shepherded the fatherless boys to Askhabad, a town in the Turkmen Soviet Socialist Republic close to the borders of Iran. They had crossed the menacing Kara Kum, the steppe of black sands west of Bokhara. It was at Askhabad that Teresa collapsed on the street. She could not rise, and as she felt she was about to die, she consigned her children to a group of Poles carrying on toward Iran. Then she lapsed into unconsciousness. When she came to herself she found herself in a hospital a victim of spotted typhus.

Gradually, she came back to life, and in time she was able to leave her cot and walk about. Her hair had fallen out and her body had become wisp-like. Bald and wasted as she was, she would not remain in Askhabad. With a group of weary stragglers, who helped each other on the way, she succeeded in reaching the far side of the Soviet frontier.

It was to Meshed, Iran's shrine city, that she came. At another time, it might have been of interest to many of the Poles that they were passing the tomb of the fabled Haroun-al-Raschid, but nothing could penetrate the generalized daze of anguish and weakness. She passed through Isfahan, where, less than six hundred years earlier, Tamerlane ordered the massacre of seventy thousand citizens as a warning to other cities. Pyramids of their skulls were piled on top of the city walls. The exposed bones around medieval Isfahan were hardly more numerous than the barely covered skeletons, including that of her husband, that marked the passage of the Poles through Siberia and Central Asia.

In Iran there was help. The Polish ministries, the Polish Red Cross, and Catholic Relief Services had installed personnel and supplies in readiness for the bedraggled caravans. In New York City I once was shown a few feet of film, taken at the moment when a group of Polish deportees stepped from the house of bondage into Iran the land of rescue. They walked with slow, weary steps, across a stretch of desert. It must have been filmed in the summer months. The women were barefoot. Their heads were wrapped in kerchiefs tied at the back of the neck in the manner of women who work in the fields. Some were carrying children and some were holding them by the hand. The barefoot children wore rags of clothing. They looked like little gangs of beggars such as one sees on the streets of refugee-filled Calcutta. One little boy was bare from the waist up, and a black cross stood out sharply against his bony ribs. All of these helpless creatures were gathered for shelter and help.

Through the Polish Red Cross, Teresa learned that her children were no longer in Iran. They had been taken with a children's convoy to India. She herself joined the next convoy of three hundred children which wound its way through a remote landscape. They arrived by bus at Quetta, Baluchistan, then British India, and made their way to Karachi. Like someone resurrected from the dead, she appeared before her children. She was in time to be a part of the transport to Mexico.

9. Polish Postscripts

The Bremen enclave became an American staging area for migrating displaced persons in the British zone of Germany. Camp Tirpitz, a camp for displaced persons, was located so as to be convenient to the port area of Bremerhaven. Crowded into a bare room of the camp were one hundred and forty-nine Polish children, the majority of them between ten and sixteen years of age. They were to sail the next morning for Canada on the army transport *General Stuart Heinzelman*, one of the ships chartered for use by the IRO, the International Refugee Organization.

They had originated in eastern Poland and they might well have been on the same deportation trains as the people of Colonia Santa Rosa. Their most recent home had been an orphan village, one of the many Polish villages in Uganda, Kenya, Tanganyika and the Rhodesias. The driven Poles who had survived the frozen tundra of Siberia now learned to withstand the fiery breath of Africa's winds at the foot of Mount Kilimanjaro, and along the shores of Lake Victoria. The movement was under the auspices of the British Military Command. These villages were formed by the tens of thousands of Poles who had spilled over from their first asylum, Iran, into Palestine and the whole Middle East. CRS had begun in 1943 to organize a network of aid.

As new settlements were set up, the Reverend Aloysius Wycislo, later a bishop, arranged for the setting up of welfare centers similar to the one at Colonia Santa Rosa. He later stationed a Polish-American social worker, Joseph Wnukowski in East Africa to plan programs and distribute agency relief supplies, from recreational and school equipment to cooking utensils.

For the children in Tengeru, Wnukowski ordered musical instruments and equipment for a vocational school. The Polish children's orchestra became a feature of Polish life in Kenya. Boy scout troops marched over the roads and forest paths of what was then Tanganyika as they marched over the Mexican countryside. Other settlements were filled with the incapacitated and convalescent. Some villages, housing the more able-bodied, put up their own little hospitals where the newly-arrived Poles went when struck down by malaria. Medicaments and hospital equipment came through our agency program and from the Polish-American community.

After a year or two, the Poles painted their homes of sun-dried mud in bright Polish colors. At Koja, on Lake Victoria, Tanganyika, they made a replica of a Polish wooden church. The children's village of Tengeru clustered around a church of stone and wood, complete with carvings in the style of the Zakopane mountaineers. Masindi, Tengeru, Kondoa, Kidugala, Ifunda were all African settlements where Polish sounds filled the air and where the dwellings and churches were made to look as much as possible like the villages around Lwow. These settlements faded away after World War II. For six years the young people in Camp Tirpitz had been living in Tengeru, then British east Africa.

The boys and girls from Tengeru had traveled to north Germany by way of Italy, and had been sheltered briefly in an Italian camp—the D.P. Transit camp located in Salerno. For these children, all but five of them complete orphans, the whole world must have seemed a succession of camps. They were a tiny remnant of the same great deportations from eastern Poland to the Soviet Union which had filled the Colonia Santa Rosa. The Soviet Union to them had been a place of camplike existence in the *sovkhozy*, state farms, or *kolkhozy*, collective farms. And now, their last view of Europe was a D.P. camp at the very edge of the Atlantic.

There was no place for the youngsters to sit, so they stood to hear a speech of farewell from a pale, tired woman who had been with them for eight years. Their next move, to Canada, was to be their final one—no more camps, but a beginning of permanent homes. Mrs. Eugenia Grosicka, who was speaking, had helped gather these children together in the towns of central Asia to shepherd them into Iran. She stayed with them for the African years. Through the closely interlocked planning of voluntary societies (Catholic Relief Services and Catholic Immigrant Aid Society of Canada), a governmental organization, the Canadian Immigration Commission, and the intergovernmental agency, the International Refugee Organization, a haven had been arranged in the North American continent. Mrs. Grosicka was telling them goodbye, for now that their future was settled, she was going to England where her son was waiting for her.

The faces of the children were quite composed. Many of them seemed to me undersized for their age, though a surprisingly large number were strong-bodied, healthy teenagers. They were dressed in wearable but rather makeshift clothing, picked up, I supposed, en route at the various camps. Most of the boys wore pieces of grey Polish scout uniforms or of cut-down army khaki. As Mrs. Grosicka went on with her farewell talk, her composure began to leave her. She talked on, trying to enunciate her words calmly, when unexpectedly the tears gushed out and rolled down her tired cheeks.

Suddenly the quiet faces of the youngsters underwent a change and a palpable agony broke through. The room was filled with the sobbing of the girls, not the crying of children, but the racking sobs of grown women.

Standing in the front line was a little girl with a bent back, whose face was so distorted with blazing misery that I turned away. Her name was Bronislawa and she was being separated not only from Mrs. Grosicka, but from the group about to sail. She was one of nine children refused a visa at the last moment because of active tuberculosis. Altogether, the emigration of twenty-six children was in the balance, but it was likely that all but the nine would follow in about a month when technicalities had been resolved.

During Mrs. Grosicka's final words of farewell, words mangled by quick sobs and efforts at control, most of the boys, except for a very few of the smallest ones, stood like men of stone. Not for an instant was their totally unnatural composure shattered by an expression of feeling. Mrs. Grosicka stopped speaking, the tears running unchecked down her tired cheeks.

A Franciscan priest, himself a deportee, who had been a shepherd and healer of the wounds of the children in Africa, knew how to heal the situation. He led the youngsters in a hymn. As it drew to a close, the sobbing of the child exiles subsided.

The next morning, the Franciscan, Fr. Lucjan Krolikowski, O.F.M. Conv., celebrated a special mass for the children. Displaced persons from the whole area learned of it and took part. They came with gifts for the children, pathetic articles of clothing, sweaters, shirts, blouses that they could not really spare.

Before the ship left Bremen, I had a chance to learn more about the individual youngsters.

Bronislawa, whose short body and twisted back made her seem no more than a six year old, was in reality twelve years of age. She and her seventeen year old brother were the sole survivors of a family deported to Siberia. The brother was eager to work and make a home for the little girl in Canada. Then came the rejection for tuberculosis.

Dorothy Sullivan, the social worker of Catholic Relief Services who had conferred in Canada and then had traveled to Salerno to expedite the migration of the children, broke the news to the two children in the office of Camp Tirpitz. She explained that Catholic Relief Services would arrange for Bronislawa to go to Switzerland for a possible cure and that both could remain in Europe if they wished. She talked over all the possibilities with them and answered all their questions. Then she suggested that they talk the matter over and decide what their course would be. The two little people with the weighty decision to make went over to a corner of the office and pondered on their future. Some time later they returned to Miss Sullivan's desk.

"We have talked it over," said Bronislawa. "My brother will go to Canada, and when I am strong I will go after him."

"And," said the big brother, "if I want to come back to Bronislawa here, Canada is a free country and I can always leave."

That was his way of saying that he knew that the little sister might never be cured and he would face up to that eventuality if need be.

Stanislaw, a lad of sixteen, sat and told me the story of his family. His father, an engineer, was arrested in the fall of 1939 by the NKVD in eastern Poland. It was not long before the family was informed of his death. "I was next to the oldest in my family. I had three brothers. They took my mother and all of us and put us into a big railway car with about sixty other people. We were all in the same car about two weeks."

Stanislaw was clear about the accommodations awaiting them in Siberia. "Each family had a stall, not like a room. All of the men and some of the boys like me had to go out into the forest to cut down trees."

After the "amnesty," the family made its way to Bokhara, but the youngest boy died in a box car en route. The second youngest boy died right on the Kagan Station near Bokhara after dragging himself out of the car. Stanislaw and his elder brother were immediately carried off to a Bokhara hospital. Their mother left them there in the evening and promised to come back the next morning. The elder brother died beside him in the bed and Stanislaw waited alone for a mother who never came. Someone informed the sick child that his mother had died.

A similar tale was told by Zofia, a blond girl of sixteen. She was the only survivor of a family of eight. Their place of deportation was near Novosibirsk where the father labored in the forest and the mother gathered mushrooms and any other plant or berry that would help keep the family alive.

One day, the father did not come back from his forest labor. After a search, his body was found frozen into the hard Siberian earth. According to the usual pattern, it was the breadwinner who perished first. One by one the other members of the family died on the journey southward or shortly after arrival. Zofia, a lone emaciated child of eight, was added in Bokhara to the group of orphan children who eventually were taken to east Africa.

Zofia seemed content to go to Canada. She wondered what it was really like. "I have seen films of the United States," she told me. "But they are not true. No country could be like that." "Like what?" I asked, not knowing what films she had seen. "Cars and rich people and singing. That is not real—is it? The people are not like real people." I agreed with her.

Many children remembered very little. Andrew, ten years old, could recall only that in some cold place, he did not know where, his mother had wrapped him in a red blanket. He often talked of his mother and the red blanket—but could remember no other member of his family. That must have been the time that his mother died, since he was picked up and cared for until he could be turned over to the Polish Red Cross.

We stood on the dock at Bremerhaven and waved at the children congregated on the deck of the General Heintzelman. All one hundred and twenty-three of them seemed to be waving goodbye to us and to the continent from which they had started their wanderings. Their shepherd, Fr. Krolikowski, stood with them. Up until the last moment, two members of the Polish Red Cross hovered near the children, still maintaining that they belonged in Poland because of the right of "parens patria," and because if a search were made, relatives could be located within Poland. The Warsaw government had tried in Rome and again in Germany to divert the children from resettlement in Canada. Even though only a rump Poland survived, and the eastern provinces where the children had originated were by then incorporated into the Soviet Union, they still tried incongruously to call into play the right of an officially non-existent homeland over children thrust out of that homeland.

* * *

1960 NEW YORK

Helenka, the ten year old who had escaped with her family from ice-bound Arkhangelsk, wanted to talk about her two-week visit to England. A poised twenty-six-year-old secretary in a New York publishing house, she had taken the trip to visit her brother Rafal.

The oldest brother, Marek, had been killed in the Italian campaign and had been buried in the Polish cemetery in Monte Casino. Her mother who had seemed enduring and resistant as a rock, had literally toppled before her daughter's eyes at the news of the death of her firstborn. She struck and bruised her head.

The disconsolate woman mourned many months and was cared for by Helenka and her younger brother Witold. Rafal had found work in England, but in a few years things seemed to have gone badly for him. His letters ceased coming and his friends wrote that he had gambled away any money he had. All attempts to have him join the family in the United States failed. In the end, all hope of a reunion was shattered when a notice reached them that he was a "certified case" in an English mental asylum.

"The asylum was near Manchester, a sad-looking place," said Helenka. "The doctor let me see him every afternoon. I sat next to him and talked to him. He always sat in the chair in the corner of a big room.

"I would say, 'Rafal, Mamusia sends you her love. She wants to see you.' I tried every way to make him talk. I would mention things about the family, about Arkhangelsk, about Pahlevi, about our father. One day I mentioned Marek, thinking perhaps it would bring him back to life, even if he would cry. Rafal and Marek had been together when Marek was killed.

"But nothing happened. He was like a dead man still living. His mind, how can I say it, was completely gone."

Tears rolled down her face as she spoke, but she went on to finish her story.

"I talked with the doctor. They had given him all sorts of treatment, even many shock treatments. But nothing happened. The doctors could not give us any hope for him.

"On the last day, I said 'Goodbye, Rafal. I am going back to Mamusia.' He did not have any expression in his eyes."

When I visited Helenka in the little flat she shared with her mother in New York's lower east side, I saw the photographs of Marek dead and Rafal dead-to-life looking out from brass frames on a table covered with old-fashioned lace. A vase of blue artificial flowers stood before the photographs.

The mother spoke little English. After greeting me, she sat quietly as though lost in rumination. There were colorful images of the Mother of Jesus and St. Francis on the wall, as well as a large crucifix.

I dared put a question to her. Why, I wondered, did God allow such sufferings as deportations to fall on innocent people?

Helenka translated.

"I don't know. I don't know." She seemed to be talking to herself.

There was a pause.

"Perhaps we were guilty of some things and we had to pay in this way. This is how we suffer—always asking ourselves if we will see our home again. Will we stay here or will we have to move again—people never feeling at home anymore?"

There was a more prolonged pause.

"But God chastises the people whom he loves. He makes those people he loves suffer during their life down here. But God is just in the end."

She got up and turned on the radio. A devotional service in Polish came over the air.

Helenka's grey-green eyes managed a smile. "Mamusia listens to that station every day no matter who is here. The Franciscan Friars give very good sermons in the Polish language."

Wherever they found themselves, the Polish exiles formed a "cloud of witnesses" against the inhumanity of mass deportation and violence. Some found themselves, like Rafal, shut away from the world, too deeply wounded by the ruin of their personal and national lives ever to know healing. Their witness was given by silence. Sometimes, there cannot be a witness whose testimony is more shatteringly loud than that of one like Rafal in a Manchester asylum, who has been rendered mute.

1979 MEXICO CITY

When a Polish-born pope, Pope John Paul II, paid a visit to Mexico in 1979, among his honor guard was a group of Polish-Mexicans.

The survivors of Colonia Santa Rosa and their children were invited to meet Pope John Paul II at the home of the papal nuncio to Mexico. They had kept in touch with each other over the years. This was facilitated by the fact that a little church in Mexico City had been dedicated to the Virgin of Czestochowa, a place of pilgrimage of the Polish people. The newly constructed church had been about to be dedicated to the Virgin of Guadalupe when Cardinal Miranda of Mexico City, who had known the Polish community from the days of their arrival, suggested that since there were so many with that dedication, there could be one church to commemorate the Mother of God under another title.

Among those who helped people board the special buses for the papal ceremony, and who formed a guard of honor for the pope from Poland, were young people holding banners announcing that they were Polish-Mexicans.

1992 KATYN MASSACRE RESOLVED

It was only after the Soviet Union was no more that the mystery of the mass graves in the Katyn forest was resolved with finality. It was the time when the files of the dread Soviet secret police were being opened to the world. What had happened in the spring of 1940 was that Stalin's politburo had specifically ordered the execution of a group that included close to five thousand Polish Army officers. The "supreme punishment," execution by firing squad, was ordered to be carried out by the NKVD. The members of the March 5, 1940, session of the politburo listed for death "14,700 former Polish officers, officials, landowners, policemen and gendarmes held in camps for prisoners of war." In addition, the "supreme punishment" was to be meted out to eleven thousand other Poles in custody, considered subversive because they were government officials, factory owners and clergymen.

A photograph in the *New York Times* showed the chairman of Russia's Archives Commission pointing to the execution order annotated by Stalin.

The document, publicly confirming at last the mass murder of his compatriots, was brought to Warsaw and handed over to Lech Walesa, president of a free Poland.

1993 RETURN TO COLONIA SANTA ROSA

The memory of Colonia Santa Rosa lived on. On July 3, 1993, a mass was celebrated in the chapel of St. Rose of Lima by the bishop of Guanajuato, Bishop Rafael García González. This was the chapel which had been reverently cleaned and restored by the Polish refugees after their arrival. That mass, on a sunny day, was the centerpiece of a reunion of the residents of Colonia Santa Rosa to mark the fiftieth anniversary of their arrival at the haven of refuge.

In the overflow congregation were forty-two Polish-Americans, chiefly from the Chicago area, and eighteen Polish-Mexicans, some from the León area, some from Mexico city.

Also in the congregation were the governor of the state of Guanajuato, the mayor of León, the consul of Poland, and representatives of the embassy of Poland and of various Polish groups and communities, including the Polish communities of Argentina and Uruguay.

Bishop Garcia paid tribute to the people of Poland, citing "their unquenchable faith in the face of dreadful sufferings. A proof of their fidelity is that they could bring to the world Pope John Paul II. We are proud," he continued, addressing the former residents of Santa Rosa, "to have you with us. In the church, there are no strangers."

At the site of the Colonia Santa Rosa, the former refugees were happy to find the Don Bosco Boys Town conducted by the Salesian Fathers. The vast old granary, the Molino, was still in use, now as a school for orphans and needy youngsters. New structures had grown up around the still-standing relic of the old "ejido."

One former resident remarked, "It is not as beautiful now as it was then." Colonia Santa Rosa was a place of happy healing memories for those who had found refuge there.

Concerts, folk dances, films of Poland, speeches and presentations were part of the reunion. All the participants received an image of the Virgin of Czestochowa with the inscription: "Lord, we offer you these fifty years of our lives. Receive them, and bless our two countries, Mexico and Poland."

A leader in organizing the events was Sra. Anna Zarnecka de Santos Burgoa who had served in the clinic of Santa Rosa. A highly-respected citizen of Mexico, and a grandmother, she had published in Spanish a powerful book on her life in Poland and in Siberian exile. In *Poland: Wind and Nightfall*, she described the terror and sufferings of her mother and sister in Siberia and in their wanderings. She alluded to them in an emotional talk to the gathering. The overpowering emotion in her talk, and in the reactions of the former refugees, was, however, that of gratitude to Mexico and to its people. The loving arms held out to them after their wandering over the face of the earth had made an unforgettable impression.

Chester Sawko, a leader of the Polish-American group, a distinguished and well-known citizen of Chicago, had experienced the same anguish as the former Anna Zarnecka and the other residents of Santa Rosa. He arrived in Santa Rosa with his mother, father and two younger brothers in what was known as the "First Transport." Chester was thirteen years of age.

The deportation of his family had begun on February 10, 1940, when three Russian soldiers appeared at their home in the area of Bialystok. The soldiers gave them orders to pack and get ready to leave their home. The parents explained that the eldest son and a young daughter were in the local hospital. The soldiers were adamant. The family had to move immediately. It was winter. With breaking hearts, the Sawko family gathered what they could of their possessions and were herded into horse-drawn sleds. In a journey of two days they reached a train station where cattle cars awaited them. Their ultimate destination was the city of Arkhangelsk.

The father of the family was recruited to chop down trees in icy weather. After three months, the eldest son, Stanley, joined them. He had survived the hospital stay but brought the sad news that the sister, Jadwiga, had died. The Sawko family also lost another child born in Russia.

After the so-called "amnesty" described earlier, Stanley joined the allied war effort as a paratrooper with the Polish Army stationed in Scotland. The rest of the family embarked on the painful trek south. Finally, together with other Polish refugees, they were allowed to leave the Soviet Union. They traveled by boat over the Caspian Sea to Iran. The trajectory then continued with stopovers in India, Australia and New Zealand. After a Pacific crossing, they disembarked at San Diego, California, where they boarded the train for León, and Santa Rosa, Mexico.

In March 1946, the family came to the United States for permanent residence.

Chester Sawko, called to the U.S. Army from his new home in Chicago, served in Korea as platoon sergeant with the combat engineers. With his savings, he founded a manufacturing company producing mechanical springs and metal stampings. He was soon the chief executive officer of a large and important company, enabling him to become a philanthropist, especially as a generous donor to scholarships for needy students. His four children were college graduates, and he himself was the recipient of an honorary doctorate.

Chester Sawko lived up to his reputation for generosity on the grounds of the former Colonia Santa Rosa. After expressing thanks from the depths of his heart to the Mexican people for their generosity, he made a return. To the fathers directing the Don Bosco Boys Town, he presented twenty-five thousand dollars. This would go to Mexican youngsters studying on the site where needy Polish youngsters had resumed their schooling interrupted by exile. A plaque was placed on the wall of the granary.

Joining Chester Sawko in the gift was his wife, Stasia Grodzki Sawko. As a little girl, she had been one of the orphans who had stepped off the train as the midday sun of Mexico beat down on the León railroad station fifty years earlier.

Chapter Two

IBERIAN REFUGE

1. Brands Plucked from the Burning

Spain followed Mexico in the work of Catholic Relief Services for the refugees of World War II. My first stop was the office of "Representation"—Representation in Spain of American Voluntary Agencies. It was a joint operation conducted by the Quakers, the American Jewish Joint Distribution Committee (AJJDC) and Catholic Relief Services. It wasn't long before Catholic Relief Services gave me permission to open an office of our own in Barcelona. I could commute between the two offices. Barcelona in those days was the closest point to "Fortress Europe." The CRS office was in a hotel on the imposing Plaza de Cataluña and was next to the office of the AJJDC. I plunged into their agonies as well as the agonies of others for whom I became, as CRS, a sort of lifeline. Europe's horrors were at their height. Human beings were being thrust into ovens, and others were being destroyed *en masse* as fire descended from the skies in implacable attacks.

People were straggling across the Pyrenees to escape the horror. One escape route was carefully planned, that dealing with child refugees. With the invasion of Europe clearly imminent, an intensified wave of dread passed over a special group whose lives were at risk, the children of Europe's Jews hidden by French families and French child care institutions. When it seemed that even these children might be searched out for destruction, an exodus to Spain was planned and executed.

As I found co-workers among refugees for the CRS office, I learned of the heroic work of the AJJDC next door. It was a highly personalized exodus, I was told, with the children being gathered in small bands to be brought across the mountains by experienced guides. Despite the fact that more secret trails had to be frequented because of the increased danger of detection, the frail line of exodus was maintained. The smaller children had to be carried the entire length of the perilous, often bitterly cold, passageway to safety. Some crossings in the remote mountain heights took five days to a week. Some guides were in the rescue operation for reasons of humanity and others for gold. The latter kept raising their prices higher.

After the children had been shepherded like flocks of helpless lambs into a safe place across the frontier, it was a comparatively simple matter to gather them together in Barcelona.

A roomy old mansion was rented for them on the heights of Barcelona by the AJJDC. I was taken for a visit by an intrepid social worker, Laura Margolis. I admired her composure as she introduced me to the recently rescued children in the various rooms of the great rambling house. Laura herself had not long returned from a series of rescue adventures in Shanghai and Manila.

Among the children we talked with were twin girls, seven years of age. They had auburn wavy hair and liquid brown eyes. I could not help but notice how careful and controlled they were in their conversation with me. The matter of our talk was ordinary. They described the permanent waves they had just acquired, and their new toys. They showed themselves very protective toward a five year old friend. She was a little chatterbox, talking gaily of her Spanish doll, of the trip to the new city, and of how she would tell her mother and father all about it when she got back to France. At this point the twin sisters looked grave but said nothing. Soon the five year old left the room.

The conversation suddenly turned nightmarish. The twins told us in careful, quiet tones that the parents of their little friend had already been deported, and probably were no longer alive. They asked the social worker and myself not to tell the little girl anything because the older children had succeeded in keeping the situation a secret from her. The unspeakable death meted out to deportees seemed to be known to the children from middle Europe as a fact of their everyday living—as burial in the frozen earth seemed to be an ordinary fact to the Polish child exiles.

Then I met Rudi, a five year old, whose parents had been so tracked by the Gestapo that he had been instructed never to give his real name lest it give a clue to their whereabouts, as well as endanger the child himself. Even after he was in Barcelona and under the care of sympathetic protectors, he would only give his assumed name. Weeks went by. Finally, recovering something of a feeling of security, he came to the point of revealing his secret name. The child enunciated it with a terribly knowing smile.

This pitiful band, remnants of families pitilessly hunted, tracked down, subjected to all manner of suffering and consumed by fire, might well have echoed the lament over the children of Israel by the prophet Jeremiah, "Pray for us to the Lord thy God for all this remnant, for we are left but a few of many."

The mansion, perched high over Barcelona, served not only as shelter but as a regular day school. Each classroom became a center of feverish activity for children of Rudi's age and older. When we visited classroom after classroom, the teachers gave us a short greeting, but our presence did not deflect teachers or pupils from concentration on learning. Whatever the subject, algebra, arithmetic, Hebrew, the children gave almost mesmerized attention. Black-haired boys, many pale and gaunt, curly-haired girls, a few sunburnt, several hollow-cheeked, maintained an intensity of gaze as though their eyes were linked with the face of their instructors by invisible steel wire. In their precarious hidden existence, many of these children had been deprived of schooling so as not to reveal their German, Austrian or Polish origin. Even those who had been able to attend school in occupied France found themselves for the first time in a security they had never known.

The teachers were almost all teenagers, or at most in their early twenties. As I got to know them, I found that they were members of the Halutzim, young Zionist Pioneers. One young Halutz taught Hebrew. He was nineteen years of age and he led his class with an authority and verve that I have never forgotten. Whatever he said or did seemed to give vent to a fire banked within.

There were many others like him, forged in their people's holocaust and impelled by that greatest of all crimes against any people. They brooked no obstacle to the "Beth Aliyah," the ingathering of Jewish exiles into Palestine.

During those spring months of 1944, before the European landings by Allied forces on June 6, the stream of child exiles kept flowing into Spain. This stream had a mythic aspect for me; it was part of that continuous endless stream of exiles taking its source in the great diaspora after the destruction of Jerusalem. Starting with the first century of our era, the stream had been flowing through time, compounded of gall, of blood, of unspeakable agonies, and was finally turning in its course. It was being bent inexorably back to the fountainhead, the Holy Land. As I saw them work, I felt that those who were achieving the apocalyptic change of course from streams of exile to a great in-gathering of the waters, were of the type of the Halutzim.

*　*　*

With the children of the Poles, snatched from death by ice, and the children of Jews, snatched from death by fire (whom I saw as "brands plucked from the burning"), I realized anew the great evil of a time which heaps suffering on the innocent and the world of the refugee.

2. Jewish Exiles from 1492

Among the refugee community of Barcelona was another group who had cheated the pyres of the concentration camps. They had been granted the right of entry into Spain during World War II because their ancestors had been part of the expulsion from Spain in the fifteenth century. They were the Sephardic Jews from the area of Salonika.

A considerable Jewish presence had been a feature of the life of Salonika, the Greek Thessalonika, from the time of the great diaspora. The AJJDC put its sheltering arm around them.

The descendants of the Jews from Spain were remarkable for their preservation of medieval Spanish culture and above all for preserving in a marvelous way the Spanish tongue as spoken in the fifteenth century.

If I had ever wondered how it would feel to talk to a person who employed Shakespearian English as his everyday tongue (an impossibility since there are no pockets of British exiles who preserved pristine habits of speech), I at least got an idea of how it might be while talking with the Sephardim in Barcelona. I remember especially one of the Sephardic refugees, a courtly gentleman with fine aquiline features and snowy hair, Señor Saportas y Cohen. I soon realized that it was fortunate that I knew Portuguese, because his pronunciation was somewhat more like Lisbon than Madrid. The "th" sound for the letter "z" was absent since the Sephardim had left Spain before this lisping pronunciation filtered down from the royal court. Words like "trocar," meaning "to change," were used instead of the current "cambiar." "Trocar" was still current in Portuguese. Señor Saportas y Cohen said that he felt at home in Barcelona. He explained that the language was a great bridge to easy adjustment. Even though there were a few words that made for difficulty, the basic language, called Ladino, was the same, and there was little problem in shopping for necessities and in giving orders to their maids and cleaning women.

The Sephardic group, it developed, found ways to live more thriftily than other refugees, and in short order most of them had made themselves very much at home in Barcelona. Many of them were employing maids at the low Spanish wage scale and were making the very best of their exile. Except for the utterly fascinating accent and choice of words, they were scarcely distinguishable in looks or dress from the Catalans among whom they found themselves. The background of the presence of Señor Saportas y Cohen and other Salonikan refugees in Barcelona in 1944 forms a unique footnote to Spanish history and to the movement of peoples in World War II.

After the occupation of Greece by the armies of Hitler, the Jews of Salonika were routed to such death camps as Bergen-Belsen. Approaches were made to the government of Generalissimo Franco to have descendants of Spanish Jews placed under the protection of Spain. Then they could be "repatriated" to the land of their ancestors.

In March 1943, Mr. David Blickenstaff of "Representation in Spain of American Relief Agencies" and Mr. Niles Bond of the American embassy were informed that the Spanish government would intervene with German authorities for the rescue of Sephardic Jews who had come under German occupation.

There was precedent for special status for Sephardic Jews. Under the dictatorship of Primo de Rivera, a group of Sephardim was extended extra-territorial rights through the efforts of the Spanish consul located in Jerusalem. I was fortunate in getting firsthand details from the consul himself when I met him in his retirement in Pamplona, Navarre. A strong Basque of the prominent Baleztena family, and follower of the legitimist or Carlist tradition, he was proud of having played a part in the return to Spain of even the Barcelona remnant. He had attempted without success to have all the Sephardim of the Middle East granted extra-territoriality at the same time. The old consul recounted that during that period a movement was launched by some Spanish leaders to invite back from their exile all the descendants of the Spaniards of Jewish faith who had been expelled more than four hundred years earlier.

At least some descendants of Spain's expelled Jews derived some benefit from Spain. Just over a thousand of the Jews of Salonika, because they could trace their ancestry to Spain, were snatched from transports bound for death camps.

3. Madrid—Statelessness as Protection

While throwing the protection of Spain over them was a way of saving some refugees, the only way to save others was to remove the power of their nation over them by having them listed as "stateless." "Apatride" was the word listed on the dossiers of large numbers of our people. A man who fought for this "cover" for hunted people was David Blickenstaff of the American Friends Service Committee, head of the central office for refugees in Madrid. This office, known by the cumbersome title of "Representation in Spain of American Relief Organizations," was supported by funding from the "Joint," and from Catholic Relief Services as well as the Quakers.

The office was made possible through the understanding and help of Carlton J.H. Hayes, then American ambassador to Spain. Consultations with Dr. Hayes were initiated by Quakers and the American Joint Distribution Committee. "Representation" was formally opened in January 1943. I was the third American staff member, a commuting member, since I divided my time between Madrid and Barcelona.

One of the chief concerns of the Madrid office was an encampment at the northern tip of Old Castile. It was called Miranda de Ebro and became the place of in-gathering for all male refugees who crossed illegally into Spain. "Clandestino" was the name given to the person who came over the Pyrenees without papers. All were subjected to arrest by Spanish authorities.

With a competent staff, largely composed of refugees, Blickenstaff and another American Quaker staff member, Lawrence Parrish, were free to make regular visits to Miranda de Ebro. The camp was Europe in miniature with every nation represented at one time or another. Frenchmen, Britons, Poles,

96

Czechs, Dutchmen, Belgians, Yugoslavs, Balts, anti-Nazi Germans and Austrians, and an occasional Armenian, Russian or Scandinavian, all shared Old Castile's blinding summer heat and bone-chilling wintry blasts in Miranda'a barracks.

Escaped prisoners of war accounted for a number of the detainees in Miranda. According to the 1907 Hague Convention, a neutral nation can assign places of forced residence to escaped war prisoners and those suspected of being so.

Blickenstaff worked with American and British officials, as well as the Spanish Red Cross to obtain freedom for the men who listed themselves as stateless. Many so-called Britishers, for example, turned out to be middle Europeans. The cloak of statelessness descended at the point of unmasking so that those who had needed the cloak of a false nationality would not be left defenseless. At that same point came protection and full material support by American relief agencies.

Our office reports from Miranda de Ebro showed a remarkable age sampling—the men were either under nineteen years of age or over forty-five. Blickenstaff smiled as he explained that word had got around that men of military age, from nineteen to forty-five, were liable to internment by a neutral power. As all of the men hoped for freedom of movement, if not speedy evacuation from Spain, they opted on arrival for a status outside of military responsibility. Up to the actual age of thirty, they were all listed as nineteen or under, the over-thirties all became forty-five years old. No one could gainsay them, for there was no way of proving otherwise. Most possessed no documentation. If they did, they did not produce it. Even if some sort of a document was produced, there was no way of checking against official records in a Europe in flames.

False national claims spurted enormously when Frenchmen rushed across the Spanish border after the German occupation of Vichy France in November 1942. The men could claim to be French-Canadian so that they could still go on speaking French and yet claim British protection. The prisons of Figueras and Gerona, as well as Miranda de Ebro, were bursting with French-Canadians far from their *soi-disant* homeland. When the burden of care and evacuation of the "Canadians" became too heavy for British resources, it was taken up by the relief section of the American embassy. The process of screening and re-establishing the nationality of this group was referred to as "de-Canning." The young consul charged with the task complained at a weekend social gathering, "It's been a rough week. De-Canning every day and hundreds to go."

There were close to two thousand stateless refugees in Spain living in freedom in 1944. Blickenstaff had liberated from prisons and detention camps more than five hundred of them during the preceding year. The liberated refugee was then served with a formal notice of expulsion from Spain. Technically, the Spanish Red Cross had the responsibility of aliens and refugees in Spain, but its budget could not be extended to refugee maintenance. The Red Cross under Count Granja turned out to be helpful in resolving refugee predicaments, especially the predicaments of detention for forced residence. Aliens were not allowed to work, so every man or woman released was put on our rolls for full care and support.

While we American relief workers took as our charge the unprotected civilian refugees, official governmental rescue missions were operating quietly at top speed for military and official personnel. The U.S. embassy evacuated more than eleven hundred American servicemen, chiefly downed airmen, through Spain. The British embassy had been working from 1940 onward for escaping military men and especially endangered refugees and resistance contacts. We heard tales of parachute raids into France as part of this massive effort which eventually freed many thousands of individuals. Spain, though nominally tilting axis-ward, had on its soil a French Red Cross operation, later openly called the Free French mission, and even a Polish mission. The latter was headed by a Catalan whose wife was Polish and who had long had the title of Honorary Polish Consul. There was even an office for anti-Fascist and stranded Italians.

Some of our poorest refugees were Mexicans who were in effect stateless since their country had no diplomatic ties with Spain. A Mexican dancer who had reached Spain ill and destitute from France received support from us. Her name was

Celia Meléndez. Thin and wispy as a bird, her classic face was framed in a luxuriant mass of dark hair. We were ready to arrange for her repatriation, when instead she entered a hospital. Her strength faded day by day, her eyes and hair seeming the only living part of a wasted little body.

When she died, I had to arrange for her burial. I found that she had traveled with a rough brown garment with a white knotted cord. It was a shroud. Lay followers of Francis of Assisi are often buried in such a habit. Celia Meléndez had told the hospital sisters that if she died, this was to be her burial garment.

There were three of us at her burial one sun-bright afternoon in Madrid's Cementerio del Este, a Spanish priest in long black cassock and low-crowned hat, a woman staff member and myself. We stood before the open coffin in a mortuary while the priest intoned prayers over the little body with shining dark hair lying unbound over the poor shroud. Our little procession walked behind the coffin to the graveside where, in pitiless sunlight, the priest led us in final prayers. Some grave-diggers courteously joined the two of us in Latin responses. It was explained to me that the grave space could only be rented, and that after a certain number of years the bones of Celia Meléndez would be dug up and stored in a stone locker above the ground.

Foreigners living in Madrid came to hear about the material advantages of being a refugee recognized by our office. Clothing was provided and the service of our full-time doctor in addition to a monthly allocation of pesetas. Word had to get about because our refugee shelter comprised a network of furnished rooms and boarding houses in almost every barrio of Madrid. Poverty-stricken Russians, Poles, Italians, Austrians, Armenians and their children presented themselves for like advantages even though their immigration to Spain had occurred decades earlier. We could not accept all of these needy people, and some of them placed real dilemmas before us. One White Russian made frantic appeals of help. He had not long returned from the Russian front where he had fought with Spain's Blue Division. He had no savings and no secure job despite long-time residence in Spain. Evidently the Blue Division had little or no benefits for its survivors. Already the slogan "Toda Europa Contra el Bolchevismo" under which the volunteers had been recruited into the Blue Division had faded from Madrid. We could not take on the Russian volunteer, despite his claim of statelessness.

4. Barcelona

What had happened in Madrid repeated itself in Barcelona. Every person I added to our rolls unearthed another who pleaded for help. Each time I flew from Madrid, a city stretched flat-out on the Castile plain, there was new fascination in the tingling life of the Catalan city, with its many hills. Looming higher than all was Tibidabo. According to Catalans, it was from this height that Satan showed Jesus "all the kingdoms of the world and the glory of them." "Tibidabo," Latin for "I will give thee," were Satan's words of temptation to Jesus in offering all worldly power if Jesus would bow down to him.

Almost all the refugees who surfaced after my arrival in Barcelona were in fact entitled to protection. Many had been hiding out in monasteries and farms in the countryside, grateful for the chance to survive, however meagerly. It was not long before our Barcelona refugee family included Lithuanians, Austrians, Italians, Germans of Jewish ancestry, anti-Nazi Christian Germans, Slovaks, Czechs and a smattering of such nationalities as Dutch, French and Belgian.

I started my search by a visit to the Benedictine monastery of Montserrat which I knew had given shelter to refugees without resources. This monastery and church are perched halfway up the four-thousand foot rock promontory that thrusts startlingly out of the Catalonian plain. The first refugee to greet me was a French priest who had been active in the French underground. He led me to a group of Catholic Austrians who had fled first to France and then across the frontier to Spain. Some of these were housed in the monastery; others had to be placed in farms around the countryside.

The only way to reach one of the remote farms was to hire a *tartana*, a two-wheeled horse-drawn cart which was the closest thing to riding a camel. At the farm the man was called from his work. He stood before me, breathless and suspicious. He was a short, dark-haired Austrian labor leader, and it was natural for him, as an illegal alien, to fear the worst when he was sought out. The shock and incredulity that flooded his face when I told him that I was an American who had searched him out to help him was reward for the rough ride.

Many of the Christian refugees in Barcelona itself had been put on the rolls of the AJJDC since it was the only refugee agency with outside funds. Dr. Samuel Sequeira, a Portuguese Jew and director of the AJJDC in Barcelona, told me that he would be sending me some of these cases. One of these was my very first visitor at the office.

He was waiting at the door for me when I arrived early in the morning, a towering large-boned man with a truly impressive handlebar moustache. When he came into my office, I saw that his hair was streaked with white and that there were deep lines in his strong, large face. I could not place him in any group, and I asked him how long he had been in Barcelona. "I have been here four years—three in Miranda," he told me in labored but understandable Spanish. "I am a sailor, but many sailors quit our ships here." His blue-gray eyes were on my face, studying me intently, and then they misted over. I put another question to him, trying to find out his nationality. Then I noticed that in the deep wrinkles of his face, tiny rivulets of tears were running down unchecked.

There was a pause while he passed the back of his hand slowly over each cheek. "Soy de los Católicos," he said finally. "I belong to the Catholics." He looked away. I explained that I represented the American Catholic agency which would help refugees formerly aided by Dr. Sequeira. He got up and awkwardly seized my hand across the desk to implant a kiss on it.

"Señorita," he said with a long wheezing sigh. "I thought only one thing when I was told to see you. You were going to tell me there was no more money for me.

"Soy de los Lituanos," he said in a more relaxed tone, "I am Antanas Samson. Here they call me Antonio. I could not go back to Lithuania. You know how things are going. And now I am past seventy and I cannot find work on any ship." He was one of the hundreds of stateless persons released from Miranda through the efforts of David Blickenstaff.

I worked out his budget with him—enough to cover his board with a Catalan family and other daily needs. He rose to his height of six feet four inches and lumbered out of the office happy and smiling.

Antonio Samson, as he always appeared in our records, was one of our agency's first "hard core" cases. Even when World War II was over, Lithuania was still hermetically sealed. We supported him for several years in Barcelona until an American-Lithuanian relief committee provided for him. When he was well into his seventies, we arranged for him to live in a home for the aged conducted by the Little Sisters of the Poor in Barcelona. Eight years later, he still figured in correspondence from Spain, and I was negotiating for a pair of specially built shoes for the old man. He was of towering size, and his feet were so enormous that nothing could be found to fit him in the ready-made market. He received his last hand-made shoes a few months before he died.

The visitors to my office were not all such clear-cut cases as Antonio. One day, a thin, dark man darted in and stood before me. He had appeared so suddenly that I knew that he must have been hiding in the corridor. I was alone. I waited for him to make a move. Furtively, he told me that a refugee friend of his had told him that he could trust me. "You will not tell the police that I have been here?" he queried anxiously. I told him I had no connection with the Spanish police, and that we were here to help people who needed aid and protection.

"Does it matter what their nation may be?"

"Generally not—the main question is one of need."

"Well, I am in need," he announced with a certain finality. "I have no protection. I am Spanish, Señorita, but I have no protection. I cannot work."

"How do you live?" I wanted to know.

"I have relatives and I have friends. They feed me. I live first at one address and then at another. Even if I could, I would be afraid to rent a piso. My real name might be found out."

"What is your past experience—that you cannot admit to your identity?"

"Señorita, I was one of the leaders of the Columnia Durruti. We were the real anarchists of Catalonia. My compañeros and I, we seized a factory and ran it for the workers. It was a just system. That factory really produced things. We were free men— the freest in the world, I think. It was a glorious thing to see, Señorita. We Catalans are 'muy trabajadores.' We do not only talk. We work." He stopped.

I said nothing, for I was picturing in my mind's eye the Barcelona of those days as I had heard about it—with the barricades up and the black and red anarchist banners sprouting everywhere. With the struggle for power between the anarchist followers of Bakunin, the Trotskyist deviationists, the orthodox Stalinists, as well as various branches of socialists and syndicalists, came the murders of those whose banners were of a different color. And these were little murders compared with the massive murder of the ongoing civil war. I thought of the hunted and the hunters, displaced again and again in history, but always moved by the same element of fanaticism and the same belief that the extinction of a life can help make things better.

The face of the hunted anarchist before me was distorted as though he was in physical pain.

"I cannot do any work here. No work at all. I could be caught at any time and put in prison.

"Are there any crimes charged against you?" I asked.

"I have committed no crimes. I only fought and killed for justice. It was against the men of the Columnia Durruti that the crimes were done. Can you help me get to the Americas—to North America, to Mexico?"

I told him it would be next to impossible, since migration for other than proved refugees was cut off during wartime.

"Then could you treat me as a refugee, and give me some help the way you give it to them? You could give me less, because I know how to manage. I am a refugee in my own province. It cannot be denied."

We had a talk about the limitations of my mission—and we branched into the nature of anarchism and the reasons for it.

He was an intense but not unreasonable man. It was clear to him that I could not be of any help at all. He rose. "I am a Barcelonan. I am suffering for justice, for my city and for people everywhere, and I must suffer without help and without recognition." He pulled his coat around him and darted into the corridor.

It was inevitable. One day a man calling himself Christ stood at my desk. His name was Christos.

That was his first name. His last name seemed Greek, and in fact, he turned out to be a gypsy originating in Greece. Tight grey curls covered his head like a wool beret. His manner was soft and ingratiating, as though he was always engaged in pleasing the world.

He had been the owner of a circus and small menagerie which traveled around the provinces of Spain.

"We had animals, Señorita, even an old lion. Our family could live not very well, but 'medio bien.' The war came—but we had nothing to do with that. We were not on the front. But then came the hunger. We could not eat, so how could the animals have enough? They died, Señorita. So the family managed—with the soldiers and all."

The whole family, including five daughters, landed at war's end in Barcelona.

"We are still here in Barcelona. And we don't get enough to eat. Could you help us, mostly with the food? We have places to live."

"How many are there in your entire family?" I asked.

"There are sixty of us," he said in a gently deprecating way. "My wife, there is, and also my sons and their wives and children, and my daughters and their children."

I caught my breath. Here was a real tribal family. I had received no instructions about caring for tribes. "How many in the family work?" I asked.

"Well, my sons and I do whatever jobs we can—all kinds of work. But it is hard to find regular jobs. It is very difficult to satisfy the hunger of all the children. My daughters suffer when the children are in need."

"I am sure conditions are painful," I said. "Can your daughters' husbands find any work?"

He smiled deprecatingly, shrugging slightly and lifting his palms in a gesture of rather charming helplessness. "You know how it is, Señorita. They are just girls."

Then, as if he were not sure that I had understood, he added, with his head to one side, "Husbands, the girls have not."

We could not take on the tribe. It was hard to turn away a patriarch named Christos. We did find it possible to supply clothing for the small army of children.

A sizeable group of Italians were helped by us through those last years of the Second World War. The larger group consisted of former soldiers and sailors who had opted for Marshal Badoglio when he became premier at the fall of Mussolini in 1943. Many were in France where they were promptly put under arrest or sent to work in the so-called Todt battalions shoring up Fortress Europe against the coming invasion. With courage and tenacity they deserted and fled to Spain, putting themselves under Allied protection. The men were of all ranks, including army, navy and air officers as well as enlisted men. All received the same subsistence allotment.

In addition to the recent Italian refugees there was a smaller group of anti-fascists who had fought in Spain for the loyalist cause and had escaped into France at the 1939 defeat. Their haven in southern France became too dangerous under German occupation, so they made their way back into Spain. They lived under a variety of aliases so as not to be recognized as having belonged to the anti-Franco forces.

Their appearances in my office were often emotionally charged as they recounted their past sufferings and divested themselves of their false nationalities. A north Italian, with hawk nose and the hollow cheeks of hunger, made light of his own hurts, his wounds in the civil war, his two crossings of the Pyrennees.

His emotion came to a pitch when he almost shouted, "Mussolini murdered my son. He ordered him to fight in Abyssinia. He was killed there. That broke my heart. I came to Spain to fight with the workers. I am not sorry for the sufferings that came to me. I made up for my poor son who had to die for that murderer."

It was an ironic footnote to the Italian situation that the same Badoglio who had crushed Ethiopian resistance in the service of Mussolini was now rallying Italians after Mussolini's fall from power.

I had no contact with the Frenchmen who were being continually processed for eventual alignment with the forces of De Gaulle in north Africa. I did by happenstance meet an American airman who was spirited into Spain after being downed in France.

I was deputed by "Representation" to travel to the north of Spain where a group of recent refugees were living at an inn in temporary forced residence. My task was to get them passes to leave Lecumberri, a village of Navarre. Four airmen arrived at the inn while I was there. Three were British and one was American.

It was a surprise meeting on both sides—I had only expected to see refugees and they could not believe that they were meeting an American in a remote Navarrese village. The American was a New Englander of Italian origin. We think of New Englanders as being on the taciturn side, but this one seemed to have an advanced case of logorrhea. As soon as I mentioned a subject, whether it was New York City, or food, or any trivial matter, he would take off in a flood of verbiage. The Englishmen smiled and finally laughed.

"Yank has found his tongue," said one of them finally, "Do you know what happened to him in France? Well, he was there more than six months, and he had to pretend he was an Italian—that was easy—but a deaf-mute Italian. Otherwise he would have given himself away. His looks pass all right but you should hear his broken Italian."

The young American broke in: "Can you imagine being dumb, real dumb, every day of the week? They were always making signs at me to tell me what to do on the farm. I'm sick and tired of people making signs at me like as if I was a real, honest-to-goodness dummy. I used to get so mad—and I had to keep it all inside.

"In the evenings, when I was finished working, yes, I could open my mouth. But this family speaks French only, see. No English, so what's the use? Boy, it's good to talk to an American again. My own language, that's all I want to hear."

The British and American flyers downed in France, they told us, were taught a few useful phrases in case they were ever stopped by German troops. They were drilled in such sentences as: "I am going to the next town to work." One of them had fallen back on this when stopped for questioning, and as there were so many foreign workers in France, he had gotten by.

The latest refugees at the Lecumberri inn were twenty young Halutzim, pioneers, heading for Palestine. I met them all, and then presented myself to the police in Pamplona for permission to take them from Lecumberri under my escort. I did not succeed, but I was assured that permission would be given within the month. In ancient Pamplona, I stood at the Puerta de Francia, the gate facing toward France. Here in centuries past the smugglers used to enter and leave Pamplona for their trafficking in the Pyrennees mountains beyond. I looked over the range of hills and thought of the contrabandistas of 1944. The old contraband items had been replaced by one item, human flesh.

The Pamplona authorities gave me a permit to take with me an unaccompanied young woman from Lecumberri. Ruth's family had fled from Austria to Belgium where her grandmother had found protection with a Catholic order of nuns. She had escaped to France, and then through France with members of the Halutzim. Ruth was only part Jewish but her future was completely with the struggle for Palestine.

Before arranging for our journey, I was called on to settle a problem. The new refugees demanded, in addition to the regular three meals, a "merienda fuerte," a mid-afternoon snack with coffee or chocolate. The innkeeper refused, saying that board bill did not include extras. The refugees were adamant. The innkeeper told me he could not meet the demand without losing money. We reached an agreement on the extra cost. I saw that the young refugees put the same vehemence into their demand for extra food as they must have put into planning their escape from an empire of death.

During the summer of 1944 I saw members of the Halutzim leave Barcelona on the first leg of the journey that was to end in Palestine. I accompanied Dr. Samuel Sequeira and the "Joint" staff to the railroad station to wave off a group of about five hundred exiles who would board a special train for Cádiz. A ship was waiting in the port of Cádiz to take them to north Africa. There, at two way stations, Camp Fedhala and Camp Lyautey, they would live until it was time for the final resettlement in what was to become Israel. I could not help noticing that all the joy and excitement was concentrated in the Halutzim who gathered in one carriage. Most of the travelers who belonged to the Sephardic colony looked glum as they stood among their possessions on the station platform.

One of the Barcelona station porters had a group around him. He was a tall lean man with almost no hair and a large nose ending in a bulbous knob. The departing Sephardim had realized when he spoke to them that he was also of the same origin. He had somehow made his way into Spain alone. It was next to impossible for non-Spaniards in those days of near-starvation to get work—but he had joined the station porters and was supporting himself without any committee relief. He was telling a knot of Sephardim that no one would make him move from Barcelona.

A woman who had been brought directly to the station from prison also became the center of a group. She had been in prison since the end of the civil war when she had been captured with a tank corps. She was only freed on condition that she be evacuated from Spain. Her name, Sofia Barzecka, sounded Polish to me and I asked her in Spanish if she were not of Polish origin.

"I am a Russian woman, a patriotic Soviet citizen," she replied, throwing her ample chest out. I came here to fight and I drove a tank with the battalions of freedom," she added. Her Spanish was perfect.

"How do you feel about a woman serving as a soldier?" I asked her. "I wonder if women should be part of combat battalions."

"You are an American, no? If your country needed you for a special work in time of danger, you would not refuse."

I was about to say that I would refuse combat, when she went on: "My country needed me for a task. I did it, and I would do it again."

She smiled at us in a gracious manner in acceptance of the fact that she was a personage worthy of attention. She was a striking woman, of more than medium height, with a strong heavy body. She seemed to be in her middle forties, and her hair, piled high in a pompadour, was fair with a few streaks of gray. Someone asked her what she thought of Franco. She threw back her head and laughed. "Be careful what you say about my protector. He's the man who gave me board and room for the last five years." She patted her broad middle. "All I will say now is that he was a good provider—just look at the proof." She guffawed gleefully and climbed on the waiting train.

Hundreds of older Sephardim climbed aboard slowly and glumly. They looked out of the carriage windows with sad eyes. Some of the women wept helplessly when the train began to move. A few waved handkerchiefs forlornly as the train cleared the station.

A little later, Dr. Sequeira received a report from Cádiz. At the last minute, a group of refugees had refused to leave Spain. They had actually staged a strike, and had to be forced to board the ship. We laughed about it in a rueful sort of way. The drama and pathos of the Sephardic return to Spain was heightened by the fact that the refugees felt it too safe and comfortable a haven to leave at that moment in history.

5. Foreshadowings

Members of the voluntary agencies who worked in Spain saw that what we were doing provided foreshadowings of what European refugee service could become after the Second World War. What we could not picture even in the wildest nightmare was the reality of the refugee condition that burst upon the continent as soon as the killing stopped. The lessons we learned in Spain were many and invaluable. Statelessness as a protection for an exile in danger of being swept up by a predatory government was a basic lesson. Perhaps the outstanding achievement of David Blickenstaff was that the "Representation" office was accepted as the "embassy of the stateless." In this, the three voluntary agencies active in Madrid foreshadowed the joint protecting function of many more voluntary agencies after 1945.

It was not long before scores of American private agencies were operating in France, Italy, Germany, and the Near and Far East. They cooperated with each other on programs and often on cases. "Representation" pioneered in the moral adventure of locating justice for the individual in a maze of legalities that might have imperiled his basic freedoms, including the right of asylum. At a later date, the American voluntary agencies continued the same moral adventure even against such targets as governments and the United Nations Relief and Rehabilitation Organization. The aim was the same, to preserve the right of an individual, even a child, against encroachments by the political authority.

The unique function of "Representation" was described by Philip Conard of the American Friends Service Committee:

Largely because this Office has never refused to accept responsibility for a "stateless" refugee, or one supposed to be such, it has come to be regarded and recognized as hav-

111

ing the "right to intervene on behalf of any and all such
cases." One is constantly amazed to find on all sides evidence of this recognition in the foreign embassies, lega-
tions and consulates; in the Ministry of Foreign Affairs; in
the police department; in the direction of prisons, the
directors and commandants of local prisons, camps and
forced residences, in the public offices, in the offices of
railways, shipping companies, and other concerns.

Antanas Samson, the Lithuanian whose exile was forever, foreshadowed and symbolized the "hard core" refugee. It was the voluntary agencies who years later took up the cause of "hard core"
refugees and displaced persons who were left behind after every
resettlement or rehabilitation scheme had been exhausted.
Samson, along with aged and sick middle Europeans and White
Russians, never left Spain or refugee relief rolls.

Joint programming and cohesion among religion-related voluntary agencies gained immeasurably through the Spanish experience. Jews, Catholics and Quakers put the same questions and
the same demands to Spanish authorities on the basis of common humanity and human dignity. No one was more gratified
by each voluntary agency achievement than Dr. Carlton J.F.
Hayes, the Columbia University professor and historian who laid
the groundwork for the "Representation" office. In *Wartime
Mission to Spain*, the account of his three years as ambassador to
Spain he wrote, "It is a source of special satisfaction to me that I,
who had long been a co-chairman of the National Council of
Christians and Jews back home, could have an opportunity to
promote in Spain this practical demonstration of sincere and
successful cooperation, for important humanitarian ends,
among American Protestants, Catholics and Jews."

Still another lesson learned from the combined
"Representation" office was that of the necessity for moral
courage by voluntary agencies—and the need to support programs dictated by moral courage with significant financial outlays. To maintain the operation of the "embassy of the stateless"
in wartime Madrid, voluntary agencies made heavy outlays, utilizing their own resources as well as funds from such agencies as

the U.S. War Refugee Board, a body created by order of President Franklin D. Roosevelt in 1944. In 1945 when the dimensions of the post-war refugee population became apparent, and when the relief needs of devastated countries began to call for massive action, the agencies needed greater resources to support the refugees in Spain.

A joint memorandum on behalf of all the refugee aid agencies working in Spain and Portugal was addressed to the director of the Intergovernmental Committee for Refugees by Clarence Pickett of the American Friends Service Committee. Pickett reminded the committee's director, Sir Herbert Emerson:

> The scope of responsibility of the Intergovernmental Committee on Refugees was broadened at the Bermuda Conference to include all those persons who had to leave or may have to leave their countries because of threat to life or liberty growing out of race, religion, or political belief, due to events in Europe; and that the functions it is to perform were at the same time enlarged to include not only negotiations with governments on behalf of those displaced persons, but also maintenance and transport.

Pickett proposed that the committee take over the residual group of refugees in the Iberian Peninsula and pointed out:

> The situation of the stateless refugees on the Iberian peninsula seems to us to exemplify the opportunities which will present themselves to the Intergovernmental Committee on Refugees in various countries in the post-war period.

Eventually, the larger number of the residual Iberian refugees were accepted for aid by the Intergovernmental Committee for Refugees, and the chief challenge of the voluntary agencies was over in that area. The combined office of "Representation" had thus shown another facet of voluntary agency activity—that of entering an area to give emergency aid so as to pave the way for a necessary governmental or intergovernmental aid operation. Again and again in the post-war situation, American private agencies rushed in with life-saving help where the feet of politicians feared to tread. Only after a "pilot project" had been launched under voluntary auspices was the umbrella of government funding opened over the project.

What to me stood out as a special contribution of our American refugee work in Spain was less pragmatic but of measureless value. We supported and defended the person at a time when the individual person was being swallowed up—by armies that separated him from the operation of his conscience, by camps that put him into slave labor or annihilated him, by governments to whom dissent or human compassion on behalf of dissenters was a criminal activity, by tyrants who decreed life or death on categories of their own devising. Our very presence told the person, cast-off or hunted, that the anonymous life of armies or the anonymous death of concentration camps had not taken over the world. We were engaged in restoring the personal, the human, the compassionate in the lives of those who had survived the most depersonalized, the most dehumanized, the most savage era of Europe's long history.

Before I left Barcelona, I was invited to a refugee party. This was a farewell gathering for several hundred Poles whose exit from Spain had been arranged by the Polish Red Cross mission. All of us knew they would join Polish troops alongside the British forces.

It was a warm night, and the party took place in the open garden of a home in a hillside suburb. The host was the Catalan honorary Polish consul whose wife was of Polish nationality. The only light came from the large yellow moon and a few bright orange lanterns suspended from two tall trees. As a chorus began a Polish tune with a pounding rhythm, a group of young men in Polish costumes bounded onto the grassy lawn from the porch of the house. On the small garden, uneven and located on an incline, they leaped in a Krakowiak dance, their white embroidered capes tossed about in the dashing movements of the dance.

Now that they were free to fight again for their country, the resilience of their spirit had reasserted itself.

I felt myself back in Mexico. It would be, I felt, a soft balmy night in Colonia Santa Rosa, and the child exiles might also be dancing a Krakowiak dance or a mazurka and singing songs of home.

As the men danced wildly, drowning homesickness and hoping doggedly against hope, I pictured in how many unlikely places of deportation and exile would Poles be thinking back of their homeland. I could see them across the world from Isfahan, Asiatic Russia and Siberia to camps in Mexico, the Middle East and East Africa, and in every military campaign form North Africa to the Italian peninsula.

Another party I learned about after I left Spain. In preparation for my leaving, Catholic Relief Services had arranged with Ambassador Hayes for a young American counsular official, Mary Louise Breen, to be released for work with refugees. She gave a description that reminded us how frail the fabric of composure of refugees was when they were transported home by a simple carol.

The Christmas party grew out of loneliness and was suggested by the refugees themselves. We attempted to keep the party a secret until our plans were completed and the invitations issued. Barcelona, however, is built like a glass fish bowl with most astonishing listening devices, and the news got around. We were swamped with offers of talent— Spanish dances by a children's group, broken-down opera singers, a crystal-gazer. The response was immediate and complete.

Permission for the gathering was obtained from the police by the American consulate. The Virtelia school, a private institution, offered its chapel and dining room. It is one of the old palaces of Barcelona, and a beautiful spot. Father Lluma, director of the school, officiated at the mass. Two Austrian refugees were mass-servers; the Catalan choir sang the Latin mass and at the breakfast following gave a special program of Christmas carols in Catalan, Andalusian, French and German.

We gave each "apatride" a small present and fifty pesetas, with small toys for our five children.

The breakfast was Catalan in every detail (heaven help our foreign stomachs); Spanish chocolate thick as pudding, ensaimadas (Mallorcan bread), barquillos, turron (honey and almonds), sweet and sticky pastry, a glass of sherry or cognac.

There were flowery speeches, most extemporaneous, in the most horrible slaughter of the Spanish language ever perpetrated in public—including the one given by this representative—but there was fellowship and remarkable good will. An Austrian baron took under his wing our decrepit Lithuanian sailor, both chatting happily in Russian. Two Armenians gathered up the leftover pastry and went off with paper bundles. The youngest at the party was one month and the oldest seventy-four. Seventeen nations were represented.

One contingency I had not counted on occurred when the choir sang "Holy Night" and at least half of the guests burst into tears; it was moving.

All in all, it was a stupendous success. There is no doubt but that for many it was the most genuinely happy moment they had had since they left their homelands.

Chapter Three

DISPLACED PERSONS AND THE RIGHT OF ASYLUM

1. Do Not Move Westward

It was April 7, 1945, when the most gigantic pincer movement of armies ever deployed in history was beginning to close on the heartland of Europe. A communiqué of that day was addressed not to troops in the field, but to Polish and Russian civilians in the narrowing gap between the advancing Anglo-American and Soviet armies.

"Do not move westward. Stay where you are," said the communiqué issued by the Allied Supreme Command of General Dwight D. Eisenhower. "In a few days, the gap between the armies of liberation from the west and from the east will be closed. After the armies have been joined, all measures for your repatriation will be taken. Whoever moves westward will delay his repatriation. Whoever remains on the spot will speed his repatriation.

"Maintain order and discipline until the Allied Armies arrive. You are entitled to receive food and shelter from the German authorities. . . .

"Choose your own spokesmen. After their arrival, the Allied Armies will make provision for your food and shelter. Therefore your leaders must report at once to the Allied authorities. They will then receive instructions for your feeding and housing."

But it was precisely westward that almost all the Polish and Russian civilians wished to move. They wanted to be sheltered by the Anglo-Americans. They fought by every possible strategy and subterfuge to enter an ark that had been fashioned to shelter them. The ark was known as UNRRA, the United Nations Relief and Rehabilitation Administration. The ark had been launched eighteen months earlier in the already turbulent seas of international politics, seas already swirling in their depths with opposing currents. The ark, even while it was yet empty, was shivering from the buffeting of waves set off by

119

inexorable currents from the east, and ever stronger currents from the west.

Of the twelve million non-Germans found dislocated in the greater Reich after World War II—war prisoners, concentration camp victims, slave laborers—most wanted to return to their homes as speedily as possible. The Dutch, Belgians, Norwegians, French and Italians commandeered cars and trucks, jumped aboard trains, clogged the roads in their efforts to shorten the time of their reunion with those they loved. But they were all from the west. It was those from the east that posed the problem, and especially the slave laborers.

Snatched from their homelands to the east of Germany, or captured in war, they had been impressed into serving a massive machine of death. Wearing garments, or carrying slave identity cards, marked "Ost," meaning simply "east," they were dignified by neither name nor nationality in their work battalions. It was these gangs of slaves that were utilized to carry out a Nazi scheme that eventually made out of Europe, once the teeming womb of culture, an obscene charnel-house. More and more of them had been dragooned as the immense Russian war front needed replacements, as a great shroud of snow enveloped not only the German dead, but the unrescued dying, the wounded, the exhausted.

Foreign workers, originating in at least seventeen homelands outside the Reich, worked out of more than twenty thousand camps erected alongside armament works, factories and railroad yards. Germany as a warmaker was kept in motion by the great spidery cancer of the camp world, comprising not only the men and boys branded "Ost," but the war prisoners organized into Arbeitskomandos, and the concentration camp inmates assigned to the most murderous work details. Women and children were dragooned from their "Ost" homelands as factory hands and farm drudges.

When the gigantic net in which Nazi manpower commissioner Fritz Seuckel had snared millions of unwilling victims had burst asunder, the foreign workmen had escaped like a flock of wildly happy but often vengeful birds. For millions of them the words of the psalm would have been a fitting multilingual anthem: "Our soul has been delivered as a sparrow out of the snare of the hunters. The snare is broken and we are delivered." But for too many of the "Ost" workers, only dread faced them as they looked east, and as they discarded their "Ost" cards, and branded garments, they rejected the east as their home.

The twelve million workers and prisoners melted away to somewhere between a million and a half and two million persons. These managed not only to reach the Anglo-American zones of occupied Germany and Austria but to escape repatriation transports. These were the displaced persons. They demanded the right of freedom of choice; they demanded the right of asylum against one of the victorious Allies.

The ally in question, the Soviet Union, had foreseen this eventuality before any other power. While unable to prevent the formation of UNRRA, the Soviet Union had done its best all along the road of negotiation to "mine the route" ahead of time so that a community of displaced persons should not come into being. Even the April 7, 1945, communiqué from the Allied Supreme Command stressing repatriation was part of the careful mining of the route. Such excessive precautions on the part of the Soviet Union might have owed something to its experience with the earlier wave of refugees who went into exile after the Bolshevik revolution. Those refugees found protection under international auspices when the League of Nations set up in 1921 the office of the High Commissioner for Refugees. Fridtjof Nansen, the Norwegian who occupied this post, formalized the protection of the stateless individual by the issuance of a travel document commonly referred to as the "Nansen Passport." With this document, recognized by fifty-two governments, refugees from the Soviet orbit were able to make their way to the farthest corners of the globe.

* * *

Realizing that it was possible, and even likely, that the rights of World War II's victims of history would be in jeopardy, American voluntary agency personnel embarked on a moral adventure. It consisted in taking a clear stand whenever human rights were threatened and in finding ways to outwit those whose policy it was to annul or trample on these rights.

I took part in this moral adventure and relate it as a part of the D.P. story that is little known.

This part of the story had the elements of spy activity, the decoding of official documents that couched in "officialese" destructive political aims, attendance at UNRRA meetings and the following up on "leaks" to the higher policy makers in the American state department. The tale was only fleshed out later when I met those who had been rescued by our efforts.

Prior to November 1943, when the original agreement of ten articles for the United Nations Relief and Rehabilitation Administration was formally established, it became obvious that the organization would of necessity be highly politicized. Many of us, because of special experience, were anxious to see whether immediate help could be rushed to refugees wherever their location, even within Russia. We were certain that homeless people falling under the western Allies would be the recipients of speedy aid.

One concern was the Polish refugees still within the Soviet Union, especially the children separated from the family group by death or other cause. Article I of the UNRRA agreement presaged future conflicts in the United Nations which was still to be born. In point of fact, the first use of the term "United Nations" was in the UNRRA agreement. It contained a carefully inserted veto over any relief or rescue activities not wanted by the host government in the innocent wording: "The form of the activities of the Administration within the territory of a member government wherein that government exercises administrative authority and the responsibility to be assumed by the member government for carrying out measures planned by the Administration shall be determined after consultation with and with *the consent of the member government.*"

We knew immediately that, with these words, access to Poles, Balts, and other deported peoples within territory controlled by the Soviet Union was blocked.

It was natural that governments would be called upon to give their consent before the entry of relief missions, but it was significant that the agreement stressed the rights of the sovereign state, and not the right of needy persons to receive aid. Significantly, the right of asylum or the right of freedom of choice of victimized people wherever they might be was not mentioned.

From the beginning, UNRRA gave consideration to its future relationships with voluntary agencies such as those of the major religious groupings, since these were already deeply involved in refugee assistance in many parts of the world. While UNRRA was concerned with relief and rehabilitation programs within countries from Yugoslavia to China, I shall deal here with its relationships to refugees and displaced persons in Europe. Incidentally, the term "displaced persons," as contrasted with refugee, seems to have stemmed from the overall plan of SHAEF, Supreme Headquarters of the Allied Expeditionary Force, for needy civilians likely to fall under its control. In discussions of June 1944, it was decided that United Nations nationals, outside the borders of their countries, were to be designated "displaced persons," while the term "refugee" was to be reserved for those people displaced within their own national boundaries. Those who had been persecuted because of race, religious belief, or activities on behalf of the United Nations were to be considered as displaced persons regardless of their place of origin. Jewish persecutees and other concentration camp victims fell within this category.

In its "Policies with Respect to Assistance to Displaced Persons," as drawn up by a sub-committee in 1943, UNRRA recognized that its services might be needed in liberated or conquered territory by people displaced from their homes and homelands, by exiles, and by prisoners of war. UNRRA had already initiated its refugee work by assuming the operation of camps for Yugoslavs, Greeks and Albanians in North Africa.

The Yalta Conference, which was to have fateful consequences for large groups of displaced human beings, was held in the spring of 1945. From the beginning, UNRRA showed itself a precarious instrument for the protection of displaced persons whose rights might be in jeopardy. Poles and other refugees in the Middle East asked in 1944 if they could, when necessary, claim the protection of "statelessness." An UNRRA spokesman stated to voluntary agencies in New York in March 1944 that the policy would be *not* to extend aid to such refugees if they claimed to be "apatride" or "stateless." Naturally, the Yalta agreement was worded so that it applied equally to its signatories, but the total effect was to give the Soviets the opportunity to extend an Iron Curtain even over its citizens who were outside its borders.

The agreement of the Allies on proposals that cut to the heart of human rights aims of the war effort was partly due to the power of blackmail held by the Russians. This power stemmed from the presence of numbers of Allied troops in captivity in areas expected to be controlled, or already controlled, by Soviet arms. A few extracts from the agreement entered into at Yalta in the Crimea on February 11, 1945, indicate its totalitarian character. Man is understood only as a political entity to be herded wherever the state commands.

Article 1 specified: "All Soviet citizens liberated by the forces operating under the United States command and all United States citizens liberated by the forces operating under the Soviet command will, without delay after their liberation, *be separated from enemy prisoners of war and will be maintained separately* from them in camps or points of concentration until *they have been handed over to the Soviet Union* or United States authorities, as the case may be, at places agreed upon between those authorities."

Article 2 dealt with the rights of repatriation representatives to "immediate access into the camps and points of concentration where their citizens are located," and to "set up the internal discipline and management in accordance with the *military procedure and laws of their country.*" The final sentence of the second article brought up an issue later aired in the General Assembly of the United Nations: "Hostile propaganda directed against the contracting parties or against any of the United Nations will not be permitted." These articles, incredible from the democratic point of view, but perfectly understandable from the point of view of a monolithic state, were signed by Joseph Stalin, Franklin D. Roosevelt and Winston S. Churchill. Justice, as Albert Camus pointed out, is the eternal refugee from the camp of the victors. It was by these articles that people caught in the whirlwind of history were snatched and whisked away against their volition. It is only after justice itself is a refugee that persons are forced to enter the refugee condition, or sometimes are prevented even from asking for refuge.

The millions of POW's and forced laborers on German soil when the Soviet Army arrived were speedily transported to the Soviet Union. The Russians in Allied custody were another matter. From May to September 1945, over two million Soviet nationals were turned over by the western Allies in Germany and Austria to Soviet authorities. Among these were liberated prisoners of war and men of the Vlasov and other units who had been captured in German uniforms. Included were "Ost" workers and White Russian emigrés who had already acquired another citizenship. Included also were many would-be D.P.'s who would have chosen not to return had their choice been respected.

Before his death, a Russian refugee whose family had fled to Yugoslavia after the 1917 revolution told in detail how he, a Yugoslav citizen, his father, and his grandfather had been handed to Soviet authorities in Austria. All had been officially called to a conference with the commander of the English Eighth Army. At the same time, all officers of Russian origin who had opposed the Soviet forces in detachments under German command were ordered to report. Surrounded by tanks and armored cars, they were herded by the British Army into barracks and eventually turned over by force to Soviet detachments. As in all other such forced transfers, men risked death, in this case by leaping from bridges, in their attempts to escape. And as in other transfers, there followed execution, death and slave labor on the Soviet side. The young man, Nicolai Krasnov, survived ten years of forced labor; his father died in captivity, his grandfather was hanged in a Soviet jail.[1]

A first-hand account of American participation in forcible repatriation came from William Sloan Coffin in his memoir. As chief interpreter in a detention camp for Soviet citizens in Plattling, Germany, his attitude changed from one of hostility to an understanding of their refusal to return to the realm of

---

1. *The Hidden Russia: My Ten Years as a Slave Laborer*, by Nikolai N. Krasnov (New York: Holt, 1960).

Stalin. He listened to their experiences, long terms of forced labor for dissidence, executions and the horrors of forced collectivization.

The men, captured in German uniforms, should according to the Geneva Conventions be treated as German POW's. Yalta rode rough-shod over these and other conventions.

Coffin learned that the men were to be tricked into attending a morning meeting which would actually be the occasion of a round-up. They were to be turned over to the Soviet Army.

The evening before, Coffin had attended a happy camp festival, with singing, folk dancing and balalaika music. He came to the point of blurting out what was to be done to them the following morning, but stopped when he remembered that he was under orders.

Before dawn, tanks surrounded the barracks and searchlights played on the buildings. Three GI's were assigned to each Russian to force him to board the truck that would take him to the Plattling railroad station.

"I saw several men commit suicide," recounted Coffin. "Two rammed their heads through windows, sawing their necks on the broken glass until they cut their jugular veins. Another took his leather boot straps, tied a loop to the top of his triple decker bunk, put his head through the noose and did a back flip over the edge which broke his neck."[2]

Coffin found it painful to write about the event thirty years later.

"My part in the Plattling operation," he said, "left a burden of guilt I am sure to carry the rest of my life. . . . Repatriation showed me that in matters of life and death, the responsibility of those who take orders is as great as those who give them."

While the American and British forces were obeying the letter of the law of Yalta, grisly scenes occurred regularly. In Camp Kempton, Germany, Russian prisoners who took refuge in a church were dragged out and injured while being loaded onto trucks. In the concentration camp of Dachau, which served as a detention center for Soviet POW's, the attempt

---

2. *Once to Every Man: A Memoir*, by William Sloan Coffin (New York: Athenaeum, 1977).

at forcible repatriation brought on a scene of "human carnage." The crazed men were attempting to take their own lives by any means. Guards cut down some trying to hang themselves from the rafters; two others disemboweled themselves; another man forced his head through a window and ran his throat over the glass fragments; others begged to be shot. . . . Thirty-one men tried to take their own lives. Eleven succeeded: nine by hanging and two from knife wounds."[3] Among the four thousand repatriated from the United States was a contingent from Fort Dix, New Jersey, who were tear-gassed by military police to force them into waiting vehicles. Three men succeeded in hanging themselves and were buried nearby. Those who were wounded in the resistance were sent with the contingent to Plattling to be turned over to the Red Army.

* * *

After the officers had been forcibly turned over to the Soviets through the trickery of the conference call, Coffin recounted, their families were informed of the fact. They were told that it was now their turn to be repatriated.

The Hidden Russia related some of the details regarding the disposition of these relatives and family members who could not or did not flee to the hills and remote villages of the Austrian countryside around Linz: "From June 1 to 3 the process of repatriation progressed to the accompaniment of English tanks, machine guns, rubber truncheons. . . . Defenseless women, children and old men were forcibly sent "home." Many committed suicide. Mothers threw their children into the Drau River and jumped in after them. Some, who chanced to have firearms, shot themselves. Why was it that these people, once having left the Soviet Union, did not wish to return? That was a question no one asked."

In Linz, Austria, a cemetery holds the graves only of Russians whose names have been placed above their resting places. In their despair at being turned over to the regime of Stalin, they took their own lives.

---

3. *Pawns of Yalta*, by Mark R. Elliot (Urbana: University of Illinois Press, 1982).

*   *   *

UNRRA's role was influenced by the Yalta commitments, since the Soviet Union was one of UNRRA's founding nations. By UNRRA's rules, Soviet repatriation missions had access to camps. They tried and often succeeded in getting the registration lists of camp inmates. In point of fact, it was not until the spring of 1949 that the Soviet repatriation mission finally ceased operating from Frankfurt, and then only under U.S. pressure.

UNRRA, while caring for those declared eligible, chiefly persecutees, Poles and nationals of areas incorporated in the Soviet Union after September 1939 (namely citizens of the Baltic countries and Poles and Ukrainians from eastern Poland), could not serve as the agency to promote overseas resettlement. The logical agency to assume the resettlement task was the Inter-Governmental Committee for Refugees (IGCR). This agency, which grew out of the 1938 Evian Conference called by President Franklin D. Roosevelt, was already caring for the refugees, many of them non-repatriable, in Spain, Portugal, France and other European countries. The voluntary agencies, as well as military occupation authorities and some UNRRA leaders, depended on the IGCR to initiate the overseas migration of non-repatriating refugees. A very cleverly placed land mine exploded all such plans. Late in 1943, a clause had been inserted by the Soviet Union which stated that "where a government is itself able and willing to look after its own nationals who have had to or may have to leave their country of residence, the Intergovernmental Committee will not deal with such people without *consultation with and agreement of that government.*" A delegate of the Soviet Union was on the Intergovernmental Committee. Any real program of resettlement by the committee was effectively blocked long in advance of the fact.

When the D.P.'s showed their utter unwillingness to return to their homelands, the western Allies determined, possibly in desperation, to rid themselves of the heavy burden of the D.P.'s by other means. While UNRRA's teams ran the camps, and maintained internal order, supplies and funding came from SHAEF sources as well as local requisition. As the larger number of D.P.'s congregated in the American zone, the cost to the U.S.

was considered heavy. A decision was made to close all D.P. camps except the relatively few camps housing the persecutee group. Originally this group included the Jewish survivors of persecution and concentration camps—less than a pitiful twenty thousand in Germany, seven thousand in Austria.

The United States was not prepared to turn over openly and directly the remaining displaced persons to the satellite regimes of eastern Europe. The compromise reached by the military and the State Department was one that would not technically violate the right of asylum for innocent persons. It would, however, be an effective step in removing from Allied responsibility a group of people who were a festering wound on U.S.–Soviet relations. The decision was taken at a time when the refugee problem was being raised in the United Nations and while the fourth session of the UNRRA Council was being held.

The solution to rid themselves of the seemingly insoluble problem of the displaced persons was to close the D.P. camps.

By cutting off the lifeline of supplies, the displaced persons would be forced to return to their homelands since there was nothing for them on the gutted landscape of West Germany. In bomb-scarred towns and villages, German expellees were contending with local populations for the food and shelter that would allow them to survive.

The plan to close the camps in the U.S. zone of Germany had been taken in secret in the early months of 1946. Secrecy was broken by a news leak datelined Germany, March 1946, and carried by the International News Service. The reporter made it clear that he had obtained the news from an informant who assured him that the D.P. camps were to be closed almost immediately.

Patrick A. O'Boyle, director of Catholic Relief Services, was an official observer at the fourth session of the UNRRA Council held in Atlantic City, New Jersey, in March 1946. I was registered as an observer as well.

I came to the Atlantic City Council session armed with the clipping. I had a letter of introduction to a leader of the British delegation, Sir George Rendel.

Observers could attend the sessions, but could not make oral or written interventions. One of the resolutions discussed was the "removal of conditions which might interfere with the repatriation of displaced persons." Liaison officers "not properly nominated by presently recognized governments" were to be denied access to the camps. This part of the resolution was directed against the one hundred and fifty liaison officers belonging to the London-Polish Government. They had stayed on to assist their compatriots after representatives of the Lublin regime, the "presently recognized government," had been named as camp liaison officers.

Between sessions, I had an opportunity to discuss matters with Sir George Rendel. When I showed him the news release, he looked at me gravely, but made no comment.

"Such a plan could not be true," I remarked. "American voluntary agencies working with the displaced persons would be the first to know. We have heard absolutely nothing."

"Of course, you would have heard nothing," said Rendel. "If hundreds of these camps are to be closed, the only way to do it would be without any warning at all. As you see, the writer of this news release got wind of it only through an unofficial leak."

I was stunned by an almost unthinkable reality. I could envision the effect of stripped, defenseless strangers, chiefly Poles, on communities where German civilians and expelled people were already scrounging for life itself. What social peace could we expect where former enemies were pitted against each other for the survival of themselves and their children?

Without actually affirming the report, Rendel gave some crucial advice on how to postpone or overturn the camp closing order.

"The resolutions, even the emphasis on repatriation expressed at this session, are not too important to the displaced persons right now," he said. "The matter of the news report is extremely urgent."

"But what can we do?" I asked.

"Absolutely nothing," he replied, "by remaining at this session. It is your own government that must be approached at the earliest possible moment. Only at the highest level could such an order be postponed or rescinded."

I relayed the advice of the British representative to Patrick A. O'Boyle. He realized that his presence at the UNRRA Council session was useless. There was only one course that might lead to effective action.

Through urgent telephone calls to Washington, an appointment was made for O'Boyle to meet with the secretary of state, James F. Byrnes. When they sat down, Secretary Byrnes calmly confirmed the plan, and pointed out that the displaced persons would be the better for having to get back to work. He told O'Boyle that from reports reaching him, there were approximately half a million men in the camps of the displaced. All their needs were being met, he said, and they were living a life of idleness.

O'Boyle explained to the secretary of state that he had been misinformed, that not all the displaced persons were men, and that there would be absolutely no work for them in a destroyed country. He asked Byrnes to await a memorandum we would prepare giving facts on the displaced persons situation based on reports from our own and other voluntary agency representatives. He also explained that there were many American citizens, in particular ethnic groups, who had a deep concern for the fate of the displaced persons. We would have to inform them in particular, and in general the American public, of developments.

Byrnes committed himself to a study of the matter. He agreed that no immediate action would be taken regarding the camps. O'Boyle agreed that no public announcement, of great possible embarrassment to the U.S. government, would be made by the agency in the meantime. In a communication to O'Boyle dated April 1, 1946, Byrnes wrote that he had taken under advisement the facts brought to his department by O'Boyle, but that the closing of the camps in the near future was still the considered policy of the American authorities. The time had come, early in the post World War II period, for a voluntary agency to use all the resources at its command to fulfill a task that had been thrust upon it, namely to become the "embassy of the stateless."

The memorandum which I was called upon to draft was dispatched by the head of our agency to the secretary of state. It said in part: "I have your communication of April 1. . . . This memorandum, dealing as it did with displaced persons camps, left me concerned and troubled because the two points which I, in company with many other Americans, consider the most essential and most vital were completely omitted from consideration.

"The problem of basic human rights so inextricably bound up with the problem of displaced persons received no mention. It might be well to remember that there were more than ten million displaced persons in Germany at the liberation. The Frenchmen, Belgians, Dutch and Norwegians went home as fast as transportation or their own legs could carry them. A group of unfortunate Lithuanians, Latvians, Estonians, Poles, Ukrainians and Yugoslavs did not return to their homelands when given the choice. These people are not staying behind to take advantage of a glorified WPA set up by the American Army. The ties that join them to their homes and to their relatives are just as strong as those that bind Frenchmen and Belgians and Netherlanders. What keeps these people behind in Germany is fear for their lives, for their freedom, or for their religious liberty. Any action that would force these people to return to their homelands is an infringement of their basic rights as human beings and a betrayal of the ideals for which we as Americans fought. We have a duty to provide for these people *freedom of choice* as to their future and to preserve for them the *right of asylum*.

"It is a basic misconception to conceive of these camps or assembly centers as containing mainly or only men. In the memorandum of April 1 the displaced persons were referred to as 500,000 men. There are many women in these camps who came either as slave labor or as refugees. There are more than 100,000 children in these camps and an uncounted number of teenagers. What reputation would America get in the world if these women and children are turned out of the camps and assembly centers and left to roam without shelter or aid because the Americans did not think that they liked to work? If there had been banditry and thievery among the displaced (and there is no doubt that there are delinquents among these as among all groups), this would not justify turning out all of them to a life of such uncertainty that 'banditry,' to quote Philip Noel-

Baker of the United Kingdom Foreign Office, 'would be their only means of livelihood.'

"Refugees from many nations had stepped into UNRRA as an ark of safety, perhaps an insufficient ark, but the only ark in sight. The protective beams of that ark were being assailed not only by thrusts from eastern totalitarianism but also by a sudden attack from the direction of the strongest victorious democracy. If the refugees were tossed overboard into the great deluge of need that was afflicting western Europe, any question of the preservation of their rights would be purely academic."

The memorandum did not touch on the one subject to which Secretary of State Byrnes and other spokesmen for the Democratic Party were most susceptible, namely the political effects in the United States of closing of the camps and of the complete abandonment of the displaced persons. This point was dealt with "viva voce."

The so-called ethnic vote, particularly that of the Polish Americans in such cities as Chicago, had long been a pillar of the Democratic Party edifice. That pillar, which had begun to crumble after the revelations of the Yalta agreements, might crumble very rapidly should the circumstances of the projected closing of D.P. camps be made public. Some other voluntary agencies, notably the Polish-American War Relief organization, had got wind of the plan to rid the United States of the burden of the eastern European D.P.'s. Many people were ready to make a public outcry to forestall any action by U.S. authorities in Germany, but our agency prevailed upon them to restrain their voices until our memorandum had been studied.

We knew that the highest echelons of our government were rethinking the whole matter when Secretary of State Byrnes asked the director of our agency to return to Washington for consultations. He and his aides seemed sobered by the vehemence of the response to their quiet plan of liquidating the greater number of D.P. camps and by the fact that a public outcry was only being delayed because the matter was being restudied.

The agencies waited for ten days after our director presented the memorandum. Headquarters offices were in constant touch with informants and staff in Germany and knew that no action was being taken to implement the proposed plan. On the tenth day, the State Department made it known to our agency that the decision to close the D.P. camps had been reversed. We informed the other concerned people-to-people agencies. No announcement of any kind was made to the press either in the United States or in Europe.

The ark sheltering the displaced persons had been saved. The personnel of voluntary agencies had aided at a crucial point in averting a tragedy that threatened one of the most helpless assemblages of people on the face of the globe.

But threatening sounds continually reached the refugees from international assemblies; dire rumblings and threats were voiced at UNRRA Council meetings and at the United Nations. There were also reassuring pronouncements. Refugees were a subject of the First General Assembly of the United Nations. The Third Committee, charged with Social, Cultural and Humanitarian Questions, was commissioned to make the report to the Plenary Meeting. The Committee's official report noted:

> To more than one Delegation the ordered attempt to solve the problem of uprooted people, including the unrepatriables, appeared as the first opportunity presenting itself to the United Nations to give practical and concrete evidence of faith in the human rights and freedoms enshrined in the Charter.

2. Some Nations Protect the Nationless

During 1946, displaced persons could not help but feel the ark crumble as reports filtered through to them that UNRRA would be dismantled as of the last day of the year. The successor organization was at that time only in the discussion stage. At these discussions, the United Nations continued to serve as a sounding board for blasts from the Soviet Union and its new satellites against the non-repatriables. As our agency, along with the other voluntary and Red Cross societies, had concluded agreements with UNRRA on July 31, 1945, we were anxious to be as close as possible to all new developments.

I was present at the United Nations session held in Lake Success when the Soviet delegate made a historic intervention on the subject of refugees. It was November 6, 1946, and Mr. Andrey Vyshinsky took the floor to discuss the draft constitution for an International Refugee Organization—a document which had already been circulated among the member nations of the United Nations.

The wily old Menshevik with the finely chiseled face and sharp fox eyes was carrying out to the end the carefully planned campaign—to get control over Soviet citizens who were outside of Russia's borders, and to help Soviet satellite regimes to achieve the same end. Such control would be preliminary to herding them back within those borders without reference to the choice or rights of individual citizens. The Yalta agreement had seemed to promise the Soviet leaders exactly what they wanted with regard to their citizens—surrender on demand. Up to a point, the western Allies had succeeded in "rising above their principles" to the extend of turning over groups of Russians without giving them freedom of choice. Numbers of

135

Russian soldiers, who had defected and turned against their own leaders, were captured in German uniform. Under the terms of the Geneva Convention, to which the United States and Britain were signatories, these men could, and perhaps should, have been treated as all other prisoners in German units.

When the Allies began to return to their own principle of the right of asylum, they balked at turning back men who attempted suicide rather than enter the Soviet orbit. The Soviet Union, which had a conception of the individual citizen completely opposed to that of the American, British and French Allies, had scored an enormous victory in forcing through agreements which embodied its politicized concept of man. Soviet representatives fought to the end so that their concept of man and citizen should prevail. In sum, they wanted to preserve the complete power of the state over the individual that had become part of the Soviet system. Political dissidence, as evidenced by large groups of refugees, was not to be tolerated, and the dissidents themselves were to be turned over for whatever treatment their state wished to mete out to them. It was against this background that Vyshinsky talked that day in Lake Success.

For over three hours we wore the headpieces of simultaneous translation while Delegate Vyshinsky extolled the heroic patriots of Russian history, the heroism of Soviet resistance to fascism. He began to fulminate when he finally came to the problem of refugees. The great masses of the refugees, he announced, were anxious to return to their countries of origin, but were prevented from doing so by the terrorism and false propaganda of fascist elements in the camps.

The draft constitution of the proposed International Refugee Organization (IRO) contained an objectionable "loophole" that would provide aid for refugees in re-establishing themselves overseas. People who refused to return to their native countries should not receive such aid, he pointed out, since their countries of origin were to be members of the IRO.

The purpose of the IRO, Vyshinsky version, should be to return all refugees to their native lands, and not to ship them from Europe to distant lands such as Canada, Australia and the Union of South Africa where they would be condemned to a "wandering existence and a dependent position under alien living conditions."

Delegate Vyshinsky's white mane began to toss furiously when he came to the "fascist groups, the military and paramilitary formations" that were intimidating the masses of refugees, and by threats of violence holding them captive in the camps of western Europe. The list of organizations conducting "provocative activities" came to a climax with the mention of "the Polish emigrant army of Anders."

He demanded that the camps be closed to all propaganda against repatriation and hostile to any member of the United Nations. Such propaganda, he shrilled, was the work of fascists who were furthering their own sinister political aims.

The Soviet Union had served its own ends very well by assigning this task to its former attorney general. I understood why this man had been so effective as prosecuting attorney of Moscow's lethal purge trials of 1936 and 1938.

He was mouthing angry and outraged eloquence as though the displaced persons were represented before him in the dock like the Bukharins, Radeks and Zinovievs he had prosecuted. If the D.P.'s could have been subjected to prolonged questioning by Vyshinsky, he would have succeeded in forcing them into one of two categories—either dupes or traitors. They could be for him only repatriates, or, if not, then candidates for the supreme administrative penalty meted out to traitors.

He belabored the fact that in the camps were men who had the blood of thousands of innocent people on their hands. As I watched the stormy indictment, the flailing arms, I became increasingly aware of a shocking contrast. While the throat was hurling out passionate phrases, the pale eyes were totally unmoved, coldly and piercingly calculating. The face never lost its motionless, ashen whiteness.

Not only the delegates to the Third Committee but a considerable gallery listened almost hypnotized to the end. Then the delegate from the United Kingdom wearily pointed out that the spokesman for the Union of Socialist Soviet Republics had taken three hours and twenty minutes of the nine hours allotted to this section of the debate, and that most of his statement was irrelevant to the matter of the IRO constitution.

The split which plagued succeeding sessions of the United Nations had exploded in a special way over the heads of the refugees. The demands of Delegate Vyshinsky on the cessation of propaganda in the camps were countered by Mrs. Franklin D. Roosevelt, the U.S. delegate, and by other delegates, as unacceptable because they violated the right of freedom of speech.

It was the question of the fundamental rights of human beings that divided the delegates into opposing sides. After a debate in which the Soviet delegate was adamant on the rejection of aid to political dissidents, the delegate of New Zealand made the point that to refuse assistance to such refugees would undermine the basic principles of the United Nations. He observed that the Third Committee of the General Assembly was now divided into two blocs which voted in accordance with differing political sympathies.

*   *   *

Those of us who attended the series of meetings as observers saw the two blocs tilting verbal lances at each other from irreconcilable positions for more than a month of meetings. Almost every intervention by the delegates of the United States, Britain, the Low Countries, and members of the so-called western bloc dealt with the inalienable rights of the individual, while the statements put forward by the eastern bloc emphasized the rights of the state. At one point, a member of the Soviet delegation announced that the extension of aid and protection to political dissidents who would not recognize the lawful government of their countries was tantamount to questioning the legitimacy of those governments.

The delegate of the Byelorussian Soviet Socialist Republic demanded that since ninety percent of the refugees originated in five areas (the USSR, the Byelorussian and Ukrainian SSR, Poland and Yugoslavia) the governments of those areas had the "moral right" to see that the problem of refugees should be resolved in a way that would not harm the national interests of these states.

As the debate proceeded, the gap between the opposing

sides became unbridgeable. A delegate from a Middle Eastern nation, caught in the crossfire of words between the opposing sides, interposed a philosophic commentary to the effect that the grave problem of refugees was symptomatic of a disease of civilization. The ultimate causes of the disease would have to be sought out in order to prevent recurrence.

When it became clear that the constitution of the International Refugee Organization would not be the political instrument that the eastern bloc wanted, and which it had engineered to some extent in UNRRA, an attempt was made to limit the life of the contemplated refugee agency to one year.

Despite the great gulf which yawned between the eastern and western bloc, the resolution approving the IRO constitution was passed. On the last day of the year 1946, by a vote of eight nations, the Preparatory Commission of the International Refugee Organization (PCIRO) came into being. None of the five members of the eastern bloc were members of the new organization. When fifteen nations became members and financial supporters of the agency, it assumed, in August 1948, the title of International Refugee Organization. When the PCIRO took over the task of care, maintenance and resettlement of over 700,000 displaced persons on July 1, 1947, it took over the assets and personnel of UNRRA and of the Intergovernmental Committee, without the legacy of Soviet intervention and of Yalta commitments which had hampered the other two agencies. While IRO's purpose was nominally to "encourage and assist in every way possible" the return of D.P.'s "to their countries of origin," it did establish in practice the right of asylum. No D.P.'s were to be forced to return to their country of origin unless specific criminal charges had been lodged against them. Some, few in number, managed to evade the screening net by concealing past crimes and associations.

The measure of the confidence reposed by the east European refugees in the new organization is the fact that while it started its four-and-a-half-year-term of service with the 700,000 clients mentioned, it eventually aided over 1,100,000 persons. Besides adding the 200,000 postwar Jewish escapees from satellite countries, it extended help and protection to a large number of eastern Europeans who had been fearful of entrusting themselves to UNRRA.

White Russians and Ukrainians, Hungarians, Rumanians, Czechs, Slovaks and Croats came up out of the cellars of the bombed-out streets of German towns to ask for help in settling overseas. Then began in earnest the combing of the D.P. camps by migration missions from the far corners of the free world. IRO prepared for the great rush by gathering records englobing vital statistics, occupational and medical data.

It was as a result of their confidence in the trustworthiness of the IRO vessel that thousands of these displaced persons were later carried to new lives overseas in a whole fleet of ships operated by I.R.O.

The "Ost" workers, once marked only according to their eastern origin, fanned out north, west and south, over the whole globe. Ukrainians and Poles became "new Canadians," Balts and Yugoslavs became the "new blokes" of Australian labor, Russians took on the citizenship of the Argentine and other Latin American lands.

It was an inescapable fact that Europe would have to cope with a refugee problem for a long time to come. Sixteen European nations met at the end of 1951 to map out a response to the problem and in February 1952 set up the Intergovernmental Committee for European Migration. ICEM was charged with the transport overseas of a steady stream of migrants from Europe. It was ready when there were spectacular breaches of the Iron Curtain, like that of the Hungarians in 1956 and of the Czechs in 1967. In its first twenty years of moving refugees and migrants, ICEM assisted 1,800,000 individuals to reach countries where they could put down new roots.

3. The Displaced in Person

It was as a guest of the IRO, just after its sturdier beams had replaced the trembling boards of the UNRRA ark, that I first met Jewish, Polish, Ukrainian, Baltic and other D.P.'s. I was serving for a time as guide for three officers of the National Council of Catholic Women. As leaders of a nationwide organization that had affiliates even in the smallest parishes and communities, they were in a position to be channels of information regarding D.P.'s. With them I began to meet victims of uprooting, such as Tatiana whose family was driven over the entire Eurasian land mass before finding refuge in the new world.

The emphasis had ceased to be so heavily on repatriation and had been shifted to overseas resettlement by the time of my first visit to the camps in September 1947.

Selection of displaced persons for work in mines and farms was already underway in scores of camps. The resettlers were chosen by strength, by muscle, by the fact of being single, or of being willing to travel without the encumbrance of a family.

"Cattle market deals," said welfare workers as truckloads of able-bodied males rolled out of the camps for Belgian mines and French farms. But realism told us that war-depleted countries could not begin any immigration scheme with a welfare approach.

The fall of 1947 was a still point in the D.P. story—a hiatus like the deadly quiet eye of the raging hurricane. In that hiatus the Jewish D.P.'s were marshaling their forces to batter down the closed door of Palestine, while the masses of eastern European D.P.'s begged insistently and desperately for sanctuary. I started the trip to D.P.-land in the IRO office in Rome.

My very first European D.P. camp was Ciné Cittá, Rome's Hollywood. In its wildest pre-war days, Ciné Cittá had never

141

churned out such drama, such incisive tragedies, as it did in those days of 1947. Jewish infiltrees from communities of Rumania, Hungary, Poland, from the camps of Austria and Germany, slipped across frontiers, swept over the Alps in guided groups, and found incongruous shelter in the great movie studio.

The golden Roman sun beat down on the teeming life of this way station on the path to Palestine. Broad stages were screened off into cubicles for families and bits of families that had somehow escaped consignment to the death camps of Auschwitz and Treblinka. Earlier arrivals had the privacy of actors' and stars' dressing rooms. If suddenly the teeming life, the busy preparations had stopped, and each refugee at Ciné Città had acted out his own drama of persecution, humiliation, loss and liberation, who, I wondered, could serve as the scribe of so endless a saga of human cruelty, who could stand the anguish of being a spectator?

Farther up the boot of Italy, in a Milan school, was another way station for Palestine. On the walls were posters and painted signs depicting an arm grasping a rifle. Under the picture were two stark words: "Soltanto Così," "Only Thus." A young man stopped and pointed to the sign, "No one can stop us now. We will win Palestine." The wave of Aliyah Beth, the second return, that I had met in Spain three years earlier was sweeping past me now in an inexorable course to the Holy Land. Ships crowded with Jewish exiles were moving eastward in the Mediterranean, their destination a country that had ceased to be a homeland for their people since 73 A.D., when Titus captured Jerusalem, leaving "not a stone upon a stone." Some of the Jewish D.P.'s made their way to Rome's ancient Forum to gaze on the still-standing Arch of Titus, erected to mark the fall of Jerusalem and the end of the Jewish war. It was then that the defeated Jews were driven out and dispersed among the nations; it was then, as a bas-relief inside the arch showed, that the Romans carried away the seven-branched candlestick and the sacred objects from the temple.

We entered Germany from Switzerland by crossing a thin, white line on the road. The four of us—three Catholic women leaders and myself—were greeted by the Rev. Fabian Flynn, the CRS representative in the French zone of occupied Germany.

"On one side of the line, order, Swiss order, food, staid normalcy," said Flynn. "On this side, chaos, hunger, a broken world."

* * *

As I began to see the signs of a fragmented world, I saw behind it the fragmented human beings who caused it. Ordinary human beings they were, with no more nor less of the marks of that primal sin which wounded all of humanity. By placing his conscience in the keeping of the state, the modern soldier or civilian had fragmented himself in a manner most dangerous, and even lethal, to his fellow men. In a world where man was not keeper of his own conscience, how could he be his brother's keeper—except when he was ordered to be so in the custodial and punitive sense? The stones around us had been fragmented as part of a system of terrible obedience—an obedience based on the presumption that the individual cannot question the decisions of a government which alone is in possession of all the facts in the international situation. I later felt that the whole horror of the trial of Adolph Eichmann, who had helped direct the organized transport for the organized massacre of the Jews of Europe, was justified by one phrase. That phrase, used by Adolph Eichmann to describe his role during the war years, was "corpse-like obedience." The obedient soldier or functionary, separated from his own conscience, was not a complete man; he became a thing manipulated by others. In turn he made other men into things, slaves to be utilized, or corpses. Sadly, I had to admit that the moral trap, of using human beings as things, awaited both sides in a total war. The D.P. camps were a sign that our side had succumbed to that moral trap.

An occasional car sped by us on the rutted road. TOA was on each license plate. "Territoire Occupée Allemande," explained Flynn. "The German translation is 'Tyrannie Ohne Adolf.' The French are occupying this zone along the lines of the German occupation of France—minus the executions. Don't look for peace yet."

I decided I would try not to look at or for anything as we drove

toward the American occupation zone where the International
Refugee Organization had "laid on" a special tour of D.P. camps.
I wanted to keep some part of me unmoved, some part of me
undrained, for the camps.

All four of us of the tour group grew silent. Battered main
streets of towns showed signs hanging crazily before non-existent stores. Bäckarei, Metzgerei, Frisör. Where were people getting their bread, their meat? Did anyone bother with beauty
parlors in a land of death and hunger? September greyness
turned into a beating rain. The only people plodding along the
road as we left Freiburg were haggard men drawing wooden
carts after them, and women, heads wrapped like mummies,
hugging string bags of vegetables.

We looked at one another as we saw our first rough wooden
cross planted in the ruins of a house in a row of ruined houses.

An evergreen wreath, with what looked to be a framed photograph of the deceased, hung on a broken door frame. The
bodies must have been pulverized and mingled with wood and
stone.

One of our group broke a long silence.

"It seems a terrible thing to be so callous driving by these little houses. It's not just the ruins. They're tombs." She turned
away and I think she was weeping.

A deputy director of IRO met us in Heidelberg. We lunched
in a Schloss above the undamaged "open" university city. IRO
was in the process of taking over the D.P. camps from UNRRA.
His organization had accepted the fact of non-repatriating
D.P.'s, the task of emigrating those who could not be persuaded
to go home. Five out of the seven hundred camps bequeathed
to IRO in tri-zone Germany were listed for our visit. IRO, still in
its preparatory commission stage, needed every good word
from every side—especially from the American public. The leaders of the National Council of Catholic Women were ready for
the task. For a week we found ourselves VIP's, billeted in the
best of requisitioned hotels.

We were to make a tour of the people caught against their will
in the "stormwinds of history." Their windbreak against the
political hurricanes of the time—hurricanes which might have

blown many of them back into the orbit of tyranny which they dreaded—was the IRO. Sixty percent of the charges handed to IRO were Poles and Ukrainians, eighteen percent were Balts, the rest Jewish survivors, Yugoslavs and a few smaller ethnic groups.

Our visits had been carefully planned to present the spectrum of D.P. life in the American zone of occupied Germany. The nationless D.P.'s were clustered carefully in national camps. We were to see camps of Jewish, Ukrainian, Baltic and Polish D.P.'s, as well as a center for unaccompanied child D.P.'s.

While awaiting our visit to a camp of Jewish D.P.'s, we were lodged in Frankfurt. We drank coffee on the high balcony of an Army snack bar while we took in the view of the wrecked rooftop of the still-operating railroad station. The spidery twisted steel of the former roof was a surrealistic design. The ride by car to Zeilsheim was a short one. As we drove into the camp of a thousand Jewish D.P.'s the blue and white flag of Zion rose before us, the flag of a nation yet to be born. For all of us, the words "Exodus 1947" trembled on the air. *Exodus* was the name given to an aged and battered Chesapeake Bay steamer purchased by the Haganah, the Jewish armed force of Palestine. A fortnight earlier, the more than four thousand passengers of that historic vessel had been debarked at Hamburg. The press of the world presented the heart-stopping spectacle of the gunned and rammed Exodus being towed into the Haifa Harbor by British cruisers while the course of the Jewish refugees was turned back in three small vessels to the Europe they had left.

The very word *exodus* reminded the whole world of the liberation of the children of Israel from their bondage to the pharaoh of Egypt. The goal of the exodus, then as in 1947, was a country held by others, described to Moses as "the land of their pilgrimage wherein they [the people of Israel] were strangers." For weeks on end millions of people identified themselves with the travail of the refugees who refused to debark in France, and had to be forced off the vessels in the port of Hamburg.

While the Zionists were throwing aside the national flags under which they had existed hitherto, their new flag, I found, did not rally all the Jewish displaced persons.

A survivor of the Warsaw ghetto helped guide us around Zeilsheim—a lawyer, tall and spare, with a long narrow face and inexpressibly tired brown eyes. Swirls of fine dark lines circled the eyes—a tragic personification of a Klee drawing.

We talked in an open space in the center of the camp. He explained that he himself was not a Zionist. I studied the shaft of stone near which we stood. It was a memorial, raised by the survivors, to the millions murdered in the holocausts of the death camps. I saw every ordinary detail of the camp in the shadow of that pillar, symbol of the most massive extermination ever perpetrated on a people.

"You are Americans. The American visa is the dream of refugees. But I think I would not want it—an American visa. The tempo is too much for me. I would do best in Canada. It is a bit less pushing. Most people here wish for Israel. But I'm too tired to be a pioneer."

His first wife had died in the ghetto massacre. A Polish family had hidden him. His second wife and small child were with him at Zeilsheim. He was one of the large stream—more than a hundred thousand—of Polish and eastern European Jewry who fled their homes to find haven under Allied occupation.

The almost complete disappearance of thousands of Jewish communities in central and eastern Europe—symbolized by the stark memorial shaft—was made final by the flight of such people as these in Zeilsheim. Everything in Zeilsheim had an apocalyptic overtone.

The man from Warsaw managed to be quiet and rational.

"When you see the kibbutzim you will see why it is too late for someone like me to throw myself into a life of pressure. One can stretch oneself so far. I have applied to Canada. I hope they will take some who are not manual workers. It is hard for a lawyer to transplant himself to any place."

Across the road, a hundred young D.P.'s had segregated themselves into a collective, for both working and living. They were Spartan types, teenagers and people in their early twenties, who could not be bothered with the interruptions of visitors. One light-haired young man, short and muscular, took us on a quick tour of the settlement. He, like all the others, was a post-hostility refugee from Poland. The United States was of little concern to him except insofar as it could further the setting up of a Zionist state. We saw his home, a small dwelling requisitioned from a German family. The typical German billowing feather beds and cluttered walls made the rooms seem busy and effete for the bare-kneed landworker. His wife was holding a tiny baby, one of the precious crop of children born in the days of liberation and destined to grow up in the promised land.

Our guide's attitude showed his lack of interest in the snug little house, and in the row of such homes in which his co-workers lived.

He led us next into a common dining room in a large shed. Young men and women, many of them parents of the small children who were playing in a garden, sat down at two long tables for the midday meal. They were dressed in work shorts as though they had just come in from field work.

This was a kibbutz, a community ideologically and nationally committed. It was one of close to three hundred such communities—including the famous Nili kibbutz, which by ironic justice occupied the estate of the sadistic leader, Julius Streicher. The kibbutzim, gathered in tight knots of farmers and workers all over D.P.-land, were the shock troops of the Aliya Beth, ready to organize illegal transports to Palestine on orders from their high command. It was from their number that key leaders, for such ships as *Exodus 1947* and SS *Redemption*, were drawn. The captain of the *Exodus*, Yelqiel Aronowicz, was only twenty-three years old. The young kibbutzim and their leaders were referred to as redeemers, those who were pledged to restore the kingdom of Israel.

How poignant was the word *redemption* used in the temporal sense to one like myself accustomed only to the spiritual sense. To the Jews, threatened by extinction under alien flags, redemption would occur when their own flag flew over Palestine. The earthly exile would be over in a redeemed nation. The mighty evil which had assailed their race would make it hard for them to even glimpse the concept of a redeemed world—in the sense in which I had been accustomed to use the term. How hard it would be now to convey a sense of a redeemed world to those for whom a tyrant had changed the sign of a Passover to its opposite. Once the mark on the door of the household of the children of Israel meant that the angel of death would pass it by and Passover became a symbol of eventual liberation. During Europe's travail, the Jewish household was marked for ghastly imprisonment and almost certain death. Later I read what the philosopher Martin Buber said about the spiritual sense of redemption, a sense which excluded the precarious exercise of free will in a redeemed world. "In our view, redemption occurs forever, and none has yet occurred. Standing, bound and shackled, in the pillory of mankind, we demonstrate, with the bloody body of our people, the unredeemedness of the world."

For the young "redeemers" of the Zeilsheim kibbutz, "Next year in Jerusalem" had a literal meaning, and they defied the Allied power that had helped liberate them to make it come true.

As I watched them leave their shed and their playing children to go back to work, I could imagine them sailing as crews on the refugee ships, and guarding their crops in tracts of earth wrested and won from the desert.

One part of Zeilsheim sheltered only children. This section brought me back to the Jewish child refugees at Barcelona, to the Polish child survivors of Siberian deportation. It was a center for unaccompanied Jewish children. Here they were gathered and processed for overseas migration. Most of them were from Poland.

Jewish welfare agencies took complete responsibility for the child D.P.'s. No government of origin would refuse to sign a release for a Jewish child whose migration had been arranged. Non-Jewish unaccompanied children were often snatched back regardless of the interests and welfare of the individual child. The Zeilsheim experience in child care showed how necessary it was for voluntary agencies to have experienced personnel and significant amounts of funds ready to search out and protect the children who otherwise would have become the pawns of political forces. The Jewish voluntary agencies, alone among the religious groups, foresaw the necessity to put a protective arm around every unaccompanied Jewish child.

As I saw the children in the Zeilsheim center, healthy,

assured of their future, I could only echo the Old Testament: "According to the greatness of thine arm, take possession of the children of them that have been put to death." The children of others who had lost their lives were not so protected.

* * *

A trip to a Ukrainian camp was a vastly different experience.

The Canadian Immigration Commission, one of the first to go through the camps, had just left the D.P. camp at Ettlingen when we arrived. Jubilation rose over the camp as though someone had sent up a flare as we made our way into the rows of heavy barracks of a former Wehrmacht officers' training school. Camp rolls listed over two thousand D.P.'s.

Heavy-shouldered men with lined faces and greying handle-bar moustaches looked shyly at us. Knots of shock-haired young men stood talking excitedly. Having lived through the obscene camp world of the war years, they were liberated by Anglo-American arms. Then, in bitter irony not lost on them, they returned to a camp world to await a new liberation. The visit of the Canadians was a first sign of a second freeing from bondage.

In the jam-packed rooms of the blockhouses there was excited shouting and singing. Five priests, three Catholic and two Orthodox, cared for the spiritual needs of the ebullient peasants, about evenly divided between the confessions. Here we had to resurrect our German.

"I hope we can all go to Canada," a tall gaunt priest told me. "Such camp life is not good for our young people. We have about five hundred children under sixteen here. You see how they are mixed in with the grown-ups in these rooms. Do you think our chance will come soon? What about the United States? Do you think perhaps the commission will come here soon from America?"

"Oh yes," I answered quickly. "I am sure of it. But a law for displaced persons to come to America—it will take a little time."

He looked at me inquiringly. I tried to explain that the tours of D.P. camps by U.S. senators and congressmen were a preparation for a new law—but not a mission to choose immigrants.

"Thanks be to God the Canadians are quicker. They will start picking people right away, is it not so?"

"Yes, they can go right ahead. But the United States won't be far behind. We have Citizens' Committees for Displaced Persons in cities all over America. Our people want a good law."

I was trying to put the best face possible on a yawning gap in U.S. policy. Since December 1945 when a presidential directive allowing 42,000 displaced persons, including orphans, to enter the U.S. as immigrants, nothing had been done to provide haven for these deadlocked people.

It was not until the senatorial committee had returned with a controversial report, and legislative haggling had embittered the atmosphere, that a D.P. bill, reluctantly signed by the president of the U.S., became law. Only in August 1948 did a U.S. displaced persons commission come into being, charged with administering a law that allowed for the admission of up to 205,000 of the European displaced.

The priest led us to the camp chapel. It was painted by peasant hands in wonderfully barbaric colors, bright blue walls, splashes of red, green, yellow. Here was no good grey creed but a faith of hope against wild hope. He stopped and pointed to the altar. "God's Mother," he said simply. "Our icon is from Kiev. She will guard us here or over the seas. She is comforting our people, our priests, in Siberia."

*   *   *

All that fall, in talking with the D.P.'s, we had to temporize, to explain in measured terms why the machinery of our democracy often had to grind slowly.

While over Zeilsheim hung a flag for a nation yet to be born, there hung over the entrance of the D.P. camp at Hanau a colorful bouquet of three flags belonging to three small nations that had ceased to be. They had disappeared into that graveyard of nations, the Soviet empire. The bars of orange, green, red, blue, black, white and maroon streaming in a lively wind above our heads were signs of uninterrupted national existence—if only in the consciences of the exiled.

Under the flags of Estonia, Latvia and Lithuania, nationals of the three countries elected camp officials, welcomed us with grave courtesy. We felt at home with them. They spoke smooth English. We did not have to unlimber our school German. More than a thousand Baltic exiles were proving that their little countries were advanced in democracy, in culture, more advanced in literacy than perhaps our own country.

As opponents of communism who reported on the 1940 Soviet occupation, as people who had often made their escape with fleeing German troops, they had been called fascists. We could see, could we not, pleaded their leaders in poised, careful speeches, that they would make good citizens anywhere in the world. It was hardly necessary for them to point up their arguments. The camp was as clean and orderly as a convent boarding school. Squares and triangles of purple and gold autumn plants and pale yellow flowers grew beside the walks and at the angles of the barracks. The proportion of intellectuals and professional people seemed high—two of our guides were lawyers—but there were skilled workmen in the camp.

The camp display room and store was filled with fine handicrafts. Embroidered women's blouses and children's dresses awaited our interest and orders. Exquisite wood inlay was presented in boxes, bowls, crosses. Intricate designs were painted on hand-carved wooden wall plates. Here was the work of disciplined, organized people. Our first reaction was one of balking a bit at a glib advertising pitch. Hanau's camp of Balts was obviously a showplace. It seemed too calculated a way to "sell" the D.P. predicament. But the insistent, unflagging eagerness of the aging Lithuanian lawyer, his bald pate breaking out in sweat with the earnestness of his presentation; the tremulous pride of a broad-faced, faded Latvian woman in her handmade blouse; the anxiety of the men to prove to us that they had made their tools and woodworking machinery as well as the artistic wood pieces—all these changed our attitude as we lingered in the hall.

These displaced persons were selling themselves in the enormous display room. They saw themselves as being exhibited in the form of heaped-up woodwork and piles of embroidered cloth. But they sold themselves and their cause with dignity, without loss of face. It was to me a mighty lesson in poise. Every now and then the Lithuanian lawyer who was chief spokesman seemed to show a twinge of fear as he mentioned the hopes of the Hanau Balts for overseas migration—and more specifically for opportunity to emigrate to the United States. But the loss of aplomb was momentary. All the order and unremitting work, we felt, was an overlay above a general desperation. They came from helpless small countries. They could point to no tremendous armed battles with Germany or Russia, no fierce resistance movement with legendary leaders, no soul-stirring uprising against invaders.

The Balts were as helpless as the little countries that had been swallowed up and might not be disgorged in their lifetime. Many of them had just escaped the second Soviet occupation of their homelands. Their desperate anxiety was to make an effective appeal on this rather than on an emotional basis.

Before going to the next camp, we stopped at Hanau to view the supply warehouses of CRS—alongside the massive buildings housing UNRRA stocks. From these warehouses our Catholic Relief Services staff trucked out clothing, supplementary foods, recreation kits, books and religious supplies to most of the camps in western Germany. While material aid was distributed without regard to creed or race, migration aid and sponsorship was asked for and given by agencies to their own religious or ethnic constituents.

In Babenhausen, a second Baltic camp which served as another step in our careful descent into the camp world, 260 Estonian guards and drivers who had been employed by American Army installations were trucked into the camp during our visit. Their jobs were finished. They filed out trim and orderly in their dyed navy blue uniforms and settled grimly into waiting for migration missions to start picking them out.

The Latvian camp leader lost no time in telling us he had been chosen in a democratic election by secret ballot. Then we were shown a placard affixed to a large board just inside the camp entrance. It was the address of the Soviet liaison officer for the area. Nothing was said, just a bitter smile exchanged.

*   *   *

At that time, more than sixty percent of the displaced persons were Poles. One of the largest Polish camps was on our tour.

Irene Dalgiewicz, of Colonia Santa Rosa, joined us. She was

working out of the CRS Hoechst headquarters on a special assignment for child D.P.'s She now wore an army uniform without insignia, as did all American voluntary agency D.P. staff in Germany.

"We're headed for Durzyn. It'll be the Mexican camp all over again for you and me," she said. "But here they have suffered different things—or maybe not so different. Slave labor, imprisonment, does it change much from Uzbekistan to the Reich?" The Poles accepted the local name of Colonia Santa Rosa in Mexico. They never questioned it. Here they refuse to call the place by its German name, Wildflecken. So they have christened it "Durzyn."

There was the same turbulent life at Durzyn near Fulda as we had known at the Colonia outside León—but the backdrop had changed. The approach through a swampland, the cactus clumps at the Colonia entrance, the palms and the orange-bright dust gave way to a setting of orderly rows of dark green pines. After a stretch of forest road we suddenly came upon a bald patch, an enormous sheared section of naked brown earth. Endless rows of troop barracks were lined up before us.

"The cleared acres were military proving grounds— Guderian's Panzer Divisions roared about here, the refugees tell me," said Irene. Then she added thoughtfully, "Now they are proving grounds for Polish patience. Durzyn would be a good-sized Polish country town—twelve thousand people. Seven hundred children in grammar school."

The chaplain, Father Marjan, and the assistant camp director, a D.P. Pole, were waiting for us. The large camp chapel was the first step of the conducted tour.

"This was a stable but we have converted it totally." The priest's smiling eyes traveled over the walls, and up to the ceiling. Primitive, bold paintings covered the wallspace. A fresco painting which I recognized as the stylized Black Virgin of Czestochowa looked down serenely from the ceiling.

In the vestibule were several rough pine coffins, the outsides painted black, The covers were laid neatly on the side.

Father Marjan saw our surprised glance. "We have made more than three hundred of these since our camp was opened.

Three hundred funerals. You know what our people had to undergo here during the wartime."

"How many priests help you with so large a parish?" someone asked.

"I have four assistants. We were all liberated from Dachau together. We are lucky to be alive to serve."

"Father Marjan," said Irene, "was one of the priests injured in torture sessions. Some that you will meet were suspended by hooks during the questioning periods in Dachau."

"The marks of the meat hooks and other instruments are still on the carcasses," said the priest, casually striding past the blockhouses teeming with people.

"But the carcasses are still very much alive," I put in, trying to match his long steps.

"The priests who survived must be very much alive—for the sake of these men and women, these children. You knew that only one out of two of us Dachau priests lived through it. In the camps they broke our bodies, but they tried to break these people in another way—by humiliating them."

Older children were in a secondary school and in commercial school classes. Younger children were bunched into blockhouse classrooms reciting their lessons in Polish, bent over copybooks and textbooks supplied by Polish-Americans. We were reminded of the patio classes at Colonia Santa Rosa.

"And yet, after all these children went through in Poland and Germany, dislocation, slave labor, interruption of schooling, you know what happened last year," said Irene over the children's voices.

In an incredibly obvious move to make the Poles repatriation-minded, UNRRA had sent out a directive threatening the imminent closure of all Polish schools in D.P. camps. The order was sent out quietly, without publicity. It seemed to be one of the many efforts to make the Poles feel less comfortable, less secure in the west.

The order profoundly shocked the Poles who had set up a network of schools, largely on their own initiative. The cultural organizations which had somehow survived in prisoner of war camps were ready to withstand all Allied pressure.

The Displaced in Person

It was at a public meeting of non-governmental organizations in New York that I raised the question of this directive with Fiorello La Guardia, then director general of UNRRA. He had asked for questions after a warmly sympathetic address on the plight of the D.P.'s.

"Wouldn't you say that the order announcing the closure of all camp schools for Polish D.P. children constitutes an unfair pressure on their parents?"

The dynamic little man seemed to teeter forward to balance on his toes. "Unfair pressure?" he asked.

"Unfair pressure in favor of repatriation to Poland." I explained.

"Who put out the order on the closing of Polish schools?" he asked.

"UNRRA—Germany," we answered.

"I am the director of UNRRA here or there," he laughed, "and I assure you there was no such order."

"Nevertheless," I insisted, "I have a copy of it."

"Well," snapped the ebullient little man, "you know things about UNRRA that its director seems to have missed."

There was a wave of laughter.

The execution of the order was delayed—perhaps because groups of American Poles were waiting, poised, to raise a cry of protest.

In due time, the strictures against the Polish schools became a dead letter, and joined UNRRA's dead file—a file of non-events that only seemed to have happened. At least, they were denied when they were brought up in discussions.

The Polish schools were in full function in September 1947, as were the workshops. A mountainous display of handwork awaited us in a drafty, whitewashed hall—rough-hewn furniture that resulted from forays into the pine forest backdrop, lasts and forms on which shoemakers were already turning out hand-made shoes, tailored suits, embroidered blouses, and drawn-work tablecloths. In one corner of the hall was displayed only metal work, heavy black iron candlesticks, religious objects, ash-trays, of every description.

"All this metal—fragments of weapons, pieces gathered by the workmen," said Father Marjan.

He picked up a round object, about a foot and a half in diameter, poised on an iron stand.

"This monstrance for our chapel took a long time to make. You can see the work to join those metals. Shrapnel, who knows what else."

He held it up—a marvelous round receptacle with space in the center to contain the eucharist when it is held up for the veneration of the people. In concentric circles designs of shining steel and brass radiated from a base of cast iron. "Weapons of war into things of worship," I remarked. "What good could plowshares do the people in camp? It is doing Isaiah one better."

Nearly half of the people at Durzyn were from farming families, the rest woodcutters, tailors, shoemakers, a scattering of skilled mechanics. When we met one of them he would ceremoniously take a hand in his corrugated work hand and bring it to his lips. There were no smooth speeches.

Irene's voice was sad.

"Of these twelve thousand Poles, only a tiny part, less than five percent, are intellectuals, professional people. The leaders, political and otherwise, have been wiped out. The other D.P. groups may give a better impression because they have more skilled spokesmen."

"I know what you mean," I replied, "but those percentages speak loudly enough by themselves."

In all the febrile atmosphere of the crowded camp, both children and grown-ups seemed to be making up for lost time. They were pouring out energy into a provisional, even unreal, world. Poised between a past of destruction and cruelty and a future blurred with threats and uncertainties, they channeled their intensity into the moment. I had heard someone talk of the sacredness—the sacrament—of the moment. The concept was epitomized at Durzyn. The U.S. and Britain, hoping to be rid of the Poles as soon as possible, worked to give their lives an even more provisional character by such devices as the order to disband camp schools, by the supply of reassuring films about the new Poland, by a notice posted on camp bulletin boards, and by "Operation Carrot."

It was Irene who translated the notice from Polish for us. The burden of it was that with the dissolution of UNRRA and the lack of a sure successor organization, there was no certainty of the continuance of camps and assembly centers. Because of these eventualities, every Pole who could remove himself from camp life and return to his homeland should do so. We wondered how many times the Poles had read and studied the implications of the foreboding message. They doggedly refused to be frightened by such veiled threats into boarding a repatriation train.

I had seen at a Washington UNRRA Council session the UNRRA-made film to stimulate repatriation to Poland. An actual train drove through jubilant Polish communities, flag-bedecked and hung with signs of "Polska Was Wita," "Poland Welcomes You." Evidently the welcoming embrace of satellite Poland did not impress too many of the exiles.

"Operation Carrot" was more of a success. The carrot held before the noses of deprived and doubtful Poles was the massive and precious bulk of a sixty-day food ration. During the final three months of 1946 thousands from this camp had come forward to claim the rich bounty that could be exchanged for the return to life in gutted Poland. In early 1947, the pretenses of a democratic election in Poland had been stripped away, the Peasant Party leader Stanislaw Mikolajczyk had fled to exile, and many of the repatriates were back in Germany.

Under the busy work of camp life, I sensed the seething despair of the trapped. We had come at the still point of the D.P. story. The Poles especially looked to the United States to make a moral affirmation of the D.P.'s right to resettle overseas by unlocking for some of them its golden door. The United States had participated in the decisions that had made them exiles. This they could never understand, they told me. But at least America could show that it felt some responsibility for its past actions. As we said goodbye to the chaplain and made our way through the now dark pine forest, I said to Irene, "These Polish D.P.'s are as densely ringed by thickets of international maneuvers as they are by the forest around them." Hope, and big movements of resettlement, were only to come later.

* * *

Our fifth camp was not a military barrack, but a former center for Germany's delinquent minors. An ornate multi-storied building, Aglasterhausen had been placed on our tour at the suggestion of Irene Dalgiewicz whose special assignment was with displaced children.

One hundred and ninety children, under eighteen, of various nationalities had been gathered at Aglasterhausen. In the parlance of UNRRA-IRO international social service, they were unaccompanied children. In the parlance of such sovereign states as Russia, they were the subjects of parens patria, the all-powerful parent state, the mother–father–big–brother state with the power to demand the surrender of any of its subjects beyond its borders. To those who saw them being repatriated by UNRRA and IRO without reference to their personal needs or welfare, the children were political pawns, even sacrificial offerings.

It was lunch time when we arrived. The director of Aglasterhausen, an American woman with a warm, frank manner, had us talk to the children as they left the dining room. A thin youngster stood looking at us nervously. He did not approach us, nor did he move away. I went over to him. He was sixteen years of age. He was from Poland. In fact, he had not long before returned from the Polish border.

The boy spoke German but I brought Irene Dalgiewicz over to talk to him in his own tongue.

He looked at her from under his eyelids. He must have decided she was not from the Warsaw regime. Then he told her: "I was here during the war. My parents are dead. I jumped off the repatriation train when it got to Poland. Then I was so hungry I came back here. I had no other place to go. Now they will send me back again."

He lost his nervousness. "I'll jump again. I'll disappear. I'll manage."

"You know," said Irene in her gentle social worker manner, "that when you reach the age of eighteen, you can choose for yourself whether you will be repatriated or not. You are getting on toward eighteen, I think."

"There are other D.P. camps besides this one," I said, "Don't you know any Polish D.P.'s?"

"No," he said. "I only know the people in this home and the German family where I worked." There were ways, I had heard, of slipping into camps and getting on camp registers.

I wanted to take him to another camp right then and there. But I did not want to endanger the presence of my agency in the zone.

We talked with a Serbian boy from Yugoslavia. His father had been an officer of the Royal Yugoslav Army. His black keen eyes were despondent.

"If my father was not dead, they would be searching for him. Someone told me he was a wanted man.

"And you. What plans have you?"

"I am lucky. No one is trying to send me back. I will become eighteen later this year. They have promised me that I can stay here until my birthday. Then. . . " he shrugged.

The young man could probably find entry to a camp of Yugoslav D.P.'s one way or another. It was a future without immediate fear, and without much hope.

Five children were sitting on a bench. They were Polish children who had just been brought in from a German child care institution—a row of pale, listless blondness. They could tell Irene their names, but not much else. German was their language by now. They had been located through the child tracing service. The Polish Red Cross, representing the Warsaw government, was arranging their early repatriation.

Already one hundred and fifty Polish children had been repatriated from the Aglasterhausen center alone. A large number of Croat, Serb and Slovene children had been returned to Yugoslavia. Even if there were no immediate relatives in Poland or Yugoslavia, as was more likely in the case of small children, they were claimed on the basis of "parens patria." Even where relatives overseas wished to adopt the children and remove them from a Europe still in ruins, the missions of the respective governments refused to give permission to move an unaccompanied child.

The only children not repatriated in this way were the Jewish children presumed to be orphans. After being located in homes and Catholic institutions, chiefly in Poland, they were nursed to health and protected in child care centers such as that at Zeilsheim. In due course, they were emigrated without the necessity of permission from the mission of the country of origin. To the surprise of the director of Aglasterhausen, two Polish Jewish children had just been sent to her for repatriation to Poland. It was a valid case of family reunion since both mother and father were alive and had traced them to the Jewish child care center.

The only way to have made possible a case study on each individual Polish or Yugoslav unaccompanied child (whose parents or close relatives might eventually have turned up on the rolls of the displaced) would have been to set up separate centers with voluntary agency funds. As this was not done in 1945 shortly after the cessation of hostilities, the children who were declared "unaccompanied," or who were discovered by the Child Tracing Service in the canvassing of German homes and institutions, were marked for speedy repatriation.

Aglasterhausen was one of the thirty-four "way stations" set up by UNRRA for child repatriates. As we left the big forbidding-looking building, a short wiry teenager came over to us. "I'm Alec," he said in a vaguely southern accent. "I'm waiting to go stateside. Can you girls give me a hand?"

"Well, you're certainly ready for the States with your language—and your uniform, too."

He had a cut-down G.I. jacket, and was twirling an overseas cap.

"The boys in my unit went stateside. Somebody was going to send for me. How do you get to the States anyway?"

"Well, it's a complicated thing, but if you have a friend. . . . "

"Alec was a mascot of an American unit near here," the director cut in. "He's twelve, but he finds it hard to be with children. He speaks German, French and Croat as well as English. His father is supposed to have been an Italian. Who knows?

Perhaps one of the men will sponsor him. Meanwhile, there's no place for him to go.

"Things are much simpler here now. There was a time when we had children of twenty-four nationalities—from Norwegian to Dutch—an international community of waifs and strays."

This was the last camp on our official tour, and the three women leaders left Germany. Now I became voluntary agency staff, with the right to billets, a special identity card, and an indescribably precious PX card entitling me to purchase supplies at the Army post exchange.

* * *

I went to our CRS offices in Hoechst, outside Frankfurt. We had several floors in a dull brick office building set in the midst of the Farben industrial compound. James J. Norris, our European coordinator, the Reverend Stephen Bernas, D.P. service director, and a considerable staff were strengthening a network of agency field offices throughout the three zones of Germany. We were gathering data on the D.P.'s for the Canadian and other missions, and also in preparation for any U.S. immigration legislation. Meanwhile, an extensive supply scheme for clothing, supplementary foods, recreational and vocational equipment was in operation.

Irene and I sat down to compare notes. The IRO car and driver had been withdrawn when our three guests left. "You realize," said Irene, her grey eyes crinkling up in fun. "that as of this afternoon, you have ceased to be a VIP."

"I gathered as much when I saw my billets with the tiny coal stove in the corner," I laughed. "Well, let's get to work. After Aglasterhausen Center my nerves are raw. Is that what's happening to most of the D.P. children without families?"

"No fear. It's true that a few Polish and Yugoslav children have been traced and repatriated automatically. Once they are in a children's center there is little we can do. But do you think most of the children ever reach these centers? They are taken by a family and just added as one more child. No one knows how many. There are accompanied 'unaccompanied children' in every Polish, Baltic, and Ukrainian camp that I have visited. It may create problems, you know," said Irene thoughtfully.

"When immigration papers have to be drawn up, I can see the difficulties—but we'll meet that later."

"The Polish boy today. It was grim, I thought. Are there many like him?"

"Fortunately not, but even one is too many. These children brought in at twelve, separated from their families, forced into all kinds of work, are old beyond their years at fifteen or sixteen. These above all should have a choice, a say, at least, about their own future. Everybody has failed these children. Our government, army authorities, UNRRA, IRO, we as voluntary agencies. If a family does not accept the care of such a young person, there is no one to help him."

"So 'parens patria' is balked after all—by the charity of the refugees themselves. Do you remember, Irene, it was Dr. Emmanuel Sassen who questioned the right of 'parens patria' in cases like this. He told the United Nations that decisions should be taken for the welfare of each child. Thank God for clear-headed, stubborn Dutchmen. They pound home a principle even in the face of huge opposition. I hope he knows he has cohorts in the camps."

In succeeding weeks, I drove with Irene Dalgiewicz to D.P. child centers in the British as well as the American zone of Germany.

Much of that fall was grey and sunless. Perhaps it seemed greyer than it was because the D.P. camps were, in the main, dun-colored, nondescript barracks. They were the left-over, ill-used accommodations, since, in general, the better installations had to be turned to the uses of the occupation armies. It seemed a huddled world, somehow. Metal stoves had been placed in hundreds of drafty barracks, and as October gave way to November, the women and small children would be found clustering around the stoves wrapped in layers of variegated garments sent by American agencies including our own.

Compared with what we were seeing outside the camps, the D.P. world, grey and static as it was then, seemed a protected, even rather a cozy world. The daily food ration was assured. The battle for shelter and food had been won—while on the outside among the more recently expelled, the struggle for the basic necessities of life was never won.

Irene said to me, "One fear people have now more than ever before is the fear of this coming winter. People pray that it will not be icy." She was probably thinking of the D.P.'s. I was thinking as well of the German population and the expellees, who lurked in the cellars and half-ruined houses where at night lights mysteriously appeared.

One journey took us to Prien, like Aglasterhausen a "way station" for the young people being sent "home." A tow-headed Slovak teenager, an orphan, was being readied for a second repatriation. I felt utterly helpless. Since we had not balked when UNRRA officials arrogated to themselves the right to turn over lists of children to repatriation missions and government representatives, we could not upset the machinery at this point.

One of the child centers was reported to be located in a lonely house in the Harz mountains, near Hannenklee. It was so remote that no one had visited it from our agency—and no one was sure of its existence. We turned up unexpectedly, Irene in her U.S. uniform.

We were greeted with guarded formality by a handsome Latvian woman: "I am Dr. Utynas, director of this home. Whom did you wish to see here?"

Her manner softened visibly when we told her we were voluntary agency representatives. Tucked away in this secluded spot was an entire Latvian orphanage of eighty children, evacuated before the return of the Soviet armies and kept intact. Dr. Utynas had taken no chances with her charges in the days of mass repatriation. By now IRO had issued directives that Baltic and Ukrainian children were not to be turned over for repatriation. The Latvian children were put on the list for agency help and were registered for overseas migration. This became a happy eventuality a couple of years later when all of them tumbled from a plane to a group of welcomers at New York's Idlewild airport.

Our visit to a British Zone child center at Bad Lippspringe came just before a small group of Polish children were scheduled for return to Poland. The Polish houseworker drew Irene aside. "The girl near the window is not Polish at all. She is Ukrainian. Talk to her."

Irene, who spoke Russian and Ukrainian as well as Polish, started a conversation with the child. The warning seemed to be true. The child's name was certainly of Ukrainian origin.

A British voluntary agency worker ran the home under the mantle of the British Red Cross. She resented any questioning of the planned repatriation.

"I have seen the documents of this child. I am convinced that she is Polish."

"If I could see them, I might be able to learn a little more," said Irene. "There may be an indication of her mother's birthplace. This would help clear up the matter."

"It is not possible to show you any such documents," we are told with cold politeness. There was nothing we could do.

The whispered words of D.P.'s houseworkers and secretaries were not to be treated lightly. As D.P.'s themselves, they knew and cared about what had been and was being done to child D.P.'s. During lunch at a Frankfurt mess, an Estonian girl leaned over Irene's shoulder. "I just saw the papers—eighteen children marked for Russia. They are Balts and Ukrainians."

Irene knew what office to dash to the same day. She asked the U.S. military man if he had checked the transport of children listed for Russia. He was annoyed with the prying voluntary agencies. Many military men were annoyed with us in those days. Troublemakers, they termed us. "Of course, all the parents' birthplaces were listed inside Russia. Where else could we send these children?" asked the captain.

This time Irene insisted on seeing the documents. She studied each place name. Right enough, they were inside the new borders of Russia, but they were all within the Baltic area or in the Ukraine.

This children's transport was stopped. It was natural for countries which had lost so many children to want as many as they could get. It was natural for a welfare worker to try to save these victimized children for carefully-chosen homes in the United States that were waiting to welcome them.

As voluntary agencies representing various ethnic groups

were enabled to send personnel into Germany, they made their own direct contacts with the displaced persons. Polish Americans, Lithuanian Americans, Russian Americans were all engaged in the moral adventure on behalf of people with whose fate and anguish they identified completely. Numbers of Polish orphans located in Germany—even those not adopted by individual families—never came to the attention of UNRRA or repatriation missions. A sizeable group was united and shepherded by the American Polish Relief Organization to Barcelona, Spain. After a decade of continuous agency care, the group, by then teenagers, received visas for the United States.

Irene Dalgiewicz proved correct on the matter of migration complications with regard to informally adopted unaccompanied children. Under the D.P. Act of 1948, families who had taken in an extra child or children were often blocked in their attempt to obtain U.S. visas. It was not until 1950, when the D.P. Act was extended, that easement was provided for the entry of children who had been sheltered by the warmth of human adoptive parents against the cold net of the parent-state.

4. Railroad Junction

The Hoechst office of Catholic Relief Services, as thronged with unrelated people as a key railroad junction, was often referred to by that name, "Hauptbahnhof." Hundreds of camp chaplains made their way to it. Nearly eight hundred Polish priests had been liberated into the zone from Dachau—less than the number that had perished inside. Most of them stayed with the D.P.'s. They pleaded for any kind of help for their people— but mostly for words of hope. The individual D.P.'s began to converge on Hoechst—professors, farmers, woodcutters, Poles of course, Blats, Ukrainians, Croats, Slovenes, an unending stream of would-be travelers without passports, travel documents, funds or destinations.

To deal with the visitors, we had, besides our American staff, D.P. staff members who could cope with any necessary language.

The secretary to the mission director, Tatiana, spoke Russian and German. She was not technically a D.P. since she had papers listing her as "stateless." Tatiana was a tall girl of Russian origin, just twenty years of age.

She had long black hair and deep, melancholy brown eyes. There was something Byzantine in the perfection of her elongated oval face. Tatiana, as a staff member of an American organization, was assigned quarters in American billets. "My first language was Chinese," she told me one day in her clipped British speech. "I am Manchurian born."

She saw my puzzled look. "I am one of the Harbin Russians. We call it Kharbin. My nurse was Chinese. She taught me her speech before I started to say Russian words."

As she told me her story, I realized that Tatiana was a descendant of the great wave of Russian exiles, who had scattered over Europe, the Middle East and the Far East after the Bolshevik victory of 1918.

166

"My grandfather took his whole family to Harbin. You know that many anti-Bolsheviks fled to there. But he did not have so far to flee because he lived in the maritime provinces, near Khabarovsk, you know. His only son was killed by the Bolshevik forces, so he took my grandmother and my mother to safety. They could take nothing with them. They had a time of hunger. My mother was only eight years old. Have you ever heard of the Amur River? My grandmother's family had a shipping company for Amur River boats."

"And your English," I asked. "It is so fine. Where did you study it?"

"At the English school in Shanghai. Of course the teachers spoke in the English manner. My grandfather moved the family to Shanghai, where mother met my father. My father also came there. He came there to escape the Bolsheviks—but he came all the way from Tsaritsyn (later Stalingrad and still later Volgograd). There were many Russian exiles in Shanghai. I think he is still there. I haven't seen him since I was five."

One day she told me the events of the trajectory between Manchuria and Frankfurt, Germany.

After her mother's divorce and second marriage to a German business man in Shanghai, Tatiana was brought, along with her stepsister, for a visit to Germany. It was 1939, and the outbreak of war cut off all chance of return to Shanghai.

"Then I realized what being 'stateless' meant," Tatiana said. "My mother was now a German citizen because of her marriage to my stepfather. My little sister, Margareta, was German, of course. But I was a Russian who had never seen Russia. I had to stand on line every month with the Ostarbeiter and other foreigners to get my papers stamped. My food ration was lower than my little sister's, but more than the ration of those poor workers from the east.

"The American soldiers liberated the town in Thuringia where we were living in 1945.

"I was eighteen. We were so glad. To have lived through hunger and bombings—it was something. It was a June day in 1945. I was walking home from the bank where I was doing translations when I saw the American soldiers trading things with soldiers in other uniforms. They were Russian soldiers.

"I rushed home to tell my mother. We only had one room in a German woman's house. My mother had heard things, and she put Margareta and me in the cellar.

"The German lady began answering the door to Russian soldiers. I could hear them. They were asking for cooking pots and then other things. She told my mother that plenty of Russian soldiers were moving in. They were going to take over the town from the Americans in three days.

"Then my mother let us out of the cellar. She was talking to a Russian officer. He was a major and a doctor. He had taken a room in the German woman's house because the Russian military was opening up an army clinic in the school opposite the house where we lived.

"The major told us that no other Russian soldiers would knock at the door—but he told us to keep out of sight. The clinic in the school was a VD center, he told us.

"Then my mother got panicky, for me especially. I could be sent to the Russian interior. My mother and sister were safer.

"The major said to my mother: 'Take your children to the American zone of Germany. It is not far away. Then try to go to America. You may have a few years of peace there.' He was standing at the window when he said it, looking out into the street. It was twilight. We have never forgotten that moment. He was a Communist—but he gave us advice for our good.

"My mother talked with the German woman who was very afraid for us. She said that there was only one chance for us to escape. She persuaded us to go with her to the Red Cross hospital.

"American and German military men were there and it was filled with German soldiers. The whole hospital was going to be evacuated the very next day.

"We sat in a room with the military men and the German woman pleaded with the Germans to take us with them. My mother spoke with the Americans. She speaks English as I do.

"The officers were making the final arrangements for the moving of the whole hospital. They did not want to be bothered with our troubles, naturally—but my mother fought like a tiger for us. She cried and she begged. She told them what it meant to be a 'stateless' Russian.

"Finally they said she could have a paper for the evacuation convoy—as a member of the German kitchen staff. That would cover Margareta too. They tried out my English. They could not give me any paper but they would give me a headband like an American nurse. We had to report at six o'clock the next morning.

"We were there in good time as you can imagine. Of course we had no baggage. I was put in the cab of the truck next to the driver, a Texas boy. He knew my story. In the back of the truck my mother sat with the kitchen personnel. All had papers. Margareta was hidden under a blanket.

"We started off. Our truck was first. Then came about a dozen other trucks. Finally, we reached a spot where we all stopped. Two Russian sentries stood in the center of the road and behind them was a new *schlagbaum*, a wooden roadblock.

"They came up to look at everyone's papers. The Texas boy put his arms around me. He had given me gum to chew and I was chewing it hysterically. 'Honey,' he said, 'act as if you don't understand a word of German.'

"'Papers,' they said to me in German. 'You must have papers.' I said nothing and went on chewing gum. I tried to smile at the driver. Then one Russian said to the other in Russian, 'She chews gum like a cow, she must be American,' and they went to the back of the truck.

After a while, I could hear my mother's voice. Then I heard Margareta crying. They must have pulled the blanket from her, I thought. Then I heard many German voices screaming something about shooting, or being killed. I tried to get out of the truck, because I was sure something terrible was happening to my mother. But the door was locked and there was a chain across it. An American officer walked up to the cab and said sternly to me, 'Pull yourself together or you'll get the whole convoy in trouble.' Then I was sure something awful had happened and I cried like a baby.

"Suddenly the driver took off and I remember seeing the trees like a blur at the side of the road. We seemed to be flying by.

"I cried and screamed and pulled at the door and begged the driver to stop the truck. But he just kept on driving and told me to quiet down. I was sure my mother was not with us and I didn't care what I did or said.

"After about an hour, he suddenly stopped the truck. He almost carried me to the back of the truck. There was my mother and there was Margareta, hugging her and crying.

"My mother and everyone began talking at once. Everyone else's paper had a Red Cross stamped on it, except my mother's. The Russian soldier had been told to check this on every paper. Mother was ordered to get off the truck. She would not do it. They told her again, and she kept on talking, explaining how it was just a mistake that the mark had been left off.

"Then the Russian pointed his rifle at mother and told her in broken German to get down off the truck right away. It was then that the other people shouted to her, 'You will get shot— get off, get off.' Margareta pulled off the blanket and began to cry 'Mutti, Mutti, don't leave me.'

"My mother was terrified but she didn't get off the truck. She knew that would be the end. Instead, she pulled off her wristwatch and gave it to the soldier. He looked at it and roared 'Gehen Sie,' waving the truck onward. It was then that our driver took off like an airplane.

"We always say it was almost a miraculous inspiration on my mother's part. We were put down at Arolsen near the Diaconessen home. They gave us shelter. My mother was almost too exhausted to move.

"I went to the American Army hospital for a job. They said I could wash floors. My pay would be three meals a day, and at night a bucket of food scraps to take home. This was a wonderful salary, because money was almost worthless to buy food. Every night I came home with my little bucket filled with food for mother and Margareta.

"Then one day, the doctor discovered I had studied chemistry and biology in the German gymnasium. I was given a job in the hospital laboratory.

"I had only one dress. I shall never forget the day I was measured for two white laboratory uniforms. Then my mother got a job in the hospital personnel office.

"My mother wanted to go to Frankfurt so that she could try to get news of my grandmother and grandfather in Shanghai. She was given a position in the American consulate and I came to work with the Catholic D.P. office in Frankfurt-Hoechst. My mother did get word through to Shanghai. She got the news of grandmother's death, and a few months later of grandfather's. We had thought of trying to go back, but now we have no reason to go back to Shanghai."

Then I put a question that provoked further journeying for Tatiana. "Would you be interested in going to the United States?" I asked.

"If only I could," she said in her gentle voice. "And if only my mother and sister could qualify."

That was the beginning of Tatiana's metamorphosis from an officially stateless person into a D.P. Her home and job assurance were mine, and she joined eventually the stream of D.P. emigration moved forward by the CRS office.

* * *

Another member of our D.P. staff gave an Irish name.

Nellie O'Brien de Lacy, a blond and distinguished young lady, owed her name to one of the migrations of the wild geese of Ireland. She was the daughter of a Polish father and a White Russian mother. Her family had taken refuge in Poland and then in Germany. It was the first time for me that an Irish name had assumed an exotic quality. The Polish, Estonian, Ukrainian, Lithuanian names of our indispensable auxiliary personnel seemed rather ordinary by comparison. Nellie's name assumed an even more exotic tone in an Argentine setting where she married a Croat refugee.

Strange things happened outside as well as inside the office. Activity was soon reinstituted in the Farben chemical works which surrounded us on all sides. Several evenings a week, a thick yellow-green miasma settled over our section of Hoechst. Sometimes it was so heavy that we had to walk home like blind people, feeling our way along the streets. Eyes smarted, throats

grew dry as sandpaper. "Parfum Hoechst, Canal Number 5."
Father Stephen Bernas would say serenely as he saw the jaun-
diced green cloud come surging toward us like smoke escaping
from a furnace in hell.

"Something special for us today, the heavy unforgettable
scent of Canal Number 17. Free to all."

We laughed off the strange pall that surrounded us at intervals. But one night, alone, I got completely lost in the acrid fog.
I walked more than a mile before the air cleared enough for me
to see to what part of Hoechst my blind wanderings had brought
me.

We often felt ourselves as surrounded not only by the strange
chemical pall, but by stranger shadowy events that it was better
not to look into. One fogged-in evening as I was clearing up a
report in the office, a light knock came to the door. We opened
it to find two very tired looking young men staring at us. Frayed
woolen coats were wrapped around thin bodies. Caps were in
their hands. With great effort one of them slowly formed the
words, "Vo-ca-tional gui-dance."

I looked blank.

The second young man took it on himself with even greater
effort and precision to repeat the same words, even more slowly—like a child attacking his first polysyllabic utterance.

"V-ca-chunal gui-dance." I looked at the two pale young men,
ghosts echoing one another.

I turned to William Sullivan, recently returned from
Czechoslovakia.

"Not my window of the Hauptbahnhof," he said smiling.
Czechs infiltrating into the zone for refuge came regularly in
search of Bill.

I asked Tatiana. "Vocational guidance, they want. At this
hour!"

"Oh, Vocational guidance." She laughed reassuringly. "I did-
n't hear them. It's in that basement. The light's still on."

She smiled at them and spoke in Russian. They answered in
Polish and went on to the basement. I dropped by the lighted
basement center on my way to meet friends at the army mess in
the Hoechst Casino.

The two young men were talking animatedly to a knot of people. I looked at the long bare cellar, with a few typewriters and a few nondescript machines placed haphazardly about the rough floor. Then they saw me and there was consternation and silence.

"Just thought I'd look in. I'm interested in," I formed the words like a child speaking English, "vo-ca-tional gui-dance." Something had dawned on me. This was a Hauptbahnhof for new arrivals in an underground railroad.

"Vocational guidance" was a password known all the way to Poland, perhaps to Poles in Italy and Austria. The Poles were taking care of their own. A Polish liaison officer from the London exile government was staying on to help infiltrating refugees slip into camps. I inquired no more. Officially and actually we did not have the facts. It was not up to us to regulate the type of vocational guidance offered to dislocated people trying to be displaced persons.

The same liaison officer, I discovered later, took part in a rescue project for non-Polish D.P.'s. Russians and Ukrainians in danger of forced repatriation took the cloak of Polish nationality, and were certified by the liaison officers as bonafide co-nationals.

One did not question the whole flock of White Russians who posed as Ukrainians from the Polish Ukraine—and therefore passed into the D.P. category—nor the Ukrainians who thought it was safer to label themselves Poles. Their identity had been used against them. They were now using identity as a shield.

5. Magna Carta of the Refugees

The Magna Carta of the refugees came in July 1951, when twenty-four member nations of the United Nations adopted a convention on refugees. The convention asserted the principle of no forced return, termed "non-refoulement." It laid down that a refugee cannot be returned (*refoulé*) "in any manner whatsoever to the frontiers of territories where his life or freedom would be threatened on account of his race, religion or membership of a particular group or political opinion." Thus it was that refugees knew that the United Nations Declaration of Human Rights was not a dead letter in their regard.

One of the articles of the convention stated that refugees must be given free access to courts of law in the country of asylum. Originally, the convention was to apply only to those who had become refugees as a consequence of events prior to January 1, 1951. The cut-off date was never rigidly enforced; in 1967 a protocol was added to the convention formally broadening its provisions to include later refugees regardless of dateline.

The Office of the UN High Commissioner for Refugees enunciated the rights embodied in the convention not only for the refugees it served directly, but for refugees anywhere who managed to reach a country of asylum.

Actuated by a basically divergent concept of the relationship between the individual and the state, as shared by the other signatories, the Union of Socialist Soviet Republics did not sign the convention. There was no doubt that eastern European refugees were dissenters from the Soviet system and from the post-war regimes in such countries as Czechoslovakia and Poland. Where the nation-state had gathered to itself social, political and economic truth, dissent was a criminal act, punishable by separation from the community by prison or labor camp. As long as there existed the profound difference over the right of asylum, it could hardly be expected that the USSR would join with more open societies in such a convention.

As the influx of refugees presented problems to this or that receiving country, a further refinement of the Convention on refugees was called for. In December 1968, the UN General Assembly adopted a Declaration on Territorial Asylum. It asserted that the granting of asylum, "being a peaceful and humanitarian act, cannot be regarded as unfriendly by any other state." Recognizing that the situation of the person seeking asylum was of concern to the international community, the declaration stated that the community should "consider appropriate measures to lighten the burden on states granting or continuing to grant asylum."

It took three years for the Convention on Territorial Asylum to obtain the necessary signatories to come into force. After that, the adherence of governments grew speedily. It was hoped that the USSR, its strictures against movement across its borders mitigated, would join the signatories.

It might be that being a signatory would not mean that a government would always live up to the ideal in practice, yet the very existence of the convention achieved two important ends: it would give a government pause before violating it; it provided for the individual refugee, or group of refugees, the knowledge of a right guaranteed by one hundred and six nations of the world.

* * *

Had the right of asylum for the innocent not been protected in western Europe in the years immediately after World War II, many more tragedies would have taken place than did occur. One tragedy might have been that the displaced persons would not have been saved for eventual resettlement around the world.

Chapter Four

PAPER WAR FOR THE D.P.'S

1. Matching and Compassion
2. The Hard Core
3. World Refugee Year

177

1. Matching and Compassion

The United States, a nation of immigrants, experienced its first truly planned wave of migration in the resettlement of the D.P.'s. The great movement of people, though under federal auspices, and supervised by a Displaced Persons Commission with headquarters and twelve branch offices in Europe, depended ultimately on voluntary effort. No D.P. could hope to touch the American shore unless he was matched with an assurance. The assurance consisted of a formal signed document that a U.S. citizen or a voluntary agency was committed to provide a home and job placement for the migrant and his family. The sponsorship of a D.P. which resulted from such an assurance was a serious responsibility—but a moral rather than legal one.

Matching became a major activity of voluntary agency personnel. A farmer from Nekoosa, Wisconsin, sending an assurance for a farming family, would begin readying a six-room tenant house. A farming family in "Durzyn" fitting the needs would be chosen by our staff. After security and health checks, the Polish family, stateless as far as government protection was concerned, would receive an entry visa on an IRO travel document. Then came the move to the reception center at Bremerhaven to be ready for the next sailing of an IRO ship.

Assurances, offering homes and jobs for the D.P.'s began to flow in. A massive "Papierkrieg," or "Paper War," for human happiness was on. Some of the assurances were for a named relative or friend. Most of the assurances that came to our agency left the name space blank. Every other detail, type of work, type of housing available was exact and clear. The agency had to "match" the assurance with a person or family in a camp in Europe. Such assurances only came forward from Americans because they trusted in the integrity of the agency administering the program,

179

and because their compassion for the plight of the D.P.'s over-
came their hesitancy at sponsoring an unseen foreigner.

The D.P. Act of 1948 which began to operate on August 27,
1948, was extended in 1950, and closed its operations on
August 31, 1952. During that time, some 370,000 refugees were
processed and brought to the United States.

It was the voluntary agencies, notably Church World Service
with a score of cooperating agencies, the National Lutheran
Council, the Hebrew Sheltering Aid Society, United Service for
New Americans, and Catholic Relief Services—NCWC, which
took the brunt of the task in promoting assurances among their
constituents. International Rescue Committee focused on the
placement of professional displaced persons; ethnic groups of
Americans stressed cultural ties in resettlement efforts. The
agencies, especially those representing the great religious groupings of the American people, penetrated deep into local communities with the D.P. story. To link the D.P.'s with the historic
founders of the nation, they were often referred to as delayed
pilgrims.

Among the vast pile of paper assurances added to the arse-
nal of the paper war was one that I deposited out of a sense of
personal responsibility. The little document brought to the
shores of the United States the young Russian girl who had
been born in exile in Harbin, on the shores of the Yellow Sea.
Manchuria-born Tatiana, the secretary to our Frankfurt mission
director, needed a sponsor. She had no American relatives to
help her take advantage of the D.P. law. No unnamed ready-for-
matching assurance had come to our resettlement office indi-
cating the need for an English-German-Russian-Chinese
speaking office worker.

On the day of her arrival, I joined one of our welfare teams
as it set itself up on the long pier of the New York Harbor dock
to meet an IRO ship, the S.S. *Mercy*. Armed with records, cabled
confirmations of names of passengers, plane and train tickets,
and travel allotments, our teams set themselves up before tables
at the end of the pier, immediately outside the customs barrier.

The team worked with lightning-like speed, but the D.P.'s
were restive—impatient to get off the line. Weeping reunions,

cries of joy, all had to wait the orderly process of record-check-
ing. This was the last time they were to line themselves up as
D.P.'s. When we had dealt with their needs, they were free to
scatter, one by one, or family by family, to go their separate
ways as inhabitants of a country to which they had been award-
ed a permanent visa. As Tatiana walked toward me, and as the
other D.P.'s left the pier line, they left the road of exile forever.
My assurance for Tatiana provided her a job in our resettlement
division, where her languages and experience were of great util-
ity. Her mother and sister soon joined her. And a family transplanted from Manchuria via Austria and Germany settled into
life in the United States.

Perhaps the most unique transplantation under IRO was that
of the remnant of the golden horde of Genghis Khan. They
were known as *Kalmucks*, a word which signifies "remnant."
These were the Mongolians who had settled along the Don And
Volga Rivers. Faithful followers of the Buddha, they had maintained their religion and separate identity even under the bitterly resented collectivistic hand of Marxism.

Some had fled Russia with the retreating German armies;
some fought with the Germans. Stranded in postwar Europe,
they finally were given the shelter of D.P. camps in Austria and
Germany.

Two American voluntary agencies united to give the Kalmucks
their chance at resettlement. The International Rescue Committee
provided the funds, while Church World Service provided the
organizational links in Europe and in American communities.
Blanket assurances protected this time, not only families of
Mongol origin, but saffron-robed and shaven-headed Buddhist
monks. Five hundred and seventy descendants of the Golden
Horde, an exotic and pathetic remnant, were brought to communities in New Jersey and Pennsylvania.

The new language of international charity gained currency:
"home and job assurance," "matching," "call forward" (for consular interview), "in the pipeline."

The matching, basic to the succeeding steps, gained speed.
The "Papierkrieg" threatened to vanquish our staff utterly. The
documents were eventually systematized by a commercial com-

pany. As the agency had a target of one hundred thousand persons, the New York staff was raised to nearly three hundred persons. Fixed into a great bedrock of corporate charity, an edifice of skill and scientific planning was carefully set up. As skill and science had been bent to the destruction of family and community, so similar scientific skills had to be put at the service of reintegration and resettlement.

A network of local contacts to weed out impractical assurances and to help in the reception of incoming displaced persons was organized in one hundred and twenty diocesan centers. A diocesan director of resettlement, usually a person engaged in social welfare, headed the work.

A National Catholic Resettlement Council was founded to coordinate the efforts of local and national groups. It became the umbrella for sixteen organizations, including the National Councils of Catholic Men and Women, the National Catholic Rural Life Conference, and organizations of Americans of Polish, Hungarian, Ukrainian, Lithuanian, Italian, Estonian, Slovenian, Czech and Slovak origin. Thus broadly based, the Resettlement Council played a crucial role in reaching into American communities to implement the program of D.P. integration.

In Europe, the arrival of more and more assurances gave rise to the greatest and most unique matching operation that was ever achieved in a humanitarian cause. IRO registration files were an aid in the total task, but each voluntary agency had to accumulate enormous filing systems on human lives. Our own agency, for example, from a headquarters office in Frankfurt, organized a network of twenty emigration offices in Germany and Austria. A special autonomous office was set up to deal with refugee problems in Trieste, and six offices operated in Italy. At the peak of refugee movement, under the U.S. D.P. Law 778, the overseas staff, American and international, of one agency, Catholic Relief Services, numbered three hundred and eighty persons.

Where individual assurances were lacking for deserving D.P.'s, our field staff was permitted to include them in the agency corporate blanket assurance. When the blanket assurance cases arrived in the United States, the resettlement network somehow found placements for all of them.

Was there much mismatching in so stupendous task, one never done on such a scale by voluntary agencies—or by any agencies—before this time? Of course there was. The chief reason—compassion. A field staff worker, knowing the needs of refugees in nearby camps from frequent visiting and long-term material aid programs, was often moved by pity and love—no matter how coolly scientific his social welfare training had been. In his hand was a paper with a blank space that needed a name; a person with a name desperately needed to be inserted in that piece of paper. The simple act of filling in his name gave him release from the bondage of camp, gave him a shelter, a country. A Polish forester became a farmer; a Lithuanian bookkeeper became a lumberman; a Ukrainian peasant who knew his wheat fields became a dairyman—all on paper. But on the whole, matching was as exact as any human equation could be. From the mail sacks of assurances delivered regularly by plane, boatloads of D.P.'s materialized at U.S. ports. As the IRO ship took off from Europe, cables were dispatched to the resettlement office listing the names of all refugees processed by our agency. From that list, we sent wires to spons︿rs and made travel arrangements from portside to points of destination. Teams of staff members and volunteers met each ship to expedite its human cargo. The aim was to put all refugees on their way inland on the day of arrival.

While the refugee was in mid-ocean, we often received word of cancellation of the assurance by the sponsor. The refugee was not aware that at some point in his trajectory over the Atlantic, he had become orphaned, and that our agency blanket assurance was gently lowered over him. His only inconvenience, and it was not at all painful to him, was that he would remain in a New York hotel while a new placement was found for him through the many-fingered National Catholic Resettlement Council. The delayed refugee became the envy of his fellows who were whisked out of New York after a quick view of the dock and of the railroad or air terminal.

Toward the end of the D.P. Act, New York City became host to so many delayed refugees that for a period of three months we had the equivalent of six small D.P. camps under agency care. It happened at the end of 1951 and the beginning of 1952.

A few thousand people depending on our agency lacked individual assurances. They were "in the pipeline" and there were dossiers and preliminary correspondence regarding many of them. These people, for whom the golden door to America was already ajar, might be condemned to untold years of homelessness, to the prolonged bitterness of missed opportunity once the D.P. law ran out. The director of our agency jumped into the breach. He wrapped them all in the security of the "blanket assurance." Thus protected, the last few thousands of the D.P.'s to qualify under the U.S. displaced persons law stepped aboard ships and planes for the port of New York.

A midtown hotel, once a fusty, Victorian-type residence, became, for three months, a jam-packed D.P. camp in the heart of Manhattan. Walking through its lobby and halls one heard Polish, Ukrainian, Lithuanian and most of the tongues of eastern Europe. I had never thought to see a refugee camp in New York—much less a mingling of the camps I had seen in 1947. At this hostel a few blocks from our office I had the impression of revisiting Ettlingen, Hanau and "Durzyn," now rolled into one.

It was close to the Christmas season of 1951. People were too busy with their own lives to make way for unexpected strangers.

Diocesan directors and local committees sent out appeals for new homes and jobs. Some lay people and priests spent the weeks before Christmas going from door to door to explain the plight of the D.P.'s in New York. One priest saw with satisfaction a score of families spend Christmas in American homes as a result of his efforts. As soon as he made his plea, listeners saw a certain parallel with another homeless family. He wrote to us after the holidays: "I was never so exhausted, but it was the happiest and most meaningful Christmas I ever spent."

But unlike what had transpired with the holy family, there was room at the inn in New York. In fact, when the first hotel refused to take another person, a second hotel was enlisted. D.P. movement out of New York was far slower than the IRO ship arrivals—and a third, fourth, fifth and sixth hotel filled up with D.P.'s for a week or month. The fabulous delights of New

York paled somewhat when the newcomers realized the reason for their free holiday. Cash outlays for room rents and meal tickets mounted inexorably, crossing the million-dollar mark.

We had to reassure anxious D.P.'s that his was not the beginning of a new type of camp existence. Baby carriages blocked hotel corridors. Children became ill. Agency workers wore haunted faces, explaining, reassuring, waiting for word of placements from local committees.

The pleas made at Christmas and New Year on behalf of our New York D.P.'s yielded a flock of new placements. By March the hotels were emptied of D.P.'s who fanned out to communities from coast to coast. For our agency, the U.S. displaced persons law had ended with a bang. The million dollars overspent had to be made up in the following year's budget.

We finally added up the reckoning in terms of people—a reckoning made possible by incredible charity on the part of Americans offering assurances, by fantastic faith on the part of the D.P.'s themselves in our motives and plans for them, by the scientific systematizing of Remington Rand, by the work of 650 paid staff and thousands of volunteers at ports and in local communities. Our agency had helped bring to our country 135,550 D.P.'s as well as 15,387 refugees of German ethnic origin and 957 orphans.

Other agencies had undergone similar experiences. Both in Europe and in the United States, the American voluntary agencies met regularly on every aspect of the D.P. migration program. When necessary, the agencies, through the American Council of Voluntary Agencies for Foreign Service, made joint representation to departments of the U.S. government. At the American council, agencies with religious or ethnic constituents and nonsectarian committees met in confidence and frankness to find solutions to problems that arose in serving the homeless overseas.

Before the last D.P. had entered the United States under the D.P. Act, the International Refugee Organization had gone out of existence. The organization turned over some assets and funds to voluntary and other groups continuing to serve the refugees, and officially closed its books as of the end of June 1950. Movement of refugees under IRO auspices continued through January 1952. The migration task accomplished by IRO, buttressed by the U.S. displaced persons law, by specific agreements with the governments of receiving countries, and by the unremitting activity of voluntary agencies, was a magnificent contribution to social peace and to the moral cohesion of the world community. In its four and a half years of life, it had played a crucial part in the resettlement of 1,104,000 refugees in a score of countries.

Few organizations of the United Nations accomplished a mandate more definitively and clearly than the IRO. Its activities had also served as a corrective for certain moral traps regarding the basic human rights of freedom of choice and right of asylum into which earlier international efforts had fallen.

The first three countries in the list of receiving countries accounted for 643,999 displaced persons in the final report of the IRO. The United States led the list of receiving countries with 370,000 persons. Second on the list was Australia. Third on the list of receiving countries was a small nation which for its own people set up absolutely no immigration restrictions. It promoted an in-gathering of the aged, the broken in health, the broken-spirited, the orphaned, the remnants of families. These were welcomed in Israel, which accepted 132,000 persons by IRO's final tally. They were a precious, rescued portion who could repeat the biblical words of Azariah: "We, O Lord, are diminished more than any other nation."

The bending back of the course of the people of the diaspora into the land of their far origin was at the same time a bending and changing of the course of history. The Near East became more than ever the crucible of history.

In the end, the SS *Exodus* and the SS *Redemption*, though unsuccessful in their first attempts at passage, did prove to be prophetic forerunners. There came the day when there was no more turning back of refugee ships. The great exodus did finally reach the land of promise, and the exiled of the diaspora were redeemed in the temporal order after the creation of Israel in 1948. The "in-gathering of the exiles" was an accomplished fact. The president of the state of Israel reverted to the evocative terminology of redemption in his book, *The Exiled and*

Polish refugees deported from their homeland during World War II line up for temporary housing at a CRS-sponsored center in Iran. A million and a half Poles were sent by cattle cars to central Asia, then fled by foot to neutral Iran.

Preparing for transport overseas, Polish refugees break camp in Iran. Nearly fifteen hundred adults and children eventually found a home at Colonia Santa Rosa in Mexico. Other thousands were located in camps in Africa until the end of the war.

The end of World War II left more than ten million "displaced persons" in Germany and Austria. Others escaped to Allied zones from the east. Much of their time was spent just waiting, like this couple.

The author visits a displaced family at a shelter in Germany. Special efforts were made to keep refugee families together.

People expelled from Yugoslavia, Hungary, Czechoslovakia and Romania also crowded DP camps, such as this one in Friedland, West Germany.

The political division of the Indian subcontinent in 1947 forced an estimated twelve million persons from their homes. These refugees received emergency shelter and care at a camp in West Bengal, India.

A Korean woman makes milk with powder from the United States. CRS is one of the largest suppliers of America's agricultural abundance.

Bishop Edward E. Swanstrom, executive director of Catholic Relief Services, with a young girl at an orphanage in South Korea.

Eileen Egan, right, with a Maryknoll Sister and a Chinese refugee mother in Hong Kong. With the help of CRS, the American nuns founded one of the first housing projects for people fleeing to the British colony.

Msgr. Joseph J. Harnett of CRS helped these Vietnamese fishermen, refugees from the north, to resume their calling in South Vietnam.

Getting back home is always the goal. These Montagnards prepare to return to the Pleiku during a lull in the fighting in Vietnam.

the Redeemed: the redeemed were those who had been part of the great in-gathering, and had become citizens of Israel.

In the temporal sense also, the great masses of the D.P.'s had been redeemed, bought back from the limbo of camp life for productive work in the farthest corners of the world. There were about 125,000 D.P.'s who had been turned down by every migration mission. They were left behind in the limbo of a landscape they had not chosen in the joyless clusters of humanity's losers, know as "hard core" camps.

2. The Hard Core

It would have been simple for voluntary agencies and governments to put the "hard core" cases of the displaced persons out of the forefront of their consciences. Refugees were springing up in other parts of the world, including Africa, and there was the immense problem of iron curtain escapees in Europe and the Asian refugees of India, Hong Kong and Korea.

By this time, the United Nations had followed the example of the League of Nations in setting up the position of the High Commissioner for Refugees. Its mandate was broad enough to include not only refugees existing at the time of its inauguration, 1950, but also those who might become refugees in the future. So enormous was the continuing challenge of the world's displaced that the services of voluntary agencies, and even of charismatic individuals, were of crucial importance in maintaining unflagging concern for the long-term refugees while responding to newer streams of the displaced.

An individual European was so moved by what he saw in a "hard core" camp of World War II displaced persons that he made himself their champion. He dramatized the needs of the remaining D.P.'s as discarded human beings left behind in camps that could be called "cemeteries of the living." He was Georges Pire, a Belgian Dominican monk of febrile energy and a keen practical outlook.

He began by establishing lines of contact between individuals in western Europe and the inmates of "hard core" camps in Germany and Austria. This activity came to be known as the "Europe of the Heart." Through such personal contacts, which necessarily bared the anguish of the D.P.'s, he hoped to break down what he termed the "iron curtain of western egoism."

So successful were the impassioned appeals of Georges Pire

that out of "Europe of the heart" grew eight European villages, complete with small comfortable homes, conveniences, roads. Many near-forgotten D.P.'s received keys to brand-new houses and settled into Europa-villages named for such leaders as Albert Schweitzer and Fridtjof Nansen. When his work was crowned with the Nobel Prize, Pire put the prize money at the service of the D.P.'s and expanded his efforts to include what was then called East Pakistan.

The name given to one of the European villages for "hard core" D.P.'s was that of Anne Frank. The girl whose shining youth was poured into a secret diary before it was extinguished at Belsen concentration camp was the prototype of all innocent victims of history. She was a fitting symbol for help to D.P.'s who were still history's living victims.

Despite the dramatic work of Georges Pire, of voluntary agencies of many nations, of permanent solution grants from the UN High Commissioner for Refugees, of residual funds from IRO which went into homes for aged and infirm D.P.'s the lot of the very last of the D.P.'s was a bleak one. Basic care came to them from German public assistance, to which the D.P.'s had equal rights with German citizens. Many of the less resilient among the D.P.'s remained a people apart from the German community. Too much humiliation still scarred their spirits, and despite having their needs met, they still fed on the dreams of exile. As Aeschylus said in the fifth century before the Christian era, "I know how men in exile feed on dreams."

One of the "hard core" D.P. camps was in Landshut, Bavaria. On a bright October day in 1955, we drove into Landshut, a medium-sized town planted in solid comfort in rich Bavarian farmland like a middle-aged woman settled placidly in a richly-carpeted, old-fashioned parlor. When I saw the Hoehnkaserne, I realized why such camps had been called the "cemeteries of the living." The cozy stolidity of Bavarian life gave way to unrelieved bleakness. The entire camp consisted of an enormous antiquated military barracks structure of gray stone. It was on the dark side of the street and permanent winter seemed to have descended on it. The blind windows, bare of any signs of habitation, faced on the town. The interior of the building looked out on a dusty square, without a blade of grass or a tree. The space must have served as a parade ground for the successive detachments of soldiery housed in the Kaserne from before the First World War until the end of World War II. Now the drill yard echoed not the sharp click of the military step, but the shuffle of dispirited men, some of them amputees, many of them living in the paralyzed half-life imposed by the presence of "schatten" on their lungs.

The women in the camp were in a minority. Some were wives of inmates, others part of the tragic crop of unwed mothers unwanted in migration schemes. One by one the camps in the surrounding area had been closed—Memlingen, Schliesheim, Altenstadt, Dillingen, and many others. The pitiful human remainders had been carted in each case to the Landshut Kaserne, and there deposited. Here was "permanent homelessness," the end of a long line of provisional homelessness.

Landshut took me back to my days in the D.P. camps in 1947, when I had come in with a special mission under the auspices of the beginning IRO, the International Refugee Organization. In the crowded uncertain days of 1947, most D.P.'s shared mass quarters. They gained a little privacy by making walls of their soiled blankets to separate themselves from their neighbors.

Most of the Hoehnkaserne consisted of large, stone-walled, sunless barracks rooms where half a dozen men were assigned to eat and sleep. I walked through long, dark halls, inhabited by stale cabbagy smells. The large rooms, heavy with the still cold air, were like vaults for meat storage, or the disaster rooms of city hospitals reserved for the unidentified dead.

At the time of my visit, the camp was peopled by six hundred and four displaced persons of a dozen nationalities—Polish, Ukrainian, White Russian, Lithuanian, Latvian, Slovak, Croat, Slovene, Rumanian and a few scattered remnants of other nationalities to make an even dozen. Two thirds of the inmates were Polish. A pall had settled over my mind as I surveyed the shell of a building and so many shells of human beings. But as I read the roster of the inhabitants, a thin blade of triumph cut its way through the pall. It shone with a brilliant steely light as it came out into the open. Strange to feel any sense of triumph in a living cemetery—but there it was. I went back to the floodtide of the displaced persons when it had been a moral adventure to protect the right of asylum and the right of free choice for such people as these. These rights had been protected against UNRRA, against governments, against immoral agreements, against repatriation schemes. I had felt part of that moral adventure. Hundreds of thousands had benefited and had found new lives, fanning out in migration projects over the whole free world. A minority had been too broken on the wheel of life to profit from the freedom that had been preserved for them. They could only endure, and they had been helped at least to do that.

In a corner of the camp lived a young woman maintained through our agency as a full-time welfare assistant and counselor. She herself was an expellee of German ethnic origin whose former home had been in the Sudetenland of Czechoslovakia. She was one of scores of social welfare assistants placed by our agency in such permanent camps.

Supervising and guiding the resident welfare assistants was a tall, young Dutch woman from Nijmegen. Her approach was a yeasty amalgam of warm compassion and implacable Dutch practicality. Under her guidance, long-term camp workers, almost ready to resign themselves to the role of attendants at a living cemetery, sprang into purposeful activity. Work, paid work, was the saving road for "hard core" D.P.'s, and her aim was a workshop in each camp. A workshop could coax back into a confrontation with life men and women who were emotionally as prone as corpses. It would be the necessary link with the productive community around them—a proof that they had something to contribute to it and a right to some return for it.

We visited the camp workshop. It was a fair-sized room, about twenty feet square, with only one window. One glaring electric bulb hung from the center of the ceiling.

With limited funds the Dutch supervisor and her German assistant had purchased and set up four hand-operated knitting machines. Eight men and women, fearful of leaving the camp and for years totally removed from the life of productive work, were busy at the machines. They were under the direction of a woman from the town who trained them in operating and caring for the machines and then helped market the finished products. White sweaters for babies, bright blue knitted dresses for little girls and navy blue sweaters for small boys were neatly laid out. One team of a man and woman were busy turning out heavy brown socks on order for a nearby old people's home. The children's clothes were to go on display at a meeting of the wives of American military personnel in Munich. Almost all the output of the workshop was disposed of either through the personnel of the American military stationed in Germany or through German welfare institutions.

By now the protected workshop was beginning to pay for itself. Out of the proceeds, each refugee received fifty pfennigs an hour for working—in addition, of course, to the basic public welfare allotment of sixty-four marks a week from German public welfare funds.

I began to talk to the workshop refugees, a group of Poles. One of the workers was an amputee, having lost an arm at the shoulder. He was in his fifties. He had gone from German prisoner of war camp to a D.P. camp, and had not earned a pfennig from regular work in a dozen years. For eight hours of work, he was getting four DM, then about a dollar, daily. He stood up to greet me, his shapeless greasy clothes clinging to his body, his gray turtle-neck sweater hugging his sinewy neck. He was peering at me from rheumy eyes, a half-smile flickering on his lips. He spoke in mangled German and ended with a plea: "When you start to work, Fraulein, you don't like to stop so early. If we had better light, we could work until six. We could work till six o'clock, till we eat, nicht wahr?"

He had made his speech and he sat down again to murmured words of approval in German and Polish.

A Pole from Lodz, also a former POW, supported the stand taken by his comrade. I was amazed that after sixteen years in Germany, he was still using a halting, Polonized German: "If we had some lamps, not just a bulb, we could do more work—even better work."

The three women in the group agreed, "You can see for yourself, Fraulein Egan. It is hard on the eyes."

In commending them for their fine products, I told them we would supply four standing work lamps so that their good production record could continue.

As we left, the social workers emphasized that the eight people had been chosen because they had been among the most negative, the most dejected residents of the Hoehnkaserne. The thought that they really could learn something new without being hurt by criticism, that their mistakes would bring forth only kindness and patience, and that finally they could earn money without leaving the camp, had galvanized this small group into action. Most of them were post-TB cases; a few were heavy drinkers. They were beginning to save their money for radios, for flashy bedcovers, for new coffee pots. Their goals were small but attainable—at least a step farther than no goals at all.

It was only later, in World Refugee Year, when they heard on their radios that people everywhere, and even the United Nations, wanted to help them leave such camps as the Hoehnkaserne, that the goals of many of these people became more rounded, human goals.

Entering the cavernous men's barracks, I was reminded that going through a refugee camp is always the act of meeting history in human shape, in its living victims. Four or eight men were living in rooms that might have served forty soldiers. Next to each cot was a wooden wardrobe, often roughly hand-made. Some of the men arranged their cooking pots and eating utensils on side tables; others deployed them on the floor around the cot. Some of the beds were discreetly screened behind blankets. The men who worked could easily be distinguished from the non-workers by the presence of a bicycle parked near his cot. The bicycles helped give the impression of life lived in an open hallway.

An unkempt friendly man from the Soviet Ukraine told me: "I work on the harvest, and I work for the farmer when he tells me. When there is no more to do on the farm I come back here."

The look he gave his untidy corner was one of familiar affection. He had been a slave laborer, an OST arbiter, brought in during wartime to serve German agriculture. He had pitted himself against the giant forces of history that had all but engulfed him when he refused to return to his former home. It occurred to me that the act of escaping from, or of saying "no" to, repatriation officers had been for men like him so momentous a thing that it had exhausted any reserves of resilience. Without the moral support of relatives or of traditional communities, they could not carve out a new pattern of life for themselves. He was doing the same work that he had been dragooned into doing, but he could not commit himself to any farm employer lest he become a slave again. The Landshut camp was a refuge against this.

Other refugees made no more forays into the outside world. A Pole in another barrack room did not want to talk at all. His dossier gave the facts. He arrived in Landshut in February 1954 after residence in a long line of camps. He could seldom be inveigled into talking, either to the Lagerleiter or to the social worker. On his record was the date of his birth, 1926, and the date of his deportation into Germany for forced labor, 1943. He had had six years of elementary school, and had worked on his parents' small farm. Healthy and strongly built, he refused to do regular work.

He received no welfare assistance because the German authorities insisted that able-bodied men perform a modicum of work. When the spirit moved him, he would leave the camp to gather scrap metal. Selling this was his way of getting extra food and pocket money. When this source did not yield what he needed, he went out to beg. He seemed to be meting out to life precisely what it had meted out to him. He had become a being moved by forces outside himself—armies, alien masters, anonymous organizations in charge of camps, camp directors and social workers. He had been forced to live provisionally, depending on the planning of a collective "they." He was striking back by taking it all literally, by living provisionally, bound to nothing, tied by no plans, no schedule. When the camp director or social worker urged him to take a regular job, he retreated behind the only barricade he could depend on—complete silence.

Another refugee had never talked. His only means of communication was the sign language, since besides being a deaf-mute he was an analphabete. Born in Poland in 1920, he had been brought to Germany for forced labor in 1941. Not only did he refuse to return to Poland, but he consistently refused to give his consent to being placed in a German institution for deaf-mutes. There his life would have been ordered and he would have been taught a trade. In point of time, he was the senior resident of the Hoehnkaserne. He would talk in sign language of his wartime experiences, and always produced pictures of his parents and of their former home in Poland. He had the address of a brother in the United States, but no offer of a sponsorship or of help ever reached the social worker on his behalf. Meantime, as the years went by, he retreated from all work. His days were spent wandering aimlessly about the camp, cadging enough pfennigs from the working inmates to go on an occasional drinking spree. The kindness of the other inmates, mistaken as it might be, was unfailing to the lonely, handicapped man.

Behind the doors of the women's quarters, mostly individual rooms, were women from Russia, Poland, Yugoslavia. Our social worker gave me details. One woman, in her thirties, had gone the rounds of seventeen D.P. camps. Brought into Germany from the Soviet Union in 1941, when she was fifteen years of age, she had for a short while done housework as a little slavey. After that she spent the rest of the war years in a brothel. Her marriage to a fellow D.P. ended in separation after the birth of a daughter. Formerly a heavy drinker, the woman had become a model mother. Her camp room was a haven of brightness, with cretonne curtains incongruously lining the barrack window. The Russian woman was one of the displaced persons on the list for an apartment—should apartments ever be available.

In a neighboring room was another young woman who had survived a childhood deportation. At fifteen, she had been brought from Poland into wartime Germany for heavy farm work. In a D.P. camp she lived with a man by whom she had two children. When he refused to marry her, she fell into the category of "hard core" and became a case for the Hoehnkaserne. Our field staff had known of hundreds of such cases in the years between 1945 and 1950 during the great exodus of single men from the D.P. camps. As a wife and child or children would imperil their emigration, the young men already working with

Allied occupation units as guards and drivers decided to grasp any opportunity to leave Europe for the United States, Canada or Australia.

The woman's two children had been born in 1947 and 1950. Her consuming passion was to see that they took advantage of their education in the local school. The welfare funds given to her were well spent, and her living quarters were spotless. The social worker was hoping against hope that an apartment would be found for her outside the camp. In or out of camp she would have received her living from German public assistance funds.

A woman from Yugoslavia had been nineteen when brought to the Reich from her homeland in 1941. She was living in untidiness and dirt, completely apathetic to every consideration but food and alcohol. Moving from camp to camp, she had borne five children. One by one they had been removed from her by reason of her neglect of their needs. Her fifth child was still with her in the Hoehnkaserne, but steps had been taken to place it in a child care home. The woman was being put under the care of a legal guardian for eventual institutional care.

Of his charges, the camp director, a brisk kindly German, said: "Many don't want to move out of this camp for good. They don't want jobs that are permanent. They want a place to creep back to when they are hurt or tired. That is why so many of them want to work on the harvest, and then take odd jobs with farmers for the rest of the year. The Hoehnkaserne, Fraulein, may look like a cold place to you. But for too many of these," he waved his hand to include the hundreds immured in the barracks, "it is a mother."

Our Dutch social welfare supervisor said: "We have to look to the German community for the cause of some of this human waste. The townspeople have no sense of responsibility for these homeless aliens. I don't mean the original deportation during wartime. What I mean is the reactions I get when I talk to employers in the town here—and near other camps. They are quite frank. they say to me, 'We hope these people will go away. We don't want to encourage them by giving them jobs in our stores and businesses.' The farmers only use them because they have no other source of labor.

"The unkindness of the townspeople has cut too deep. What we need is protected workshops for all the so-called 'work-shy.' They could produce like the eight who handle the knitting machines. I felt repaid for all my work today when those poor people asked for more light to work longer hours."

The little Sudetenlander nodded her head reflectively. "I have been expelled from my home like these. I have been looked down on. Each one of these people needs personal attention. It must be very gentle. I wish I had more time for each one."

"For each one"—that was the key to the situation. The lives that had been dislocated and destroyed by massive anonymous orders and labor hunts could only be set right, or partially set right, by the most highly personalized of counseling, planning and practical help. Voluntary agencies such as my own had held out for the individual rights of each displaced person and had helped preserve these rights for all of them, including the most handicapped, the most humiliated—the speechless led into slavery, girl children led into brothels. This was the basis of a thin blade of triumph that cut through my heavy thoughts in surveying the leftovers of the many nations at the Hoehnkaserne. The tenacity with which the voluntary agencies and individuals like Georges Pire had held on to these rights on behalf of a dispossessed, multiracial group had laid the groundwork for the phenomenon of the World Refugee Year.

3. World Refugee Year

The shadowed, submerged world of the hard core of the dis-placed persons had faded from the consciousness of the world at large when it was suddenly lit by a giant searchlight—the searchlight of the World Refugee Year. In December 1958, at United Nations Headquarters in New York, fifty-nine member nations united in declaring a World Refugee Year which was to extend from June 1959 to June 1960. Before the year was out, the participation of ninety-seven countries and territories had been enlisted and new funds totaling eighty-three million dol-lars had been contributed for refugee projects. Well over half of these funds came as voluntary donations from the public.

A first concern of governments and voluntary agencies dur-ing the year for the world's refugees was final clearance of the hard core camps of Europe. By that time, the hard core camps of western Germany numbered sixty, and sheltered about fif-teen thousand persons, a bare one percent of the original mil-lion and a half D.P.'s. Smaller groups of hard core D.P.'s were still in Austria and Italy.

The German camps were more or less prototypes of the Hoehnkaserne. The same ragtag crowd of nationalities was left to face the cold despair of a trapped existence. Against the background of a resurgent Germany, bursting with the energy of its "Wirtschaftswunder," its "economic miracle," the hard core camps cowered like unwelcome guests who resurrected troubling memories. The uncared-for stone or wooden struc-tures, housing so many listless, often shambling people, seemed a blot on a bright new national facade.

The world refugee population was estimated as of June 1959 at seventeen million, of whom approximately five million were in desperate need.

198

The World Refugee Year, coming on the heels of the International Geophysical Year, offered proof that there could be, across national and cultural frontiers, a community of compassion as effective as the community of science.

During the International Geophysical Year, sixty-six countries were mobilized in a cooperative effort to record weather and tidal data from the earth's surface as well as solar flares and other scientific phenomena from outer space. In all, over thirty thousand scientists from both sides of the iron curtain were reported to be involved in the collection of millions of scientific facts which were expected to have such practical uses as the prediction of storms.

In the World Refugee Year, since the same moral split still prevailed which had helped cause the refugee problem in the first place, the Soviet bloc nations voted against the designation of a year to remember the refugees.

As a declaration of responsibility and concern for the most defenseless members of the human family, the World Refugee Year constituted a moral act of deep importance. The immediate impetus for such a year came from two young Englishmen in the January 1958 issue of *Crossbow* magazine. An article, on fire with emotional and moral fervor, proposed an all-out onslaught to resolve the refugee problem during a designated year. The International Journal of the Red Cross of Geneva in its January 1960 issue pointed to an earlier specific proposal: the speech of the director of Catholic Relief Services, the Most Reverend Edward E. Swanstrom, in September 1957:

To tell the truth, the suggestion to fire the imagination by devoting a year to the overall aspect of population and refugee problems—so grave for the future of the world—had already been made at the Congress of Catholic Migration Organizations at Assisi in 1957. Edward Swanstrom, spokesman for the strong Catholic organization, "Catholic Relief Services—National Catholic Welfare Conference," expressed his astonishment that humanity could not in the domain of charity achieve a formula of propaganda to stimulate its efforts, as it had known how to do in the domain of science, through the institution of the Geophysical Year.

While the brunt of the work during the International Geophysical Year fell to the experts, the tasks of the World Refugee Year fell to the ordinary citizen. Groups of concerned people formed themselves into citizens' committees for the World Refugee Year in scores of nations. It was in these citizens' committees that the ultimate fruition of the World Refugee Year's aims rested. The aims, as stated by the United Nations, were "to focus on the refugee problem . . . to encourage additional financial contributions from governments and the general public," and "to encourage additional opportunities for permanent refugee solutions through voluntary repatriation, resettlement or integration, on a purely humanitarian basis."

No one thought that large segments of the world's refugee population would cease to be refugees as a result of the effort of one twelve-month period. But of capital importance was the fact that a great human problem, in real danger of being cast into oblivion, was forced into the forefront of the conscience of ordinary citizens as well as of political leaders. Once the beacon light of the aroused conscience began to play upon the most victimized and most anguished groups in the free world, there was hope of larger solutions.

Prodded by their citizenry, governments took action on migration schemes, and made special provision for the residents of the hard core camps of western Europe.

From 1959 to 1960, teams from New Zealand, from Canada and from Great Britain combed the hard core camps for the handicapped, the amputees, those afflicted with tuberculosis, the aged. Lifetime annuities were settled on the aged who were left in Europe; intensive medical aid was given to the handicapped; homes were built for the so-called "uneconomic family units," the widowers with children, widows or unmarried mothers with children. New homes for the aged and helpless sprang up not only in Germany but also in Austria and Italy. From the camps of the almost forgotten people, groups were chosen for overseas migration on the basis of their needs and sufferings, not on the basis of their strength or possible contribution to the receiving country.

As the International Geophysical Year demonstrated the tremendous strength and unity of the community of science, the World Refugee Year was an indication of the growing strength of the community of charity and compassion. The data of the International Geophysical Year was put to work to estimate the magnetic storms that twisted compass needles and interfered with communications on the planet earth. The facts on human anguish unearthed during the World Refugee Year helped to set to right norms of morality that had become twisted, and made way for a new birth of fraternal spirit in the family of man. The moral energies mobilized during the World Refuge Year served to make up in some small measure to the displaced persons for the evils that had been inflicted upon them. Projects of rescue increased in an immeasurable way the moral capital of the whole free world.

While projects to aid refugees in West Bengal, Hong Kong, Taiwan and other refugee-packed areas grew out of the heightened activities of the World Refugee Year, this part of the chronicle focuses on the D.P.'s—the first post-war crop of refugees.

* * *

One of the "hard core" D.P.'s disinterred from a "cemetery of the living" through the heightened compassion of the World Refugee Year was Franciszek, a forty-three year old Pole. Attention was focused on him from the moment he boarded the plane in Frankfurt for New York.

The history of this short, ordinary man, impassive even facing the cameras, included experiences that made him a sort of "Everyman" of the darkest days of Europe's twentieth century. Captured by the Germans at the very beginning of World War II, he had gone from being a POW to being an inmate of a concentration camp. At war's end, he began his trek through D.P. camps and a series of rejections by migration schemes. For a decade, he worked in the rubble of a destroyed German city. Sixteen years of Franciszek's life, over one-third of his time on earth, had been spent in camps, two years in concentration camps, and fourteen years in various displaced persons camps. His two children had been born as refugees and knew no other home than quarters in a D.P. camp.

Born in 1916 to a Polish peasant family, he grew up with the knowledge that the family farmhouse had been destroyed during World War I. At nineteen he was drafted as a laborer for the construction of Polish airfields. In 1939, when he was twenty-three, he was drafted into the ranks of the Polish Army. Marching out on what he thought were practice maneuvers, he found that he was in a shooting war with an enemy that had penetrated deep into his country. In short order he was a prisoner-of-war in German custody. Escaping from his captors, he succeeded in reaching his home village. This time he was picked up and sent to Germany to work as a slave laborer on a German farm. Escaping a second time, he was caught and sentenced to two years in Bergen-Belsen concentration camp. He survived because his job was that of sorting out the piles of garments left behind by the victims consigned to death.

When his two years in the concentration camp were completed, he was assigned again to forced labor on a German farm. When World War II ended, he was on of the millions of foreign workers liberated by the Allies and one of a great company of Poles who refused to return to a Poland under an alien regime.

Finding refuge in a displaced persons camp in Braunschweig, he immediately began to organize a profitable little business. "To organize" in those days of hungry chaos meant to find your own way to a source of food or money. It was not necessarily illegal, but rather an ingenious way of manipulating circumstances. Borrowing money to finance his trip, he journeyed to Bremen where he acquired sacks of salt herring. Swinging them over his back on a heavy stick, coolie-fashion, he trudged to his base camp and then to other D.P. camps, selling the herring at a considerable profit. He developed his herring sales route and put together money for his intended migration to the United States.

At Braunschweig, he married a German girl and waited along with other Poles for his chance at an American visa. His first turn-down on the basis of the marks of tuberculosis stunned him because he seemed to be in robust health and was one of the hardest workers in the camp. In successive years, as the medical rejections became a regular occurrence, the couple began the route of the hard core D.P.'s, moving from camp to camp.

At the fourth camp in their trajectory, by now "hard core cases," the couple came to rest. It was at a "lager" in Münster, Westphalia, built just after the turn of the century as an army barracks, and later utilized as a police school. Into it spilled the rejected D.P.'s of a whole area in the same way as the rejectees filled the Hoehnkaserne in Landshut. In one-room quarters in this drafty, red-bricked barracks, two children were born to the couple.

On his arrival in Münster, Franciszek chose work which forms as telling a commentary on Europe as his job sorting and salvaging the clothing of those murdered in the concentration camp. He became a rubble clearer, sorting out for reuse the bits and pieces of dead buildings shattered in air raids.

On my visits to Germany, I, with many others, marveled at the sight of orderly squads of men and women sorting out endless piles of the debris of war. Bricks that were whole or nearly whole were stacked into neat rows and towers. Salvageable metal and wood pieces were valuable exchange items for the rubble workers. Brick fragments were fed into special rubble-reducing machines. In the very center of Germany's most punished towns I had come across the endlessly chugging machines tirelessly chewing the splinters of a fragmented country and pouring out a rough, lumpy, cement-like mixture. Out of the pulverized bones of the old Germany came the building blocks, the beginning framework of the new Germany of the "economic miracle."

For a few months short of a decade, the D.P. worked full-time on the rubble of one city. He was part of a team of steady workers employed by a rubble-clearing business company. When a town like Münster, sheltering more than 150,000 people, is ninety percent destroyed, rubble is in long supply for many years. And when the Altenstadt, the historic part of the city, is to be reconstructed as exactly as possible to its original state, there must be a long-term assemblage of significant bits and pieces. The leftover man was involved with the leftovers of a destroyed city.

Franciszek's "case" had been presented once to an Australian migration commission and eight separate times to the U.S. consular offices and displaced persons commission. Each year, a fresh set of X-ray photographs was taken, and each time he was rejected for migration because of what the experts read on his plates. Franciszek himself would have used the word "schatten," shadows, to describe his lung lesions from tuberculosis. This was the word frequently on the lips of D.P.'s rejected for migration.

But the World Refugee Year rescued Franciszek and his family from the Münster hard core camp. Despite the "schatten," which were by then under control, he was allowed to come to the United States under a home and job sponsorship by CRS.

He arrived at Kennedy Airport in New York in mid-December 1959, halfway through the World Refugee Year. A battalion of press people and television and radio representatives awaited the D.P. as he piloted his wife and two children through the last official formalities of an immigrant's entry into the United States. Much was written about him as a symbol of the accomplishments of the World Refugee Year. He was seen as the human end-product of a gigantic international problem, a late and lone straggler in a mighty D.P. army that had long since marched by.

On top of the documents that Franciszek presented to the U.S. Immigration and Naturalization Service were two film negatives. These were X-ray plates that showed what remained of his "schatten," the shadows that had kept him from emigrating nine times.

Now with his feet on American soil, he had finally surfaced from a submerged world. He felt it was fitting to surrender the proofs of his "schatten" in order to enter any country as a migrant. He evidently thought that he was putting down his "shadows" for the last time and that he would be free of them once the U.S. officials relieved him of them. But such a finality of poetic logic was not to be. The Immigration and Naturalization Service officials whispered among themselves and handed him back his X-ray plates.

They asked him instead to surrender to them five Valencia oranges that emerged large and shining from a carefully packed valise. With the same bemused incredulity with which he had probably accepted being in a shooting war as a target when he thought he was only on a maneuver, he gave up the oranges. He handed them over reluctantly one by one. They might have been a going-away present, or perhaps the first supplies with which to celebrate the approaching Christmas holiday. Slowly putting his "schatten" back into his pocket, Franciszek walked out to face the television cameras and pressmen, and by that time he had managed a smile.

Chapter Five

BORDERCROSSERS UNLIMITED

1. Europe's Fault Line—
The Iron Curtain

"We call it the death strip," said the German as we gazed at the iron curtain, the man-made boundary at Europe's heart.

Since it had been formally named in the sonorous tones of Winston Churchill, the artificial "Great Divide" had been called many things, including Europe's ideological "fault line." Borrowing from geology, the use of the latter term indicated the presence of underlying rock fractures whose movement might displace one side relative to the other. It hinted at uncertainty and fear.

A close-up view validated the description of the iron curtain as a "death strip." "Todestreif." We saw a slash, ten yards wide, which cut through the road and then snaked through the open fields to left and right. The unevenly gashed slabs of concrete taken from the remote country road had vestiges of the earth from which they had been dug. A fine fuzz of grass and weeds was sprouting from them. The scraggly grass brought to mind the untended growth of beard on the rough face of an old farmer. Not a blade of grass, however, could be seen on the smoothly-ploughed earth serving as a no-man's land in the ideological conflict that intruded itself into the countryside. On that smooth earth, every footstep would make a mark.

This was the iron curtain of the early 1960s, developing as a more effective barrier along with the developments in the cold war. I had traveled along the entire length of the iron curtain, from Kiel to Trieste, in 1947 and 1949 when it could be described as more "porous." I visited encampments that abutted the iron curtain, some sheltering expelled Germans, some receiving POW's released from Soviet forced labor, and still others serving as way stations for escapees who had fled the nations of eastern Europe.

"It was they, not us, who broke up the road. Their side, not our side, takes care to plow the ten-meter death strip." In "us," he evidently included Americans as well as Germans. By "they," he seemed to include the whole Soviet orbit, which began a few feet from where we were standing. When he said "they," he fixed his eyes on a giant skeleton-like watchtower that rose in grisly authority a few hundred feet inside the iron curtain.

I left him at the car and went up to place my hand on the famous "schlagbaum," the wooden barrier that stretched across the road. An identical "schlagbaum" stood athwart the road on the far side of the gashed concrete. Painted red and white, the barriers served as "No Trespassing" signs between two halves of a continent, in fact, between two world systems.

I rested my hand on the wood. It was a pole carved probably from a straight pine tree—no more than twelve inches in diameter. Evidently people considered this a spot where a visit should be commemorated. All along the brilliantly painted barrier there were carefully hacked out initials and names. The names Willi Danner and Lisbeth Wagner stared up at me as I took my hand away.

To get to this point from Frankfurt, we had driven through the somnolent landscape of the province of Hesse, through baroque Fulda, through such country villages as Langenbieber, Niederbieber and Hofbieber, and through towns with such unaccountable names as Lieblos, loveless. The land was poor, but showed the effects of having been respected and cared for over the centuries.

Apple trees, long past bearing age, stood alongside a section of the road. The darkened, knotted branches they raised in the moist air were bare of leaves. Trimmed to the same size, the trees seemed like a chorus line of begging, haggard crones.

It was a landscape that had preserved, despite all the tragic events of the preceding years, a certain fantasy, a feeling of having been drugged by the weight of history and ancient ways. Only the mounting number of signs as we approached the iron curtain gave a new dimension of contemporaneity—and dread—to the countryside.

Near the town of Fulda, a garish road sign announced: "Border Area—Fulda County—Province of Hesse." Green-uniformed border police of the German Federal Republic and American troops, patrolling in a couple of jeeps mounted with machine guns, reminded us that we were in an area important to international strategy. After a series of warning signs that became increasingly insistent came the one that announced with finality, "Halt—Zone Border—Republic Border." It stood almost against the "schlagbaum."

The German, who had managed to escape from East Germany, did not want to come too near the wooden barrier. When I went back to the car, he jerked his head in the direction of a giant steel watch tower. "The border police. They are always there. Fifty thousand strong—the border police. They have their telescopes trained on this place—and their machine guns. They have telephone communication with the border police all along the border."

Year by year, the curtain had hardened into an elongated barricade. Germany's death strip alone measured eight hundred and sixty-three miles, cutting its way from Lubeck to Hof at the Austrian border. Aside from a half dozen check points, where rail and road traffic could move under tight customs control, the border was a closed one. Hundreds of roads were gashed in the same way as the one in the county of Fulda; thirty-five railroad lines were blocked off, many barricaded by heavy railroad ties. Irrationally, the iron curtain cut through the center of villages, through farms, through a mill which fell exactly athwart it.

In addition to sections of smoothed earth buffer zones that showed every fleeing step, there were, in other stretches, the unforgettable dragon's teeth. These were concrete pillars, four feet high and pointed like fangs, that were designed to block off vehicular traffic at important intersections. At some points there were barbed wire barriers nine feet high. Soon the death strip bustled with booby-trap guns to injure or kill those who still tried to cross to the western side. But none of these, not the booby-trap guns, not the barbed wire, not the watch towers or border police, ever succeeded in stopping the human traffic across the iron curtain. It was this traffic, not the strategic aspect of the barrier, that was the concern of Catholic Relief Services. The reality that faced humanitarian agencies was the fact that, all along its length, the iron curtain was being continually breached by human ingenuity and because of human desperation.

2. Yalta, Potsdam and Human Lives

The woman was small and apologetic in manner. She could not contain her surprise at receiving a visitor from the United States in the dark cubicle behind a cow barn which was her home. Her round face was gray, as was her shapeless dress, her once blond hair was faded. She rubbed the backs of her hands against a frayed apron as she spoke. She and her husband, she related, had owned a farm, a little one, in east Prussia. Her husband had been called into the German Army. He was sent to the eastern front. There was no news from him for a long time.

When the end of the war came, administrators came to her section of east Prussia. She and her four children were driven from their dwelling. They had to leave everything behind; they took to the road.

"There were many other Germans with us," she explained. "It took us fourteen days to get to this place."

"This place" was Oldenburg in Schleswig-Holstein and a shelter in a brick barn behind the well-cared-for animals.

"Mein mann," "My husband," she said, and handed me a card marked with a Red Cross at the left upper corner and a Red Crescent at the right. It carried a short message that the sender was in good health.

"He was captured on the eastern front. He is working in Russia. I received this card on July 21 of this year (1949) through our Red Cross. I have not heard anymore. I pray he is still living."

Her tears suddenly gushed forth as I handed her back the strangely marked postcard. The children, between nine and fourteen, stood silent.

The little woman, crouching in a cubicle at the back of an animal barn, was one of countless simple people in whom the Yalta and Potsdam agreements had met. I was to see many

213

more. If I had mentioned the two words, through which searing anguish had descended on them, they would have looked at me with an uncomprehending gaze.

At the Crimean Conference, Yalta, it had been decided, despite Geneva Conventions, that German war prisoners need not be freed at the end of hostilities. They were to be retained within the Soviet Union to repair the destruction wrought by war. The father of these children was among them. Also at Yalta, the eastern frontiers of Poland were moved westward, giving 77,000 square miles of its pre-war territory to the Soviet Union, while Poland's westward frontier was moved further west, giving 44,000 square miles of German territory to Polish administration.

By the Potsdam agreement, signed by the United States, the Soviet Union and the United Kingdom in Berlin on August 2, 1945, the German population remaining in Poland, Czechoslovakia and Hungary was to be transferred "in an orderly and humane manner" to Germany. Exact figures on the results of the Potsdam provisions regarding civilian mass expulsions were impossible to obtain. An official statistical report by the Federal Republic of Germany carried a foreword by Dr. Hans Lukashek, the federal minister for expellees.

"After World War II," stated Lukashek, "above all by reason of the resolutions of Yalta and Potsdam, over seventeen million people have been expelled from their hereditary homes in East Germany and eastern areas. More than two and a half million Germans lost their lives in this way."

The little woman and her children were also the victims of Potsdam.

In the years immediately after the Second World War the unspeakable destruction inflicted on Poles, Russians, Czechs, French, Greeks, and most of all, on Europe's Jews made a screen of such horror that it was hardly possible for the human eye or human heart to look beyond it. The victors stopped to contemplate the fully-opened book of atrocities before they could examine what war had done to the German population. As German leaders had broken the bonds of brotherhood with members of the family of man, so, in turn, the Allied Army

Command declared for non-fraternization with the German people. The works of mercy for a defeated enemy were for a time interdicted as "trading with the enemy." The concept of "collective guilt," decried when applied by the enemy, was now tacitly accepted.

It was people-to-people agencies which broke through such policies, which consisted of carrying on the war by other means. Chiefly through the humanitarian efforts of such agencies, the non-fraternization policy foundered on the rock of human solidarity. By then, the agencies were appalled at the effects of such decisions as those taken at Yalta and Potsdam with their untold cost in human agony and human lives.

* * *

POTSDAM: ARTICLE XII

A cold Germany, beaten to a standstill, awaited those whose transfer was supposed to be "humane and orderly." Any town of major size had suffered from forty to ninety percent of destruction. When the trains stopped, the dying and dead were often handed out first, and the living crawled out afterward. It sometimes took ten to eighteen days to complete a journey from Breslau to West Germany, for example, a trip that would normally take a couple of days.

So many trainloads of human misery moved westward in 1945 and 1946 that a temporary key was set up to route them to the various areas. It was done in the same impersonal way as one would assign trainloads of vegetables to provision different regions. The Allied Control Council for Germany, to which the allocation of expellees with Germany fell, operated over a long period on the "five-three-two" plan. Of every ten trains arriving in Germany from the east, five were routed to Bavaria, three to Wurttemberg, and two to Hesse. As the French had not been represented at the conference which agreed to the expulsions, the expellees were not officially accepted in the French zone for an extended period.

When communications were held up, whole trainloads were often shunted to railroad sidings and left untended. An

American soldier on transport detail saw such a cattle train standing in a railroad yard.

"What's in that train?" he asked, according to a report.

"Bessarabians," was the answer.

"Bessarabians," he scratched his head. "Bessarabians, what are they?" He thought they were commodities, potatoes perhaps. When he found out they were people, he followed the key in routing them farther.

The Allied occupation forces took no responsibility for the expelled Germans, who came to be known as expellees. Their housing, provisioning, all their needs were the responsibility of German authorities.

* * *

The main railroad station of Frankfurt was still operating, despite the fact that it had been shattered by bombs. It was left as naked from the elements as a person under the wire frame of a gutted umbrella. The steel skeletal framework of the great roof was still there, but twisted into what appeared to be a vast nightmarish, spidery sculpture.

I stood in the station as a light snow began to fall; it fell on the platforms, on the waiting rooms and on the people descending from a train. These were people who had not bought tickets and had not chosen this as their destination. Grown-ups and children, they were gray-faced and swaddled like mummies. There were about three hundred of them; their origin, Czechoslovakia. They were directed toward a section of the station given over to the Railroad Help Mission, the Bahnhofsmission. The first aid consisted of ersatz coffee and a weak but hot soup and dark bread.

The weakest of them, who had to be helped down from the train, were taken to a shelter where they could rest for a night or two on cots before they had to continue the journey and be assigned to some type of shelter. Perhaps it would be a former concentration camp like Dachau, an expellee haven for over a decade and a half.

Every railroad station of any size had its Bahnhofsmission, staffed by members of Caritas, the Catholic Charities agency, Evangelisches Hilfswerk for the Lutheran Community, the

Burgomeister's office and other voluntary agencies. When the stream of American help began reaching German civilians, a large amount went to the railroad centers.

Before the end of the morning, most of the newcomers had been herded out of the station. Some few would be assigned to Frankfurt itself, but one wondered where, since out of the city's 180,000 dwelling units, 80,000 had been demolished. In addition, some 8,000 dwelling units had been requisitioned for the occupying forces by taking over homes and hotels.

As they trudged out of the station, I could imagine them doubling up in cellars and ground floors of houses where the upper floors had been blasted away. As one went out at night, a dim candlelight would reveal that what looked like a ruin was in fact a shelter for human beings.

Carrying as their only burdens destitution, hunger, and disease, the expellees entered destroyed cities and communities already struggling to exist in conditions of immense human need. The fight for daily bread, for warmth and shelter, for clothing, for life itself, became unendurably bitter. It was at that time that a dreadful, heart-stopping theme was heard on German lips, "Besser ein Ende Schrecken als Schrecken ohne Ende." "Better an end with terror than terror without end."

3. Orphans Uprooted

In the massive uprooting of Germans, and ethnic Germans in accordance with Potsdam, whole institutions were emptied—homes for the blind, hospitals, and child care homes of every description.

Near Paderborn was a cluster of barracks housing sightless people who had been herded as a group from their shelter for the blind in Silesia. The sightless troupe of people, men, women and children, were thrust aboard a transport of expellees headed westward. Their fellow-expellees were their only means of survival during the journey.

BAVARIA 1949

The sisters and their orphan charges, driven from Silesia, were given quarters in a requisitioned house in Garatshausen, Bavaria. The thirty nuns, Sisters of Mercy, shepherded the orphans to their new home. When unaccompanied children arrived on later transports, they were added to the care of the sisters in the relocated kinderheim. A few days earlier, a group of four children had been brought in. They had been expelled from their home in Silesia, along with their grandmother.

They stood before us, pale, haunted children. Stefi, eleven, was the eldest. Edeltraut was nine, Maria, who suffered from tuberculosis was six, and the youngest, Gerhart, was five.

"My father went to war in Russia," Stefi told us. "We do not know where he is now. My grandmother took care of us. We have no mother. We lived on a farm near Kosel.

"We were waiting for our father to come home, but he did not come. People came and took us to a camp. The beds were like this." She put one hand over another to indicate double

218

decker beds. It was in the camp, she told us, that the grand-mother became ill and died.

"The people gave us bread and soup. Every day at noon we got four slices of bread, one for each. Then the German soldiers came and took us on the train with them."

It had evidently been a transport of German war prisoners returning from Russia. The children told how crowded the car was. "We slept on straw till we came here."

The story of each child, each parentless group of children in the kinderheim, was as stark and simple as this. Almost every case in the kinderheim was a victim both of Yalta and of Potsdam.

BERLIN

The Don Bosco House, a Berlin children's home, was the scene of grim stories told in the grimmest of settings. The ruins of a gutted electrical appliance factory, Siemenstadt, had been shored up to serve as a shelter for expelled, mostly unaccompanied, children from East and West Prussia, Silesia, and Danzig. Of one hundred and eighty-five boys at Don Bosco, one hundred and fifty were expellees.

The Reverend August Klinski, a short, smiling priest so near-sighted that his thick eyeglasses turned on you like telescope lenses, took us around to meet his boys.

As we smiled and said a few words of greeting to them, the priest would outline the children's stories in English.

"Those three boys were brothers, from Koenigsberg. The father was taken by the Russians. The mother started with the children to walk to Danzig. Before reaching Danzig, the mother fell ill and died by the roadside. Russian soldiers rescued the children and took them into their barracks. The soldiers turned them over to a Polish farmer. In his horse and cart the farmer drove them to a collecting point. They were brought to Berlin with an expellee transport. Then they were turned over to me.

"In those days, I used to go down to meet the transports myself. Most of them brought children whose parents were deported, or missing, or dead. I even picked them up on the street. They became my children." He smiled warmly to a few boys he met in the corridor. An unshaded bulb made his thick lenses light up like pale flashlights. His shock of greying, curly hair stuck out like a homespun halo.

"First we lived in the basement of Siemenstadt. Straw was what we slept on. We had soup and bread—and nothing else. Then an American captain sent us mattresses and blankets. Five hospitals here in Berlin gave us some bedsteads. We have master carpenters working with us. That is how we fixed up the first and second floors of our factory home."

We were on our way to see the workshops. The Congregation of Don Bosco specializes in craft and mechanical training for the poor in every continent.

"You see that boy from Stettin. His sisters are at the girls' orphanage of Maria Schutz. His father may be alive in Russia. When the Russian soldiers came, there was the usual "Komme mit." The mother was dragged away. The children did not see her alive again. She stole back and shot herself. Our boy took her body into the garden and buried it. But first, he told me, he said goodbye in the customary way. 'Mother, bless me!' the child said. He took his mother's dead hand and traced the sign of the cross on his own forehead. This is the way parents say goodbye to their children."

The workshops for shoemaking, bookbinding, carpentry and tailoring were deserted because the boys were assembling in a huge factory hall for a band concert in honor of our visit. "Every boy," said August Klinski, "learns a practical trade, and he belongs to an activity like our band. Forty-two pieces it is. The loudest in Berlin, I think. All our boys go to the public school near Siemenstadt. They have little time to think and worry."

We went by the kitchen. Dishes from the midday meal were being washed in an old-fashioned bathtub.

"You see how we manage at Don Bosco," he said.

Then came the concert. The march was so loud and the beat so strong that I expected that the soldiers of all four occupying troops might protest the competition.

Father Klinski asked us to sign his register. His sight was so limited that he pored over each name to read it correctly.

"I have had two operations on my eyes," he smiled sadly. "Perhaps I need another operation. But I have already seen too much."

He rocked his head with its outsize shock of curly hair as though the burden of what he had to see was physically heavy.

The Don Bosco Home became a well-known institution in Berlin, and eventually moved to modern installation near Berlin's broad, breeze-fresh Wannsee.

4. Reparations in Blood

Camp Friedland stood at a point in the iron curtain where the road had not been gashed. The no-man's land consisted of a hundred feet of road with a barrier and a sentry box at each end. On the far side were Soviet soldiers. That day in the fall of 1949 was an important day for Friedland, since seventeen hundred German POW's, captured between 1941 and 1945, were to be released. Americans had not realized that one of the provisions of the Yalta agreement was for retention of POW's for forced labor in the Soviet Union. The attempt to keep the agreement secret was broken by the *New York Times* in a news story headlined, ROOSEVELT THINKS IT GOOD IDEA TO LET NAZIS REPAIR SOVIET. *Trud*, the Moscow paper, announced on April 2, 1945, that at Yalta the U.S. had agreed to the use of German labor for the restoration of districts the Germans had destroyed. In addition to reparations in material form by the dismantling of German industry, there was to be a human form of reparations, called by some to be reparation in blood.

The surrounding countryside was ready to welcome the *heimkehrer*, the returnees, with donations of cigarettes, bars of soap, and shaving cream, all prized items in the Germany of that day. There were precious tins of cocoa. There were cakes and small loaves of bread baked by the women of the area. The young priest who assembled these gifts for each transport was not "stationed" at Friedland but had volunteered to live and work there because his Rhineland home had not shared the heavy suffering of other parts of Germany.

At three o'clock we were at the barrier and we could see the men lined up beyond the "no-man's land" in what was then called the Soviet zone of Germany. The line of men stood quite still, making no sound. They stood for three hours until finally,

222

at six o'clock in the evening, the barrier was raised and the men began to stream through. I stood a few feet inside the "no-man's land." The men who passed by me were wearing remnants of old Wehrmacht uniforms four years after war's end. Most of them were dressed in dark blue outfits with Russian-type padded jackets. Under their arms or tied to their backs they carried shapeless bundles or strange wooden valises.

For more than half an hour they trudged by, and as they reached us they started shouting, "Now after five years we can laugh again." Some, seeing a priest, called out the traditional greeting, "Grüss Gott." A few shouted: "God be thanked that we are here." An old man and his daughter suddenly entered the line and put their arms around a young prisoner. Until that moment he had marched like everyone else, but he was so overcome at the sight of his family that they had to help him walk the rest of the way. Sobs broke out from him, and the old man and the girl, who I supposed were his father and sister, wept with him as they walked along.

Last on the line were the sick, who were transferred from Soviet trucks to waiting ambulances, and behind the sick there was an old bearded man wearing a Wehrmacht cap. He was a doctor. His wife, who had been standing near me, saw him just as he entered the no-man's land, and she ran all the way to the Soviet side to greet and support him. He had been in captivity five years, she told me.

As he came slowly up the stretch of highway, I could see how heavily he leaned on her.

All this time, a tired, thin man had been sitting on the opposite side of the road. He had taken off his shoes, as though he had walked a long way to get to Friedland. When the last man, the doctor, finally reached us, this man got up, and with his shoes in his hand he approached him. He wanted to find out if there were any more men in the transport. He explained that he had heard from his son, a young man of twenty-five that he would be released on this transport.

The doctor explained that he was the last of the transport and all the sick had preceded him. He asked for the young man's name. Then the tired old doctor performed that last duty of the return journey, a journey that had taken fourteen days in all, including the trip in rough wooden coaches to Moscow and out again. The young man, he explained, had died on the train and had been buried in Russian soil.

The father, who had waited all the day long, and for God only knows how many days preceding that day, did not even ask where in Russia his son had died. He walked back to where he had been sitting and sank down on the grass, his face grey.

Back in Camp Friedland, the men who were well enough were lining up for their first meal as we drove in. Some were already lighting up their cigarettes and smiled as they puffed. The sick were being served in the barracks hospital.

"Even the ones who are walking," said the young priest, "can be very sick. When they get home, they have heart trouble and kidney illness. But they are much healthier than they used to be. We don't have so many men swollen like balloons with edema. Even their heads used to be swollen."

I talked with several of the men, including a young man with a child's face. He was just twenty-one and had been impressed in the Wehrmacht at the age of sixteen. He had endured five years of forced labor in a Soviet mine. He was serene and composed because he was one of the fortunate men who had been in contact with his parents through the Red Crescent postcard service. This operated only in certain Soviet areas and permitted the men to send a message every few months to their families. The only news they could give was that they were in good health. This young man's official postcards had arrived because his family still lived in northwestern Germany where he had left them. He was to go home the very next day after his registration. This consisted of checking the files of men still missing from his army unit, and the listing of information on his comrades in the slave labor battalion.

A sizeable number of the men released that day stayed on in Friedland to wait for extensive tracing services and, if there were no results, to wait until some community or social service agency would receive them.

It was such stories as those in Camp Friedland, as those in the barn in Schleswig-Holstein, as those in expellee children's shelters in Bavaria and Berlin, that fed the revulsion against the anti-human provisions of Yalta and Potsdam.

These stories were multiplied all over Germany's landscape, mirroring the ruin of millions of lives. According to German Army figures, there had been a pool of 3,700,000 German POW's in Soviet custody. The highest figure admitted by Soviet officials was 890,000. The discrepancy was not even corrected after the returned POW's reported the deaths of comrades in forced labor battalions.

Leaders in Britain and the United States publicly dissociated themselves from the agreements signed by their governments. A British political leader, Michael Foot, appalled by the sufferings of German civilians, in particular the children, under the concept of collective guilt, addressed the House of Commons in the following words: "For women and children, creatures such as these, there is for their protection an older law than any promulgated at Potsdam: 'But whosoever shall offend against one of these little ones . . . it were better by far for him that a millstone were hanged about his neck, and that he were drowned in the depth of the sea.' If these infamies are to be allowed to continue, there will be a shortage of millstones to set beside the other shortages in Europe."

5. The Great Search

The prisoners released through Camp Friedland were served a meal, and they then went to the Red Cross barracks. The "suchtdienst," or search service, grew to be an activity of the most urgent importance to German lives, especially in Camp Friedland. By 1949, between 20,000 and 30,000 prisoners were being released by the Soviet Union every month.

A Red Cross worker showed me a library of large photograph albums with pictures of missing men. Other photographs not yet entered into the albums were copied on fliers and attached to the walls. Some of these came from family members who posted them in every available space. I saw the men studying the fliers as they waited to talk to the Red Cross workers, almost all women.

"Occasionally," the Red Cross worker told me, "a 'heimkehrer' will recognize a face and a name from a flier. He will tell us, 'Yes, Anton was my comrade in the Donbas. The pneumonia got him. He died in 1947.' It is so important to get as much information as possible from the 'heimkehrer' at each transport."

The returnees, starved for news of their families, would supply every fact that would help a tracing service. The POW would be asked if he belonged to an expellee family. In many cases he did not know. Working to exhaustion in Soviet mines and factories from the time of their capture, the men had received little or no news of the outside world.

By 1949, a teletype machine had been installed in a barracks of its own, and it soon began humming with messages to Red Cross headquarters in Hamburg. Here was kept the master file, fed by the search services of Austria and those of the Catholic and Lutheran Churches. Men whose families had lived in Silesia, the Sudetenland of Czechoslvakia, Danzig, East Prussia,

226

Hungary, Rumania and Yugoslavia often thought that they would have to make their way back to those areas to locate them. Sometimes, within a day or two, through the teletype and the meticulous filing of the search service, a returnee would find out not only that his family had been expelled, but where they had found refuge.

The young woman took time to put before me a heavy album that contained photographs only of women.

"At least 100,000 women were taken into Russia when the Soviet forces came into East Prussia and East Germany. You can see by these names and addresses that East Prussia suffered very much. We got these photographs from their relatives who reached this side. We get very little news of the women."

* * *

I paid a visit to the search service conducted by Caritas Verband, the national Catholic welfare organization. It occupied a barracks building in Freiburg-im-Breisgau, a town nearly half of which had been destroyed by bombing. In the drafty barracks a card file of hundreds of thousands had been built up. Caritas had a staff of twenty-five persons busy day in and day out with the task of locating the lost, passing on information of whereabouts or death, and listing the newly arrived expellees. An average of three hundred requests were received every day.

I saw long rows of cards listed under Opeln, Beuthen, Danzig, Bromberg, Posen, Breslau, Liegnitz and East Prussia. While I was there, a few letters were delivered from war prisoners still in Russia. Some POW's had received the news of the deportation of Germans from Silesia and the Sudetenland of Czechoslovakia. One asked for any news of his wife, mother and sisters who had lived at a given address in Breslau; another gave the names, former address and ages of his mother and father who had lived in Freudenthal, Czechoslovakia.

One of the most tragic groups of POW's was housed in a transit camp just outside Vienna. It must have served as a prison stockade in wartime since it was surrounded by a heavy fence. They presented the most anguishing problems to the search service. They were the ethnic Germans expelled from Yugoslavia.

"You know, these returnees are not ours," a welfare worker remarked to me. "They were left with us because they have nowhere else to go. Most of them come from the Vojvodina in Yugoslavia. They can only wait—and wait."

Scores of men were sitting in a cold hall that must have served as a dining and recreation room.

The men, in discolored Wehrmacht uniforms, and padded jackets acquired in Russia, sat around at the rough tables like unkempt victims of catatonia. Some had learned only on arrival in Vienna that their families had been scattered from the rich farmlands of Yugoslavia. Their ancestors had been among the German colonists invited by the Hungarian crown to settle a region won back from the Turks in the eighteenth century. Through their industry, the part of the Vojvodina they had colonized had become rich to bursting with grain and fruits and well-stocked with cattle.

The farms had been emptied of inhabitants. The rich tracts of lands built up by generations of painful and patient effort fell as rich plunder to the new regime of Yugoslavia. The men who had dreamed of putting their hands to the plow after years with the weapons of war and the tools of slave labor sat as though dazed by the great emptiness that yawned before them. These were the ones whose families seemed to have been lost without trace.

I looked around at the men left in the hall. A tall ungainly man slouched over to settle himself at the bare wooden table. His craggy face was emaciated, and though he was not old, he had the sick color of worn tan leather. As if in inexpressible weariness, he closed his eyes as we went past. Some heads were shorn and seemingly puffed in a strange way. This was the effect of extreme hunger showing itself even in the flesh covering the skull.

At the other end of the barracks so palpably filled with despair were large bulletin boards covered with notices. I went down to read what I thought might be directions for the returnees. There were a few mimeographed notices about the search services available through the Red Cross and other agencies. The other papers which filled every inch of the bulletin boards and then spread over the surrounding walls were notices of missing soldiers. Under the face of an older man would be written in a formal German hand: "Lorenz Wagner. This is my husband. He was last heard from at Rostov. He was born in 1908. If anyone knew him in captivity in Russia, please be kind enough to inform his wife." There would follow the address of a woman in an expellee camp.

Many of the notices were printed, and were posted on the walls and bulletin boards of other provisional shelters for returning slave laborers and in railroad stations. Some were carefully hand-lettered or typewritten and carried a snapshot. A young smiling face would look out from a large printed poster with such a notice as: "My son, Fritz Toth, was captured at Stalingrad. His comrades wrote that he is a factory worker in Rostov. He was born in 1923, near Novi Sad, Vojvodina, Yugoslavia. His mother begs for any news of him."

While we were studying these appeals, a stocky blond young man approached us. His manner was desperately shy. He wet his lips and looked down at the floor. Then he spoke.

"I am all alone. Could you tell me what I should do next? I have been here for weeks. I gave my name to the Red Cross, and I gave them the names of all my family. But they know nothing."

"Where are you from?" we asked him.

"Our home was in the Banat of Yugoslavia. But they tell me all the people have been driven out. Some were put into camps. I have six brothers and sisters."

He paused and his lips began to tremble. "I wanted to go back to Yugoslavia to look for them. If they were in a camp, I would bring them here. I am the eldest. I am twenty-three. But they say it is too dangerous. I came to ask you—could you advise me what to do next?"

We knew that at war's end, many, even mothers with children, had died in violent reprisals. But we said a word of hope that, after many messages and letters, someone in his family might be located. He could only wait.

I looked back at the men who had been deposited in this isolated stockade. A few of them looked up at us fleetingly out of sleepless, turtle-heavy eyes. We had not approached them, and they seemed to hope for nothing from us. Each seemed to be absorbed in staring into his own private abyss, an abyss peopled by a mother, father, a wife, brothers, sisters, little children, friends—all vanished without trace as though they had never been.

We opened the door to leave. The papers asking about the Fritzes, the Lorenzes, the Martins, the Ulrichs, fluttered in the sudden breeze. Such forlorn appeals were the most pitiful part of the great search—but they were everywhere in the Germany of the years after war's end.

6. Escapees

As Europe settled, in the second half of the twentieth century, into the actuality of two sealed-off compartments, a new wave of refugees made its appearance. It was multinational and had many ebbs and flows. A single name, "escapee," was given to all of them, though they were in fact Czechs, Slovaks, Poles, Rumanians, Hungarians, Croats, Slovenes and Albanians, with an occasional Ukrainian or Russian.

Border-crossing was simplest for the Czechs since they were closest to the iron curtain. After the Prague government changed hands in February 1948, Czech refugees escaped at the rate of one thousand a month. This average was maintained through 1949 and began to slacken in 1950. In 1951 and 1952 it fell off but never stopped. Escape just became more difficult as the iron curtain was equipped with the detecting machinery I have described.

One of the largest of the escapee reception centers was Valka Camp, near Nuremberg. It was probably the most polyglot of all the refugee camps and merited the sign that one of the escapees had lettered on a high wooden beam at its entrance: "Valka—First European City." It was one of the ironies of the twentieth century that it was homelessness that forced Europeans to live together in peace.

During the fall of 1951, I spent some time in Valka, visiting the barracks offices of Catholic Relief Services and the other voluntary agencies. The heroes and heroines of the camp were a group of Czechs who had ridden into exile by train. A dozen men and women with their families had planned to crash the train through the tracks that still connected the Czech country-side with West Germany. They commandeered the engine and crashed into the west at Asch, one of the thirty-five spots where

231

railroad tracks crossed the artificial frontier. The other passengers were given a choice they had not expected to make when
they boarded the train in Prague—whether to remain in exile or
return to their homeland. Twenty-seven of them chose to go to
Valka rather than their original destination.

Many Czechs were able to bring their children. A typical family brought to the United States through Catholic Relief Services
carried a twenty-two month old child into exile. Charles and
Giny Vachal started from Prague with nothing but a few wed-
ding pictures and a supply of pills to keep the child from making
any noise.

"Of course, we had to feed him sleeping pills regularly. We
took a train and then walked through the countryside and the
woods. That is how we got by the many check points and finally
the guards at the final border."

The "Paper War" for home and job assurances for escapees
went on year after year. Voluntary agency activity attracted significant funding from the Ford Foundation. Crucial to the
movement of escapees from such reception camps as Valka was
an American governmental effort, the escapee program,
referred to as USEP. Begun in 1952, USEP provided a safety net
for those who escaped with nothing but a dream of freedom. It
buttressed the efforts of voluntary agencies committed to the
same purpose.

Of all the eastern Europeans who succeeded in crossing the
arbitrary political boundary at Europe's heart, it was the
Hungarians who forced the most massive breach in that boundary. In their rising against a monolithic power controlling a billion lives from the iron curtain to the Yellow Sea, the Hungarians
voiced demands for "full freedom of opinion, of speech, of the
press, as well as free radio, a new daily newspaper and the
destruction of existing police dossiers."

The resistance of the Poles in Warsaw's "Polish October" had
sparked the Hungarian rising. But while the Poles, learning
from their bloody history, had stood like men of stone until they
had achieved limited changes of government, the Hungarians
plunged forward to overthrow an imposed government, toppling
as a symbol the Stalin statue planted in Budapest. After October

23, the Hungarians went into action against the most obvious enemies of their freedom, the secret police. Storming the headquarters of the secret police, they burned the police dossiers and meted out summary execution to secret police torturers.

By November 4, the reply came from Moscow in the form of battalions of Soviet soldiers and four thousand tanks. The Hungarian exodus began.

Pouring into Austria and political asylum the Hungarians were credited with inflicting "the first real wound in the body of the Soviet empire."

Fabian Flynn, director for Catholic Relief Services in Austria, after heading several convoys of help into Budapest, reported on the first moves to help the fleeing Hungarians.

"The Soviets picked Sunday to begin their offensive in Hungary.

"The Austrian border guards were marvelous; they made no attempt to stop the people, but simply permitted them to flow into Austria. It was to the city of Eisenstadt that most of the refugees were being directed by border police and border guards.

"About four o'clock that Sunday afternoon, I drove down to Eisenstadt, which is about forty miles from Vienna.

"By that time the first transport was ready at the railroad station. It had been decided to send the refugees to a town call Traiskirchen which is in the wine belt below Vienna, about thirty miles from Eisenstadt. There was a huge and empty academy that at one time had been the property of the royal Austro-Hungarian Government and during the occupation had been used by the Russians as a barracks. It was in very poor condition, but nevertheless a shelter for these people. It could hold about five thousand.

"The scene at the Eisenstadt station was one that will be forever impressed upon my mind and memory. God help us, I have seen so many refugees since 1940, in the various countries of the world, but somehow the scene, the confusion and the tragedy, and the sorrow and sadness of the whole horrible business of refugees seemed to come right up and hit me in the face again. It was as if I had never known it or seen it before. A train of thirty-eight cars was pulled up before the station and extended as far down as almost the eye could see into the twilight and the darkness that was just beginning to descend. The cars were lighted and packed to the doors with this mass of humanity, mostly women and children and old folks. Here and there a soldier, here and there an able-bodied man, but they told me that the men, some of them, had escorted their wives and womenfolk and children to the border, bade them goodbye, and returned to defend their country.

"At any event, there were not many men to be seen except the old men who sat there wondering perhaps what it was all about.

"A couple of women had aprons on, no overcoats, no warm clothing on them, as if they had just jumped up from a Sunday dinner when they heard that the Russians were approaching, ran out the door without trying to pick up anything, to "hit the road," as we say, looking for asylum. The Caritas director introduced me to the wife of a doctor of a town in Hungary who had brought with her their three children, but her husband had remained behind because he thought he would be needed to tend the wounded who would certainly begin to arrive, after the Russians had started their murderous work.

"Thirty-eight cars crammed to the doors with humanity, piled in like animals—writhing, climbing over each other, or just sitting there patiently and quietly. Almost two thousand people. An Austrian police car moved slowly up and down the platform, and over the loudspeaker came the voice of a police official: 'Stand here—go there—do this—do that—move here—get out of there.' How often these poor people would now hear this sort of thing. Now they were refugees, not human beings, refugees who were numbered and quizzed. Give me your name. What's you age? Where was your birthplace? What was you last address?

"As they sat at their Sunday dinner, or as, perhaps, they were kneeling at church on this fourth of November, they heard that fearful cry 'The Russians are invading!' And leaving everything behind, their cherished possessions, their homes, their businesses, their loved ones, they fled to asylum, to freedom, to safety.

"Now word comes out from the police car: 'Clear the platform—all refugees board the train. The train will now leave.' The engine whistles shriek several times, steam begins to hiss from the wheels, the conductor pipes his whistle, and now the train begins to slowly pull away from the station and move into the night for Traiskirchen. I said a few more words to the Caritas director who said he would wait there for the makeup of the next train.

"I got into the car and took off for Traiskirchen where these refugees would go. I got there in half an hour. It took them nearly four hours to get there by train. There were no beds ready for them. Coming in, most of them hadn't eaten all day since their flight. They all were shivering, for the night was bitter cold. They arrived dreary and discouraged, only to find no beds. Straw was given to them, and mattress covers, and they began to fill their own beds. They slept in the corridors, in drafty rooms; they wandered about looking for acquaintances, looking perhaps for their own children who had been separated from them in the melee. I don't know how much those poor souls slept that night, but I left about two o'clock in the morning of November 5, and there were still hundreds of them who had not been able to get anything to sleep on, not even straw."

* * *

As thousands upon thousands poured in, the Austrian Ministry of the Interior made available new camps, in general abandoned army barracks. Each barracks room contained eight to ten double berth cots and therefore could house sixteen to twenty people. Most of the camps had no heat. Conditions duplicated those of the worst D.P. camps of 1945. European governments and Red Cross societies met the challenge of the avalanche of human agony with help and offers of homes. Germans offered homes for fifteen thousand Hungarians. France, Belgium, Holland, Sweden, and Norway all offered asylum to sizeable groups.

American voluntary agencies threw up temporary offices near the camps—International Rescue Committee, Church World Service, Catholic Relief Services, Lutheran World Relief and the American Jewish Joint Distribution Committee. Often staff members worked, ate and slept in the offices. The Intergovernmental Committee for European Migration from its Vienna office supplied funds for travel as each of the refugees' papers were completed.

For the Hungarians admitted to the United States, Camp Kilmer, a military installation, became, in November 1956, a refugee reception center just forty miles from New York City. The camp located in New Jersey was named for the New Jersey-born poet Joyce Kilmer.

Newsreel scenes of the Hungarian uprising were still showing in American theaters when a planeload of Hungarian refugees put down at Maguire Air Force Base on November 21, 1956. The refugees were put aboard a bus and driven to Camp Kilmer to be greeted like heroes by the press, television and newsreel cameramen. A twenty foot streamer of white bunting was thrown across the camp entrance with "Isten Hozta Amerikaba," "Welcome to America," in heavy white letters.

Never had a revolt been captured in all its glory, terror and desperation on film. Students and workers, carrying banners and the sixteen demands that sparked the revolution, marched through American living rooms, via television, on their way to Bem Square, Budapest. Television viewers with a sense of history saw the demonstration as a direct continuation, not only of the massive October gathering of Poles, who stood like massed statues before Warsaw's Palace of Culture, but also of the June 1953 rising of East German workers.

The United States, though caught unprepared with an immigration law that was not geared to the needs of a time of historical crisis, rose to the challenge by passing emergency legislation. Hungarian refugees could qualify for entry as parolees. They could remain permanently if after two years their records were satisfactory.

*   *   *

Camp Kilmer made every effort to live up to the greeting over the entrance. "Isten Hozta Amerikaba," a Hungarian woman explained to me in our camp office, is not exactly "Welcome to America." "The words mean, in our way of expressing, 'God brought you.' That is 'Isten Hozta.' You speak to guests that you welcome gladly."

With its free Coca-Cola, free television and movies, free English classes, and free Red Cross telephone calls to friends and relatives all over the United States, Kilmer presented a fantastic contrast to the makeshift shelters from which they had been plucked for migration.

Kilmer's facilities for male soldiers were speedily converted for men, women and children. Quarters were modified so that family groups could remain together. In a printed statement, the American General in charge of Camp Kilmer explained: "The U.S. Army's function is to act as housekeeper for the center and to operate the center's facilities for the benefit of the refugees."

The trim wooden barracks were set spaciously in acres of grounds. In a recreation hall as large as a commercial theatre, the pastimes of American Army recruits—cards, jazz records, radios, television sets, music books—were available to Hungarians of all ages.

In the Army mess hall, the Hungarians received the same food as the American military and civilian staffs. They were given the same medical services. Each adult refugee was issued two and a half dollars weekly in pocket money so that he could take some advantage of the post exchange shopping facilities.

Seven American voluntary agencies, housed in cement-floored barracks, were working around the clock to place in homes and jobs each planeload of refugees. The aim was to send out as many of the newcomers as possible before incoming transports overtaxed the facilities of Camp Kilmer. The United States Immigration Service registered the arriving Hungarians and the U.S. Government Employment Service interviewed them in an all-out effort to match job needs throughout the country with the skills and plans of the individual Hungarians.

Catholic Relief Services was one of the seven sponsoring agencies, charged with the task of finding individual sponsors in communities throughout the United States for the new stream of escapees. Sponsors not only offered homes and jobs, but helped ease the newcomer into American life. Through the work of sponsors, schools, churches and fraternal groups opened their facilities as the Hungarians arrived in communities from coast to coast. In an enormous barracks at Kilmer, our agency assembled a staff of fifty persons, many of whom had served during the height of D.P. resettlement.

*   *   *

I could not help contrasting Camp Kilmer to the other two
D.P. camps I had seen in the western hemisphere. It was a
happy contrast, showing that the U.S. government, involved in
all three camps, had taken to heart some valuable lessons
regarding the treatment of refugees.

The Mexican Camp, Colonia Santa Rosa, described in "Cloud
of Witnesses," offered restricted movement as well as the incon-
veniences of living quarters in an antique converted hacienda.

The third camp, mentioned earlier, gave a safe haven in Fort
Ontario, New York, to Jewish refugees during the last year of
World War II. To the historic fort were brought in 1944, under
the auspices of the War Refugee Board, nine hundred and
eighty-two Jewish refugees. Many were from Yugoslavia and
Greece, and had managed to survive until rescued by American
troops in the south Italy campaign. I had seen Fort Ontario just
after the New Year of 1945. The refugees spoke to me in Ladino,
the Portuguese-sounding ancient Spanish of the Sephardim, that
I had first heard in Barcelona. They wondered how they could
change from being internees into free citizens. As they had been
snatched from Europe for emergency care, the people in Fort
Ontario had no visas. The camp was administered by the War
Relocation Authority, the agency which had the responsibility
for the internment camps for Americans of Japanese origin.

It was only in 1946, after President Harry S. Truman's directive on D.P.'s, that the refugees in Fort Ontario were free persons rather than civilian internees.

The United States was deeply involved in all three camps. It
occurred to me that not many Americans, if any, had had the
opportunity to compare these three widely separated camps
serving people victimized by different historical circumstances.
The Nazi hurricane which drove the east European refugees to
Fort Ontario had long subsided, but the Soviet brutality which
had put the Polish refugees on the long road to Colonia Santa
Rosa, Mexico, was the same brutality, that had sent the
Hungarian refugees to Camp Kilmer. It was a reckoning of history, I thought, that the United States, which had helped hide the
wounds inflicted on the Polish deportees to Siberia—wounds

inflicted by a wartime ally—now was joining the rest of the world in realizing the danger of hiding or minimizing any injustice inflicted on humankind.

* * *

One of my first contacts at Camp Kilmer was with a family of gypsies. They were near the entrance of the recreation hall. Two children with cropped shiny black hair were running around the chairs shouting to each other. A woman with a black pigtail and a wide, flower-bedecked skirt darted up and caught the children. She was barefoot. Her shoes were reposing neatly under her chair.

Our second contact also dealt with gypsies. As we were talking to Hugh McLoone, who directed the work of our agency during the seven months of the existence of Camp Kilmer, a long distance call came from Cleveland, Ohio. We could not help hearing his side of the conversation.

"You showed them the restaurant? Oh, I see."

"You explained to them they could take other engagements?" Long pause. A note of surprise entered McLoone's calm, even voice. "Tonight? but how can they get here tonight? Where are their instruments? One of them has a bull fiddle."

Short pause. "Oh, a bus. It's fourteen, isn't it?"

"Yes, we'll find accommodations. Thank you for calling."

Pause. "Yes, yes, I'm sure you did your best. Goodbye."

Mr. McLoone turned to us. "That was our most difficult placement so far. An entire Gypsy band from Budapest. They insisted on staying together, so we found a booking as a unit. A restaurant in Cleveland. When they saw it, they refused the placement. They hired a bus. They're heading back to us. They left as a team. They're coming back as a team. They'll be here this evening."

As Mr. McLoone was talking, I realized why he had been chosen to head the speeded-up resettlement effort of our agency for Camp Kilmer—an effort that eventually helped in the reimplantation of twenty-three thousand persons. While he was talking on the telephone, and when he turned to explain the problem to us, he never stopped smiling. It was a smile of faint but unquenchable delight. For him, being involved in the reso-

lution of problems never before met and surmounted was a sort
of joy.

I had a warm feeling for gypsies from childhood, a feeling
intensified when I learned of the murder of whole tribes of
these anarchic, lovable people in Auschwitz and other extermination camps. I was glad they were receiving patient treatment.
I was not there when the busload of players and instruments
arrived, but I did know that bookings were found for them in
New York City. It developed that it was nothing in Cleveland
that they objected to—it was rather being cut off from the
excitement of New York.

The Hungarian agony entered Mr. McLoone's office with the
next visitor. He was a tall, regular featured young man with
curly hair and a military bearing. Geza told us that he had not
managed to escape from Hungary until November 24.

"It is a miracle that I am here. I was an aide to Pal Maleter,
one of the leaders of our revolution. He named me head of the
Red Cross, a true Red Cross, not a Red Red Cross."

"My chief is dead. The AVH (secret police) was searching for
me. But, thank God, I reached that border. I was marked for
death."

For people bounding with energy like Geza, it was simple to
find good placements.

In a dozen smaller offices alongside Hugh McLoone's, our
staff members were interviewing refugees. There were many
cases of families begging for an extension of their stay in Camp
Kilmer until word was received from a relative presumed to have
arrived in Austria. The voluntary agencies were under pressure
to establish the refugees in placements outside the camp as soon
as possible. A line of waiting people was outside each door. In
such cases the interviews were battles of wits larded with ultima-
tums on both sides.

The diagrammatic guide printed by the U.S. Army at Camp
Kilmer to show the progression of services toward resettlement
indicated a calm, ordered process. The interviewing barracks of
the agencies, with telephones ringing, telegrams being delivered, staff and refugees being paged in loud voices, people
milling about impatiently on queues, were far from the cool

scheme envisioned in the drawing. Nevertheless, the voluntary agencies, with the aid of thousands of individuals who offered homes, jobs, scholarships and hospital placements, succeeded in resettling the stream of Hungarians who fled through the sudden breach in Europe's great divide.

7. Bought with a Price

"What are we going to do," asked General Dwight D. Eisenhower surveying the wasteland of the country he had defeated, "just to prevent on our part having a Buchenwald of our own?"

Buchenwald's hundreds of acres of pain, enclosed by two thousand yards of electric fence, gave back twenty-six thousand starved prisoners when American tanks brought in the liberators. The skeletonized men were the survivors of wave after wave of those who had been deployed in slave battalions in the arms factories and stone quarries of the Thuringian countryside. Buchenwald's acres of pain had burst into hundreds of thousands of acres in a land engulfed in bottomless misery.

It was a turnabout in Allied policy which saved the Allied forces from presiding over their own Buchenwald. Enormous grain shipments, a cessation of dismantling, currency reform and the free access of a continuous stream of voluntary personnel and voluntary aid staved off mass death by starvation and put Germany on the first step of recovery. Help from the outside was a means of regeneration for the German voluntary agencies, destroyed under the Hitler regime. The unconquerable energy, ingenuity and organizing ability of the Germans reasserted themselves, and against these qualities even the chaos of capitulation days could not survive.

It was almost impossible to imagine that the arrival of the expellees, tragic victims of Potsdam, could contribute to the regeneration of Germany. Yet they did.

In the dead years following World War II, German office personnel and intellectuals who could express their will to work in no other way did it through the assembling of massive data. Then followed the analysis of the data for practical ends. I shall never be able to forget sitting down with a sociologist retained by the Caritas of Germany to study the expellee situation. He

242

had gathered all the figures and breakdowns of figures that were available to him. Then he had made various charts, including demographic pyramids of the expellee population as compared with the German population. In the expellee group he had included the Reichsdeutsche and the Volksdeutsche. He showed me the configuration by ages and sex. In both proportion of men to women, and to people of working age over the aged and very young, the expellees had a better demographic structure. Even then, he and other sociologists and economists felt that not too many of the expellees should be lost to Germany by migration. Immigration would only siphon off the most valuable working members of the expellee group. As soon as the upturn showed itself, although it was then nowhere in sight, these groups would be needed for the recovery effort. One could marvel not only at the thoroughness of the statistical analysis, but also at the implied hope in the economic future of Germany. The real marvel was that it all came true.

The second example is that of a member of the German business community. His statistical analysis dealt with a part of the human anatomy, the leg of the post-war German woman. A Saxony stocking manufacturer, he had fled, like many another dispossessed Saxon, to a Berlin refugee camp when his stocking mills were confiscated by the Soviet occupiers.

Penniless, he was anxious to find ways of starting his manufacturing business in the west. His old business customers were willing to give him orders. Even before he had any means to produce the article, he accepted a number of orders, along with cash deposits of ten percent on the total order. With these evidences of confidence in his briefcase, he contacted a German cultural group in the United States, who supplied funds for the opening of a small plant. He began to deliver the stockings. But other stocking manufacturers were already operating in the resurgent market.

"What I needed to compete," the manufacturer explained to the press, "was an exact market analysis. I staged a competition for the ideal German leg, and it provided me with the exact measurements of ten thousand women's legs. Running the figures through a computer, I learned *that war work and wandering afoot had changed their measurements.* I matched these changes with my machines and it worked. Our stockings really fitted."

The miles of wandering about Germany, the tragedy of the search for shelter during mass expulsion, the arduousness of life in wartime, in defeat and in a vengeful peace, all became grist for Germany's resurgent economic mill. The manufacturer served the newly-ascertained leg needs so well that he shortly had three factories in operation and in time became a millionaire.

The case of the stocking manufacturer was multiplied hundreds of thousands of times in truncated Germany, when the expellees added their skills to local communities. They played their part as the German industrial system was retooled from the ground up and German currency began to be the strongest in Europe.

*   *   *

A resurgent West Germany looked eastward to people separated from them by the death strip with its ever-increasing number of booby-trap guns. The horror stories of those who tried to breach the iron curtain and were wounded and captured by the border police reminded many of them of their own sufferings on the far side of the barrier.

The concern of the West Germans was heightened when, after 1961, a lethal barrier was erected to separate the Soviet sector from the western sectors of Berlin. "The wall" was topped by barbed wire and jagged glass and a death strip was mined. In year one of the wall, a young bricklayer and a companion tried to make their escape across it. The bricklayer, Peter Fechter, was shot by guards. The companion reached safety, but Fechter lay inside the barrier, calling feebly "Hilfe, Hilfe" as he lay bleeding. The border guards of the east sector let the boy bleed unaided, while a mounting crowd gathered on the western side. They watched helplessly while he died. Peter Fechter's body was pictured in the press of Germany and of the world. Each year, men and women who attempted to escape were shot or blown up by mines. Large numbers who failed in the attempt were arrested and landed in jail cells.

The pain of those who suffered for their attempt to reach West Germany gave rise to an unparalleled work of ransom.

Ransoming the captive has been a traditional work of mercy in the Christian tradition through the ages. A congregation of monks, known as Mercederians, "merced" being the Spanish word for "ransom," was formed to ransom Christians enslaved by Muslims or pirates. West Germany had money. East Germany was in need of West Germany's strong currency as well as of goods unobtainable within its borders.

Secret communications began with an East German lawyer as a key figure. A West German Lutheran bishop took part since he had experience in the transfer east of church funds, a permitted activity. Various political figures in West Berlin and West Germany became involved, concerned not only with those arrested for failed escape attempts, but with political prisoners of many types, including trade unionists, dissident socialists and critics of the regime and of its Marxist tenets. There were prisoners of conscience of every description, ministers, doctors, poets, composers, writers and professors, who publicly questioned the party line.

A few well-known dissenters were simply deported by the East German regime, including rock musicians. Thousands who had already applied for admission to the west would have wished for no happier fate than deportation. Little-known people, like a group of doctors and nurses of the Charite Lutheran Hospital in East Berlin, were simply detained when they were caught while trying to escape. When word reached the west, they were all ransomed. At first, the price per head was ten thousand dollars. Later the equivalent in foods like coffee, and material items like steel and rubber figured in the exchange.

Thus began a border crossing of some magnitude, in which each person who came to the west from East Germany was "bought with a price."

Utmost secrecy was preserved for many years. Those who had been ransomed (if indeed they knew the details) cooperated in the secrecy so as not to endanger the continuing thin line to freedom. The ransoming of political prisoners continued despite some evidence of détente. In 1988 alone, West Germany was estimated to have transferred 1.3 billion dollars for the release of political prisoners and prisoners of conscience. It was finally revealed that the human exchange had resulted in the freeing of thirty-four thousand persons and that the West German government had paid about 2.3 billion dollars from its tax revenues.

There were some, seemingly a minority, who decried the barter of cash for human beings as brokering in human lives. To others, the rescue of human beings carried a different message. It was a testimony to the value placed on freedom. The fact that the transfer of money and material things could contribute to the achievement of a gift of infinite value, human freedom, was a reason to continue the exchange as long as it was necessary. That the testimony to freedom was made by a nation whose total denial of human freedom had helped drag the world into unprecedented carnage was a sign of hope.

*   *   *

Came the political earthquake of 1989, and the iron curtain was no more.

The fearful symmetry of the two nuclear powers which gave rise to the unnatural boundary had passed into history. The secret police records of East Germany were open to the light. All in all, the records revealed, over thirty thousand people had been ransomed from East Germany. The price "per head," known as *kopf gelt*, paid to East German operatives, had risen over the years to the equivalent of sixty thousand dollars for each person.

The mined "death strip," with its watchtowers from which guards could train their weapons on fleeing people, was no more. The watchtowers were dismantled; the gashed earth of the barrier dividing a continent was smoothed over like a healed wound.

The most powerful symbol of the consignment of the iron curtain to history was the destruction of the Berlin wall. Its barbed wire was slashed; its concrete slabs topped by jagged shards of glass were hacked away by citizens of east and west. Young people were able to climb atop the defanged wall to dance and sing. Bulldozers were then brought to the scene to tear large gaps in the concrete and finally to bring it to naught.

Eighty persons had died in attempts to breach the Berlin wall in its noxious life of nearly three decades. Unnumbered persons died or were given prison terms in trying to breach the length of the iron curtain.

The wonder of the demise of the Berlin wall and the iron curtain was that it was accomplished without violence. Innumerable acts of conscience prepared for by the patient suffering of dissenters condemned to the darkness of prison cells or the inhumanity of concentration camps blossomed forth in eastern Europe. The churches were the undergirding of the movement that caused a seemingly impregnable barrier to fall, not by violence, but by the aroused moral conscience of millions of members of the human family.

Chapter Six

UPROOTING IN THE INDIAN SUB-CONTINENT

When the Indian sub-continent became two nations in 1947, the time of carnage in which a million people perished was followed by a massive cascade of refugees across the new borders. It was one of the largest transfers of people in the twentieth century. Over twelve million people trekked from their home places, some four million quitting India for East or West Pakistan, and over eight million streaming into India. Among those taking refuge in India were the Sikhs who fled for their lives from the sundered Punjab province.

At least one in ten of West Pakistan's population became a refugee. Karachi, the capital, soon counted one million four hundred thousand refugees among its two million people. They lived in all kinds of pitiful shelters, including structures fashioned of straw, and as many as five hundred thousand lived for a long period in the open street. A Karachi murder trial revealed that the victim met his fate because he had appropriated the section of a sidewalk habitually used by another homeless refugee.

One of the agencies which plunged into feeding and medical help for the refugees was Catholic Relief Services. It worked with West Pakistan's welfare and health networks and, in addition, channeled special aid to leprosariums and clinics run by missionary groups.

*   *   *

In 1955, on the way to one of my visits to the sub-continent, I spent some time in the area with the most intractable refugee problem of all, that of the displaced Palestinians. CRS was involved solely in supplying material aid to them. Visiting the Gaza Strip, a one hundred and fifty square mile piece of land where at that time five hundred thousand Palestinian refugees were concentrated, I was made to feel at first hand the seething hostility. Foolhardy enough to enter the Strip in a car without a UN flag, but in fact with an Israeli license plate, I found that it was not long before we were faced by a group of men blocking

251

our way. I could not understand their shouting, but I saw menace in their gesticulating. The driver suddenly turned and made his way out of the Strip at top speed. He explained that the men had been threatening to overturn the car.

I pondered the infinitely tragic and near insoluble problem of rights in conflict, those of the Israelis, a victimized people in power in their homeland, and those of the Palestinians, out of power in an area they had considered theirs.

*   *   *

In Karachi, welfare ministry officials, some of them British-trained army officers, were awaiting discussions on how the agency could increase shipments which included rice, *ghee* (canned melted butter), cooking oil, medical supplies and bulgur wheat. Bulgur was prized over much of the Middle East as a form of wheat that was parboiled and fashioned into pearl-like grains. It could be boiled and combined with vegetables and whatever other food was available. Along with the Catholic Relief Services' director, an army colonel assisted me in visiting areas of need.

On the outskirts of Karachi, the more fortunate refugee families had been "resettled" in one-room shacks constructed of mud-cement blocks—with mud the prime constituent. Inside many of the shacks was a wide bed of wooden slats—bed by night, seat and table by day. In others, piles of rugs and rags served as protection for people sleeping on the dusty floor.

One of the shacks boasted a homemade chair. I sat comfortably as the family related to me, through my guide, how they had been forced to leave their work on the land. As I got up to leave, I was detained with further details. When I arrived at the next shack, the chair had preceded me. I could then be treated as an honored guest while learning the story of a Muslim family who could bring nothing with them but their cooking pots as they took to the road to trek across a new border.

I was expected to visit each of the families in the row of half a dozen shacks. Each story was essentially the same, of sudden uprooting. Some of the stories reached into a deeper well of suffering than others: a baby who had to be buried by the roadside, a child taken by disease on arrival in the new country. The black eyes of women, shining with tears as though the events had happened a week earlier, kept searching my face to see if I understood. They had had few possibilities to voice their sorrow and resentment at the fate that had overtaken them. I could not help noting that before I reached the next shack, the chair was deftly removed so that I could be invited to sit down for each story.

On the outskirts of Karachi, a large camp provided minimal but stable (no pun intended) shelter for some hundreds of the dispossessed. It was the Haji camp, so called because it had been a transit camp for poorer pilgrims on the way to Mecca. Now destitute Muslims were forced to live year in and year out in the status of pilgrim, but unable to make the Haj, so central to Islamic tradition.

In a corner of Karachi, formerly a fairly orderly and well-cared for city, congregated those who had achieved no permanent shelter. By day they thronged the city streets, hawking small objects and begging. By night they returned to the spots on the sidewalk they had staked out for themselves, many under the arcades of old marketplaces.

The refugees, existing so precariously in the Karachi of 1955, continued to see themselves as a distinct group from the people among whom they found themselves. They referred to themselves as mohajirs, refugees, and were united in protests against what they saw as unjust deprivation. They passed on their resentment to their children and grandchildren. In 1986, the mohajir resentment exploded in violence in a Karachi that was swollen to a population of eight million people. This aspect of the refugee experience is a reminder that forced-out people may be a threat to peace, an ominous presence, especially in societies beset by poverty.

* * *

The most exotic group of refugees I ever encountered was the group of young monks who greeted me in 1972 at the holy city of Varanasi, formerly called Benares.

The saffron-robed, shiny-skulled young men were Tibetans, and they walked with me to their temple. I found it garish, dusty and untidy by western standards, but to the monks it was precious beyond any ordinary decor.

I had come to tell the young monks that American voluntary agencies, including Catholic Relief Services, would increase the contribution toward their upkeep in the lamasary. They were happy at the news, but wanted to talk of their great mission, that of keeping lamaist Buddhism alive in their holy place and around the world. In the Potala Palace of Lhasa, the center of Tibetan religious life, there had been over ten thousand monks. Under Chinese occupation, there was thought to be no more than three hundred. Thousands of lamaseries were closed.

The city on the Ganges, with over fifteen hundred temples, is for Hindus the holiest of cities. Among the countless pilgrims who throng its hostels, streets, and *ghats* (the steps leading to the sacred river) are those who come there to die. Dying in Varanasi gives the highest of privileges, the release from the cycle of rebirths.

For the Tibetans in the lamasery, their exile in Varanasi had its glorious side. Only five miles away was Sarnath with the beautifully preserved Deer Park. Here the Buddha, having achieved enlightenment, preached his first sermon and thus "turned the wheel of the law." I stood before a mound of ancient stones and wondered if what I was being told was really so. It was at this spot, marked by a stupa, that in the sixth century before Christ the Buddha had actually put his teaching into words.

Not only Buddhists but thoughtful people the world over have been nourished by the four noble truths of suffering, the origin of suffering, the cessation of suffering, and the fourth noble truth comprising the eightfold noble path: right views, right intent, right speech, right conduct, right livelihood, right endeavor, right mindfulness and right meditation.

The presence of the monks at the place of Buddhism's beginning was a poignant sequel to the military invasion of Tibet by the Chinese in 1950.

Into the secluded plateau of Tibet, surrounded by Himalayan peaks, and into a theocratic kingdom where the concept of the secular had not arrived, came the overlordship of the secular messianism of Marxism. The Tibetans began to react to Chinese oppression with scattered uprisings. By 1959 the repression was general and there were fears for the safety of the Dalai Lama, the priest-king. The Chinese military suppressed the rising with great brutality, and a stream of refugees made their escape from the mountain-locked kingdom.

The extended border between Tibet and India had been traversed from time immemorial by two groups, traders who led pack trains of yaks, mules and horses laden with wool, hides and salt, and pilgrims, who traveled light. In the spring of 1959, the pack trains from Tibet carried no items for trade but instead the religious items treasured by the Dalai Lama and his followers. The refugees made their tortuous way mile after mile over the most difficult terrain known to man. Eventually, at least eighty thousand Tibetans reached India.

Never before had a refugee exodus been so well prepared for by the receiving country. With the arrival of the first Tibetans, and the news of more to come, the Indian government opened a series of way stations, actually hostels, in what was then called northeast frontier territory, NEFA These were set up by detachments of the Indian Army at twenty mile intervals. At these hostels, the Tibetans, exhausted by long treks through icy mountain passes, and by the fording of ravines, were revived by food and medical care until they could be housed in more permanent camps. The largest camp was one resurrected from use in the China-Burma-India theater of World War II, Missamari. It accommodated over eleven thousand Tibetans, including the survivors of the palace guard of the Dalai Lama. Many had died when the Chinese shelled the Potala Palace Monastery.

Among the voluntary agencies offering aid to the Indian authorities was Catholic Relief Services. Joseph J. Harnett, director of Asian programs for CRS, was one of a team who journeyed to the border area. He reported that no other refugee camp he had seen resembled Missamari. It was ablaze, he recounted, with banners and prayer flags strung on ropes from windows, poles and trees. In their free time, the refugees turned to their rosaries, to spinning their prayer wheels and to humming the sacred sound of "Om" into the echoing hills. Historians of religion could see the signs of the persistence of the old Tibetan Bon religion of magic underlying the pervading Buddhism.

Another camp visited by Harnett was a relic of the colonial

period in Bengal, a converted British fort, Buxa. The fortress, on a hilltop, gave shelter to twelve hundred Tibetans, many of them lamas. Indian civil servants were called in to provide additional aid to that supplied by army detachments. In Buxa, the hierarchical structures of the orthodox society were respected. Living quarters and cooking arrangements had to be separate for the distinct groups within the archaic, theocratic-feudal system. First came the lamas, or monks, of various ranks; then lay students, fighters, traders, family groups and the men who performed the manual work for the lamaseries. In a secluded corner of the fort was an Ani Gompa, a nunnery where twenty-three refugee Buddhist nuns followed their own schedule of devotion.

In the open field around the fort, monks with shaven skulls gathered to recite their prayers in the bass chant, making unearthly use of the vocal chords. In another part of the field, two large groups regularly faced each other. One group occasionally burst into loud clapping. Harnett asked for the meaning of the applause and was informed that it was not applause at all. It was a sign of recognition of error. A group of lamas was instructing a group of novices in the teachings of Tibetan Buddhism. When the answer of a novice was incorrect, all the novices indicated their recognition of this by clapping. To Harnett, the scene resembled a playing field in which oversized football squads huddled for consultation before a game.

It was not long before Tibetan refugees moved into Nepal, Bhutan and various sections of India. In Delhi, I saw the work gangs of shaggy-haired Tibetans as they went by truck to construction and road-building sites. For the children of Tibetan refugees, help came from many sources. A group of youngsters between fifteen and eighteen years of age were brought to Switzerland, where, in a climate not unlike that of Tibet, they could prepare for the future of their people.

The Dalai Lama himself was installed in a house atop a hill in Dharamsala in the foothills of the Himalayas. Prayer flags fluttered from the surrounding pine trees. The road to his residence had markings on every large boulder of the endlessly repeated mantra "Om Mani Padma Hum," "Hail to the Jewel in the Lotus." Around him gathered the exiled Tibetans in every type of hut or house. Many kept alive Tibetan handicrafts in the form of rugs, Buddhist wall hangings and jewelry.

While inside Tibet militant atheism was continuing its onslaught on the last totally religious society on the face of the earth, the Dalai Lama was sharing the insights of Buddhism with the stream of visitors to Dharamsala. He was aware of the forced closing of lamaseries and the burning of treasured Buddhist scriptures by the Chinese. Yet he could say, "You should have love for those people who hurt you because they are your gurus. The Chinese are our gurus." A guru is a spiritual master. "Your enemy," he stressed, "is the person who gives you the test of your inner strength, your tolerance and your respect for others. He is therefore a true teacher from this point of view. Instead of feeling angry with, or hatred toward, such a person, one should respect him and be grateful to him." In many of his talks, he interpreted for the west the teachings of his school of Buddhism. "The essence of the Mahayana school, which we try to practice, is compassion. . . . You sacrifice yourself in order to obtain salvation for the sake of other beings. . . . This kind of love is to be extended to all living beings."

One of the visitors to the Dalai Lama was a monk of the west, Thomas Merton, who led countless believers in opposition to war. His message of peacemaking and forgiveness according to the gospel of Jesus met at some points that of his fellow monk. The white-robed Cistercian sat with the saffron-robed Dalai Lama to discuss, as Merton related, methods of meditation. Then they went on to more mundane issues, including Marxism. The Dalai Lama was of the opinion that it would be possible for people of religion to co-exist with communism if Marxism meant no more than the establishment of a just economic order. He knew from experience that militant atheism meant to suppress all religion. He had made every effort to co-exist with it and had found that such co-existence was not possible.

The Dalai Lama began to be invited to give conferences around the world. When he spoke at the Cathedral of St. John the Divine and St. Patrick's Cathedral in New York City, thousands of people thronged both houses of worship. His exile and travels seemed to Tibetans as the fulfillment of the prophecy of the great sage and monk, Padma Sambava. He was the founder in 751 A.D. of the first Tibetan monastery. "When the iron bird flies and horses have wheels," Padma Sambava predicted, "the Tibetans will be scattered across the world like ants and the dharma will come to the land of the west." After the exodus that began in 1959 the Dalai Lama and many high lamas were being carried by planes—"iron birds"—about the world.

The awarding of the Nobel Peace Prize to the Dalai Lama gave him heightened opportunity to share the insights of Buddhism. One December 10, 1989, in Oslo, Norway, he said, "I believe the prize is a recognition of altruism, love, compassion and non-violence which I try to practice in accord with the teaching of the Buddha and the sages of India and Tibet." Calling nuclear war a form of suicide, he pointed out, "Violence can only breed more violence. We are trying to end the suffering of our people, not to inflict suffering on others." He paid tribute to Mahatma Gandhi, saying that Gandhi's life instructed and inspired him and strengthened his conviction that "Tibet would be liberated with truth, courage and determination as our weapons."

There was no hatred or anger in the words of the Dalai Lama, despite the fact that oppression still hung heavy on his people and the fact that he had to continue to be separated from them in exile.

About the oppressors, he kept saying, "They, too, are human beings who struggle to find happiness and deserve compassion. I pray for all of us, oppressor and friend, that together we may succeed in building a better world through human understanding and love, and that in doing so, we many reduce the pain and suffering of all sentient beings."

As a refugee, the Dalai Lama spoke for countless refugees. He was the voice of his fellow exiles, Tibetan refugees who managed through such livelihoods as road-building, shopkeeping and teaching to settle far from their homeland and found families. He was the voice, also, of exiles who found in their deprivation deep spiritual meaning, and from it drew strength.

Some refugees, seeing themselves as victims with no foreseeable end to their suffering and exile, have chosen the way of retaliation. They become victim-avengers. The Dalai Lama was among those who brought before the world in piercingly vivid words the other kind of victim, the saving victim. He has made creative use of his life as a refugee to increase the role of compassion in a century called "the century of the refugee." He gave other exile-victims a transcendent use for their suffering. In this way, he has added to the moral capital of the world in a time of upheaval and suffering.

* * *

Clear across the land mass of India, in Calcutta, the same tragically ironic conjunction occurred as had taken place in Karachi. Strangers from across a border found refuge, often their final refuge, in a setting designed for pilgrims. These refugees came across the border from East Pakistan. In both refugee-choked cities, those who came as strangers lived and died as pilgrims. In Calcutta, the refuge was the Pilgrims' Hostel at the shrine of the goddess Kali. The millions of unknown Muslims and Hindus forced to live out their lives as refugees were truly victims of a history which they had no part in making. Their fate was the end result of the colonial episode of history that went through its death throes in the twentieth century.

The "Black Hole of Calcutta" is often the one fact of the city's history about which people outside India are aware. It was an incident of 1857 during an attempt to expel the British raj. The nabob of Bengal captured a group of English men, women and children who had taken refuge in the East India Company's Fort William. He herded them into the fort's guardhouse, called the Black Hole, where most of them perished during the suffocating heat of the Bengal night. Less known is the fateful partition of Bengal into Hindu and Muslim areas in 1905 by Lord Curzon.

The effect of the 1947 partition was catastrophic for the four million Hindus who poured into Bengal, one of the poorest provinces of India. Into Calcutta, called by Rudyard Kipling "the city of dreadful night," came one million destitute newcomers.

Eight years after the 1947 partition, a "black hole" of Calcutta yawned before me. It was the Sealdah railway station, the terminal of the eastern railway, reaching Calcutta from the foothills of the Himalayas. The floor and walls of the cavernous station building were of grey-black stone. Over a thousand men, women and children squatted on the dank flagstone as if in a state of suspended animation. The steam of incoming trains mingling with the smoke from cooking pots over dung-burning bucket stoves and the odor of massed bodies assaulted the nostrils. Day after steaming day, night after stifling night, they managed to keep alive in Sealdah. As some were moved out, I learned, others crept in from the streets, or crossed over from the nearby border of what became East Pakistan, later Bangladesh. The influx of refugees had not ceased with the first big cascade of 1947.

Led by a sari-dressed woman in rough sandals, I picked my way carefully to avoid not only the massed bodies, but large beetles which scurried among them. I finally found myself near the immense grill partition of heavy iron bars which marked the end of the railroad tracks. I felt that I was in an obscenely crowded jail. Little children were staring at me, naked boys, their heads a mass of scabs, little girls covered with odd pieces of cotton. Starvlings all, many had the protruding bellies of prolonged hunger. I deciphered a word addressed to me and my guide by a few women who were holding out their hands for help. It was "Ma," Mother. It was the name they addressed to any woman who might respond to their appeal. In point of fact, the woman guiding me was known as Mother to the young women who had joined her in responding to the hunger and homelessness of Calcutta. She was Mother Teresa, whose name was to become so linked with the city that she was identified as Mother Teresa of Calcutta.

A few of the sisters were busy at two enormous vats, from which curls of steam were beginning to emerge. "We cook a gruel from the bulgur wheat, soy, oil and ghee you send us," said Mother Teresa. "We come only a few days a week. It is not enough, but it helps keep them alive."

There was movement among the people as women in dun-colored ragged saris moved toward the vats. Their brass and tin pots gleamed as they held them out for the ladled gruel they called "kidgeree."

"We also give supplies to the families so that they can cook meals over their own stoves," Mother Teresa explained.

I peered into the massed brown bodies and saw tiny stoves like little buckets. I learned that they were made of mud and were called "chulas." Dung from Calcutta's large population of protected cows, dried and made into small patties, provided enough fuel to heat a meal.

The food from the vats was being added to whatever was being cooked on the little stoves. The odor of the station was almost suffocating. The men, women and children had only the station washroom for drinking water as well as for keeping some measure of cleanliness. Mother Teresa seemed not to notice or mind the smells as she leaned over a gunnysack to talk to a woman who raised her head with difficulty or to a man with a chest so devoid of flesh that it resembled a bird cage.

* * *

I thought I had seen the worst when I became acquainted with Sealdah Station. But worse was yet to come.

The place I shrank from seeing, but which I knew I had to see, was the Home for the Dying, referred to as Kalighat. Like the Haji camp in Karachi, the Home for the Dying in Calcutta was originally intended for pilgrims. It abutted the temple of the goddess Kali, goddess of destruction and purification. Pilgrims who traveled from considerable distances to perform their act of worship, their "puja," to the goddess could rest or stay overnight. The building, a type of Middle Eastern hostel, or "caravanserai," was the gift of a devout Hindu to serve Kali's poorest pilgrims. The Home for the Dying, and the fact that there was need for it, demonstrated Calcutta's abysmal need following the onslaught of refugees. Mother Teresa's work grew out of that need. Her response gives a glimpse into the effects of uprooting.

From the outside, the ivory-toned Home for the Dying with its eight, bulbous, fluted domes topped by delicate spires, had a fanciful look. Its entrance, with its scalloped Moghul arches, gave no hint of the agony within. A small blackboard faced me just inside the entrance: "Men 72, Women 69." I entered the large hall where men patients lay side by side on pallets. They had been carried in from the Calcutta streets, maggot-ridden, covered with the filth and spittle of the gutter, and ready to breathe their last. Sisters were feeding some of the men, spoon by spoon, and young Indian men were washing the patients, cleaning sores and scabs. I followed Mother Teresa as she made her way along the center walkway, sitting down every now and then on the parapet near the pallets of the patients. When she came to a man so cadaverous that one could almost see the skull beneath the skin, she stroked the brown, stick-like arm. At her consoling touch, his eyes brightened, the only part of him that seemed alive. She spoke to others in Bengali or Hindi; a few managed a smile. In their search for consolation, many hands were held out to me, and I could only shrink in revulsion. Mother Teresa recalled the words of a man who, despite the care given him by Mother Teresa and the sisters, could not be saved. "I have lived like an animal on the street," he said to Mother Teresa, "but I die like an angel, loved and cared for."

"We could not let children of God die like dogs in the gutter," said Mother Teresa. "At least we could give them a human death."

The women's ward presented the same picture of humanity in extremis. There were gaunt women with shorn heads, women rotting with sores that were being cleaned of maggots. Others had scabrous growths on their faces and necks that were being carefully dressed. The sisters gave their whole attention to hideous excrescenses or to cleaning bodily excretions.

As some of the women looked at me appealingly, I turned away. Many years later, on successive visits, I was able to overcome or transcend my revulsion, but on that day I simply asked Mother Teresa how she could face this same human agony day after day.

"Our work calls for us to see Jesus in everyone," she said. "Jesus has told us that he is the hungry one, he is the naked one, he is the thirsty one. He is the one without a home. He is the one who is suffering." She looked around at the rows of pallets in the hostel. "They are Jesus. Each one is Jesus in his distressing disguise." Even though Mother Teresa and her sisters were able to give no more than a few days of care to the weakest of the forsaken people, it was still worthwhile. Their compassionate care served to remind the dying of their inviolable dignity and utter sacredness.

* * *

It was this view of the utter sacredness of each person, however abandoned or loathsome in appearance, that animated Mother Teresa's work, a work that brought mercy to one of the planet's most scourged cities. Her life had been intertwined with that of Calcutta and Bengal from the age of eighteen. In Skopje, Macedonia, a province of former Yugoslavia, she had decided to become a missionary nun in India. The Sisters of Loreto, who had taught schools in Calcutta and its surroundings for several generations, accepted her at their motherhouse in Ireland. In 1928, she boarded a ship for Calcutta. After novitiate training in the foothills of the Himalayas, Darjeeling, she came down to Calcutta and spent twenty years as a teaching sister. During the Second World War, Bengal was visited by a famine which took at least a million lives and brought rural people in droves to the soup kitchens of Calcutta, where many perished.

In the upheaval that accompanied the freedom of India, Calcutta became a crucible of communal violence, that between Hindu and Muslim. "Direct Action Day," August 16, 1946, exploded in violence, and is referred to as the Day of the Great Killing. The roaring streets were brought to a complete standstill except for activities of human destruction. Shops and homes were set afire with their owners trapped inside. Men and women were attacked with steel-tipped *lathis* and left to bleed to death on the street. Vultures gathered to feast on exposed bodies. The Great Killing possessed Kali's city for four days of fiery frenzy. Eventually when the bodies could be carried to the burning ghats, the smoke from human flesh filled the air. At least five thousand had died and another fifteen thousand injured.

Mother Teresa had charge of a girls' boarding school. No food had been delivered and the girls were hungry. Despite a curfew Mother Teresa made a foray into streets bloodied by the massacre of Muslim by Hindu, Hindu by Muslim.

"A lorry full of soldiers stopped me," she related, "and told me I should not be out on the street. I told them I had to come out and take the risk. I had three hundred students who had nothing to eat. The soldiers had rice and they drove me back to the school and unloaded bags of rice."

Just over three weeks later on the train to Darjeeling to make a spiritual retreat, Mother Teresa experienced a clear call, something she called "a call within a call." She was to "leave the convent and work with the poor while living among them."

*   *   *

Two years later, on August 16, 1948, with all the permissions from Loreto, Rome, and the local archbishop, Mother Teresa was free to work among the poor of Calcutta. Her work would brook no barriers of religion, race or creed. Her nun's habit was replaced by the cotton sari of the Indian poor. On her feet were rough sandals. She walked alone among the "bustees" of the city slums crowded chiefly with the refugees of partition. Arriving with nothing, they clung to the city as a mother. It was in 1955 that I first walked with her among the desolate alleyways, where sewage ran in open rivulets. It was in one of the bustees, Moti Jihl, that she used her teaching experience to start a school for the school-less in the open air. She sat on a chair, drilling the students in reciting the alphabet aloud, and formed the letters with a stick in the dust. In a few months, two of her former students joined her. They were able to rent a dirt-floored room in the bustee and children flocked to them. As other young women caught the fire of serving the dispossessed, the school grew. Mother Teresa took a dramatic step, almost unheard of among missionaries from Europe or outside India. She shed her own citizenship, and became a citizen of India. From a house where they were given shelter, Mother Teresa and the young women left early each morning for their school in the bustee. They had to walk carefully to avoid stepping on men and women who clogged the streets of the poorer sections. Some were arising to go out to beg or to menial tasks; others did not have the strength to rise, and might die where they lay.

Other rooms were rented in the Moti Jihl bustee in which homeless men and women were cared for if only for their final days on earth. A phenomenon which amazed Calcutta, and later the world at large, occurred when every year numbers of young Indian women joined Mother Teresa in going to the very poorest. In 1950, they were recognized as a new religious family within the Catholic Church, the Missionaries of Charity. By

1952, Mother Teresa's society had come to the attention of Calcutta's city fathers who offered them the use of the hostel at Kali's temple for the destitute dying.

The temple's location probably entered into the decision to give it to the Sisters. It was close to a tributary of the Hooghly River on whose banks was a burning ghat, a cremation place. It was for this reason that the Home for the Dying was referred to as Kalighat. At first, despite the care, and the food that reached stomachs long empty, most of the men and women brought to Kalighat could not be saved. Their bodies were taken to the burning ghat and their ashes scattered in the Hooghly, an arm of the holy Ganges. As time went on, more of the moribund street people were restored to life. Doctors and nurses from India and overseas volunteered their skills.

* * *

The sorrows of Bengal continued as new crises arose. Gandhi's words to Bengali officials proved prophetic. "From today," he told them, "you have to wear the crown of thorns. May God help you." It was the day that India achieved freedom, August 15, 1947. Gandhi was on a fast in Calcutta because of the agony of the mass uprooting and communal violence.

As if one partition was not enough for the sub-continent, a second breakaway occurred when the Bengalis of East Pakistan rose against the domination of West Pakistan. The glue of their common religion of Islam was not sufficient to unite people of differing languages and cultures. The two wings, one on each side of the Indian sub-continent had never coalesced as a nation. The occupation of East Pakistan by the army of West Pakistan hardened the desire of the East Pakistanis, the Bengalis, to become totally independent of the western wing.

It was during the 1971 occupation that some 9,700,000 East Pakistanis fled over an unmarked border into India's province of West Bengal. They were in the main Hindus, with a number of Christians from an ancient Catholic enclave near Dacca. Calcutta again became a city of refuge, with 250,000 men, women and children encamped at its gates. The fleeing people settled into a swampy expanse called Salt Lake. The first to arrive crept into enormous sewer pipes laid out in preparation for a new sewer system. Tents were flown in to provide some protection for the men, women and children who had made their way to Salt Lake by walking, by riding bullock carts, by fording streams and rivers in fishing craft. No one knew the number who, lacking food and drinkable water, perished on the way. Corpses left to become bloated and black by the roadside marked their passage. Many reached Salt Lake in a dying condition.

The conscience of the world was aroused. Governments, intergovernmental agencies and people-to-people agencies were mobilized to save the lives of the people in Salt Lake and in the massive camps along the area bordering East Pakistan.

Francis X. Carlin, Catholic Relief Services director for the area, remarked, "Calcutta in 1971 was the high point of my long service with CRS. We helped set up camps with about a quarter of a million people in each one. We provided food, medicines, clothing, everything you could think of. Caritas of India brought doctors, nurses, religious sisters and lay volunteers from the length and breadth of India."

Only the speedy construction of water and sewage systems by teams of engineers from inside and outside India prevented an epidemic of cholera that would have decimated Bengal. Catholic Relief Services, under the direction of Edward M. Kinney, organized planeloads and shiploads of food sufficient to help feed two million of the homeless. Medical supplies followed as cries for help came from health officials facing a cholera epidemic.

Mother Teresa and the Missionaries of Charity played a crucial role in Salt Lake, a "human dead sea" of misery. They carried their work into the tents and sewer pipes of Salt Lake and soon accepted as their own the care of the people close to death. Some were brought to Kalighat by ambulance, but soon Kalighat had place for no more.

"We were given a tent for those who were closest to death," one of the sisters told me. "No one wanted this task, but we were ready for it because we had worked at Kalighat. We sat and fed them slowly, as we do at Kalighat, but it was often too late. It was not only the older people who died, but people of all ages who had suffered too much.

"I worked very hard to save the life of a mother who had three children in the camp. She held on to life, but she was fading away. I gave her my love and care. I talked with her and tried to encourage her. The children came each day to ask when their mother would be better. I am a Bengali myself—from the Dacca side, like our people in Salt Lake. My heart was near breaking when I told them that their mother had gone to God."

When the Indian Army won its campaign over the army of West Pakistan, a new nation, Bangladesh, was declared. One of the first tasks of the new-made nation was to provide for the needs of the nearly ten million returnees who poured back from Salt Lake, from camps along the border with India and from camps farther inland.

* * *

In March 1972, back in India, I saw the last of the returnees. They had been given temporary shelter in camps outside Bengal in Bihar and Maharashtra. The dispersal of the refugees had helped stem the cholera and smallpox that had begun to streak terrifyingly through the camps along the border.

The refugees were congregated in the railroad junction of Bongaon, flanking the border with Bangladesh.

Above the stone platform rose little swirls of smoke. The haze of a warm afternoon hung over the crush of people on the Bongaon railway station. Some lay prone, some squatted, some sat around the tiny twig fires from which the smoke was rising. The fires were contained within four bricks and were watched intently by women who managed to cook rice and a few vegetables for the families strewn on the floor about them. The only railroad station that ever approached this scene of massed bodies was Sealdah in Calcutta.

Two trains were in the sidings. These had brought over 1,200 people from Manna Camp in Bihar and Chanda Camp in Maharashtra. A Sister nurse, Lily, walked with me through the maze of bodies, and huge jute sacks bulging with family possessions. A few families had suitcases held together with ropes. Cooking pans and metal dishes for eating were piled up on the sacks or wrapped in saris. A few had kerosene lamps.

Even the children looked worn and exhausted as they

crouched near their mothers. Some of the women worked up a smile as Sister Lily approached them. They remembered the white-saried team of Catholic Sisters from Krishnagar, the Sisters of Mary Immaculate, that had come to stay with them in Manna Camp. They told Sister Lily that they had arrived with the train early that morning and were waiting for a train that was to pick them up at nine o'clock that night.

One woman, except for the deep circles under her eyes, could have been a true Bengali beauty. She had a bright glass jewel in her right nostril and she was sitting by her tiny fire watching the wide metal pan in which green vegetables were cooking in a little water. The water came from a common tap in the station. The bricks were borrowed from a building site next to the platform. She got up as we started to talk to her. Two pretty barefoot girls also stood up and shot furtive glances at us.

"I only left the Dacca side after they shot my husband," she told us. "I left with four children, but now I have two. The other two died when they got sick on the way."

"Yes," she answered Sister Lily. "I have relatives in Bangladesh and I must go back to see if they are all still alive. They do not know what happened to my children and I don't know what happened to them. Whoever is left will help me."

She looked down and slowly rubbed the back of her hand over her eyes. Then she fastened enormously brilliant tear-filled eyes on Sister Lily as though asking, "What else can I do?"

One young woman was stretched out on the platform. Beside her on a piece of jute sack was a naked baby. She seemed half sunk in a coma or in sleep, but we saw her move her hand against the flies that crawled on the baby's head.

The baby, she told us, had been born in Manna Camp. Her husband was with her but had gone into Bongoan to try to buy some food. The six-month-old baby seemed of normal size and would probably survive the return to Bangladesh if he caught no infection.

Near them lay an old man with a rough thatch of gray hair above his caved-in brown cheeks. He was breathing heavily. Sister Lily put a hand on his forehead.

"He has a temperature," she said.

In answer to her questions as to where he was hurting, the old man raised his palm to his throat and chest.

"I am hurting here. I have been hurting for many days. I wanted to stay a little longer, but they put me on the train."

He breathed noisily and closed his eyes. A man of about forty came over to us.

"That is my father. What can you do for him?" He was a worn, red-eyed man in a dirty blue lungi, the wrap-around cloth that replaced trousers. He asked without much intensity as though he did not expect a response.

I slipped some rupees into Sister Lily's hand and she as quietly slipped them into the man's hand.

"There is a bazaar nearby. You have some hours before the train leaves. Buy your father some milk and Horlicks. It may give him strength for the rest of the journey. But he is very weak and ill, so watch him carefully."

The son looked a bit surprised and shook his head in agreement.

As we moved on, Sister Lily said, "I wonder if he will live. I wonder if the old lady over there will live."

The old woman, her cotton sari slipping to uncover a shrunken right breast, was breathing through a wide-open, toothless mouth. Her eyes were closed. We walked by helplessly. The train was to sweep them all back to Bangladesh in a matter of three hours.

"I have seen too many old people like them," Sister Lily said. "When they reach this point, they don't live."

We had been picking our way through the shaded part of the station platform but now we reached the end of the sheltered section and emerged into the open. It was six o'clock, but the stone pavement was still hot from a sun-drenched day. Here we found a knot of people who were refusing to return to Bangladesh. They told us trustingly that they had gone once and come back. One eager little man still had his family in Manna Camp. He had returned to his home place with an earlier group of returnees. What he saw made him want to stay in India.

"The men of my village said to me, 'Why do you want to

come back here? You have a country over there.' They told us that it would be fine for us after the soldiers left. We wouldn't have to be afraid. But they don't want us. They had started working on our fields. I am from the Faridpur District."

Then he added as though explaining everything, "I am Hindu." He added, "Ask this woman what happened to her. She is Hindu from the same place. She's a widow."

The squat dark woman had a face literally striped with wrinkles and her eyes were bloodshot. There was no telling her age, but she had five children around her and the eldest was about sixteen. That would have made her at most about thirty-five. Around her were lumpy packages wrapped in dirty saris and a few jute sacks.

"I was in Bakura Camp near Howrah," she said, squinting up at Sister Lily. Howrah is a municipality across the Hooghly from Calcutta. "I went back to the Dacca side when the camp was closed. All of us went to the office and they gave us food and clothes and some money. When I reached my house, my neighbors were there. They said, 'You give us some of the food and money. You have to share it with us.' So they took it from me. All I had was my little house. There was nothing left in it. They said, 'You have a country. Why do you come back here?'

"I said. 'I am from here. My husband was killed by the soldiers.' But they said, 'You had a country to take care of you there.' So I came on the train to here but I will go to Howrah."

She probably thought that her family would be sheltered and fed as they had been in Bakura Camp, but in my mind's eye, I could see her and her family squatting by night in the Howrah Railway Station along with other homeless families. I could see her children trudging across the Howrah Bridge to beg on Calcutta's downtown streets, being chased away from one hotel entrance after another by turbaned doormen.

The thin little man put in, "I have relatives in Calcutta."

"But people die of hunger in Calcutta," I said through Sister Lily. "I have seen them. The countryside is better. At least you can get something to eat."

He flicked his head to the side in the way Bengalis do, meaning "Yes," or simply, "I have heard you," A feeling of constriction caught my heart. The story of murder and homelessness had not yet been played out. It was a tragic irony of history that the two-nation concept, the seeds of which were sown by colonials and intellectuals, was now on the lips of peasants. It was coming from the mouths of destitute refugees lying among their poor belongings at a railway junction. They had heard what was once a rhetorical concept coming from the mouths of Muslim villagers. It was being used it to despoil Hindu neighbors who belonged to the same blood and language. Would it be played out in succeeding generations?

* * *

When Mother Teresa broke the curfew in Calcutta in 1946, she saw the dread results of the Great Killing which bloodied the streets of the city, and served as a prelude to the flooding of Calcutta and Bengal with refugees.

Frail and bent, her weakened heart aided by a little motor called a "pacemaker," Mother Teresa was breaking curfew forty-six years later in the Calcutta of 1992. Again violence between Hindu and Muslim exploded. After extremists had destroyed the mosque built on the legendary birth-site of the god Rama in Ayodhya, Muslims expressed their outrage in the great cities, especially Calcutta and Bombay. The violence of one community was met with similar violence from the other.

A Missionary of Charity close to Mother Teresa wrote to me from Calcutta: "You must have heard about the terrible riots we had. Along Ripon Street, there was looting, burning, destruction and deaths. Only the army trucks could calm them down. We sisters had to walk with raised arms. We had a curfew for several days. No food. Mother as usual braved all and went by ambulance to all the 'terrible spots,' where people needed rice, oil, bulgur, biscuits, etc. Mother was asked by several groups to pray with them for PEACE. That was very beautiful."

The Missionaries of Charity continued to go to the anguished corners of the afflicted city, to the Mother and Child Clinics, to the slum schools, and, above all, to the Home for the Dying. Other religious communities encouraged them to perform their merciful works for the poorest of the poor.

Mother Teresa was aware that while violence was scourging

India, it was destroying her former homeland, the Yugoslavia that gave her birth. The massive uprooting she had known in Bengal was now visited upon a million people belonging to the different Balkan communities. Untold anguish was unleashed as men, women and children were maimed and killed. Cities that were jewels of architecture were reduced to rubble.

In besieged cities, where power and water were cut off, the most threatened people, the old and the very young, died of hunger and cold. The shrouded bodies of men and women in homes for the aged were photographed as they were carted away. Convoys of food, medicine and supplies were delayed and often fired upon. Amputations of the wounded were conducted without anesthesia. In one day in the town of Zepa, thirty-six amputations had to be carried out with no anesthetics. Religion was used by one group to justify a ferocious onslaught on members of another faith group. The rape of women by military men became a war strategy.

A peace message by Mother Teresa was taken up by the press. It was addressed to "My Brothers and Sisters in India and All Over the World."

"We are all God's children," she said, "and we have been created for greater things: to love and to be loved. God loves each one of us with an everlasting love—we are precious to him. . . . Let us not use religion to divide us. . . .

"Works of love are works of peace — in love we must know one another.

"So please, please, I beg you in the name of God, stop bringing violence, destruction and death to each other, and especially to the poor who are always the first victims."

Chapter Seven

GENGHIS KHAN AND THE MULTI-BILLION DOLLAR MOUNTAIN

1. Genghis Khan's Secret

When in the thirteenth century the Mongol armies rode out from the heart of Asia to subdue a score of nations, the world was in despair at their stupendous mobility. The warriors seemed to be able to progress for weeks on end with virtually no food. Eastern and western Asia were never the same after Genghis Khan and his descendants, mounted on their small, shaggy horses, succeeded in uniting under fiefdoms and khanates the greatest continuous land mass in all history.

From the Yellow Sea to a border that stretched a flaming tongue into the very heart of Europe, a Mongol peace, the Pax Tatarica, bound together diverse and unwilling peoples. The Tatars who gave their name to all the invading hordes from the east became known to the Europeans as Tartars, men from Tartary or hell. They left the mark of conquest and a dread, ineffaceable memory on Russia and on the European towns of Liegnitz, Sandomierz and Budapest.

A call went out to Christian princes to take united action in the face of "the inhuman Tartars, erupting as it were from the secret confines of hell." They were presumed to be in league with the devil and to have a secret, unconquerable weapon.

Their secret weapon was in fact powdered milk.

Marco Polo, who traversed ravaged Turkestan to serve Kublai Khan, the grandson of Genghis, described the source of the unheard-of military mobility. The Mongol soldiers, he wrote, "subsist for the most part upon milk. . . . They boil the milk, and skimming off the rich or creamy part of it as it rises to the top, put it into a separate vessel as butter; for so long as that remains in the milk, it will not become hard. The latter is then exposed to the sun until it dries. Upon going into service they carry with them about ten pounds for each man, and of this, half a pound is put, every morning, into a leathern bottle, with as much water as is thought necessary. By their motion in riding, the contents are violently shaken, and a thin porridge is produced, upon which they make their dinner."

The fierce warriors, mixing their powdered milk as they jogged over the steppes of Asia, succeeded in depopulating the richest cities of the ancient world: Herat, Bokhara, Samarkand, Ispahan. Those among the conquered who escaped mass slaughter fled to the west as terrified refugees, or were deported east to Karakorum as needed artisans. Juvaini, the Persian who chronicled the exploits of Genghis in *The History of the World Conqueror*, sighed, "We have grown old in a land in whose expanse one treads on nought but the cheeks of maidens and the breasts of striplings."

*   *   *

So many people were skeptical about the tales that Marco Polo brought back from the east that they dubbed him *Marco dei Millioni*.

They refused to accept as fact what they considered his wild exaggerations. Many of us were treated as American Marco Polos when we brought back accounts of massive and widespread human need among Asia's millions, and especially among the uprooted millions. When we told the story of America's "surplus mountain," however, we were believed, since the gigantic statistics could be verified from government documents.

The image of American surplus foods, powdered milk, dairy products and grains, as a towering mountain, came from a cartoon titled simply "Sermon from the Mount." It appeared in 1950 when widespread famine in India had impelled the Indian government to appeal for American food aid. At the height of the congressional haggling that ensued, and American cartoonist etched an unforgettably symbolic scene: a corpulent American legislator stood lecturing the world from the top of a mountain labeled "wheat," while a scrawny Indian looked up at him disconsolately from the grain-mountain's base.

During the 1950s, the cost of maintaining the "surplus mountain" rose to seven million dollars a day.

It was with the sharing of powdered milk that the mountainous stocks of food first reached the needy and the homeless of the world. The people-to-people agencies became the link between surplus food at home and starvation in far corners of the globe. It was in 1950, and the barrels of powdered milk were channeled through voluntary agencies because they were classified as "in danger of spoilage."

A huge "Operation Milky Way" sprang into being. Chief among the recipients were refugees and victims of war. Meanwhile, the stocks of food kept increasing inexorably. The wartime challenge of provisioning the largest army ever transported from one nation to a great perimeter around the globe had catapulted American farmers into spiraling productivity. The U.S. government, not wishing to allow a complete dislocation of the nation's farming community at war's end, purchased the excess not absorbed in meeting home needs. This went on year after year, until the stockpiles amassed by the government beggared storage facilities. Fantastic expedients were resorted to, including the piling of wheat into tent-like enclosures in the deserts of the southwest and the loading of grains into hulls of the "ghost fleet" in watery havens from Puget Sound to the James River in Virginia.

The agencies, including Quakers, Lutherans, Episcopalians, Catholics, and Jews, instituted a campaign with the U.S. government in which they asked for two changes in the law regarding the use of surplus foods. They asked that "danger of spoilage" be removed as the reason for sharing the foods. They requested that all foods in storage, including butter, grains and beans, be released to the needy through voluntary agencies.

The chief champion of the agencies, Senator Hubert H. Humphrey, early in 1954 gave an impassioned speech in which he favored the same objectives as those of the voluntary agencies. "At a time," he said, "when we are signing one alliance after another for military security and military assistance, I ask our government not to tell the people of the world that we do not know what to do with our surpluses of food and fiber. If we do that, we are not going to build peace or strength, we are going to build hatred, fear, resentment and distrust."

Senator Humphrey, more than any other legislator, laid the foundation for the program that was to be known as "Food for Peace."

*   *   *

I saw the powdered milk, mixed in iron vats or full-bellied water pots, being ladled out to refugee children in a mud-floored schoolroom in Karachi, to displaced Punjabi families sheltered in Delhi's Red Fort, to street-dwellers in Calcutta, to Vietnamese refugees in the peripheries of Saigon, to Chinese clinging to every inch of Hong Kong as to a frail raft in a perilous sea. In Pusan and Seoul, some of the over three million Korean refugees from the far side of an arbitrary barrier were being helped to stay alive with a gruel not unlike that which nourished the Mongol warriors who overran Korea in that thirteenth century onslaught.

There was a mystery about the survival of Asian refugees who arrived by hundreds of thousands, by the millions, only to lie, exhausted and destitute, on the lanes of destroyed villages or bare city streets. Part of the mystery lay in the endurance of men, women and children inured to hunger and unspeakable privation. A part of the solution to the mystery lay in emergency mass feeding by people-to-people agencies, the foods originating in rich dairy and wheat lands half a world away.

With the needs of the Asian refugees in mind, much of the wheat was eventually turned into pearl-like beads. In the absence of stoves, or the habit of eating bread, this wheat product, already parboiled, could be boiled like rice over tiny twig or kerosene fires. This was called bulgur wheat, a product known from biblical times. Its availability for overseas feeding was the result of research and unremitting pressure from the voluntary agencies. Later came the dramatic breakthrough to noodle production. The milk in small containers could be added to any other food to provide meals for the cast-off children of a disrupted world.

During the decade of the 1950s, starvation like a horizon-to-horizon vulture filled the sky over the refugees of Hong Kong and Korea. The hungry newcomers could have brought total catastrophe to already denuded areas unless the link had been made between them and the multi-billion dollar "mountain" of North America. The availability of free, basic foods not only helped in the initial survival of countless homeless people, but also in their eventual re-entry, with incredible strength, into the productive life of the human family.

2. Hong Kong: The Perilous Rock

"You are entering the largest D.P. camp in the world," said Rev. Paul Duchesne, the director of the Catholic Relief Services program for Hong Kong, as we left the Kowloon airport. It was December 1955.

"I want to see what is behind the great mystery of the port of Hong Kong. Your're the one who can show me," I said to Duchesne who, as a member of Maryknoll, an American missionary order, had spent long years in China before settling in Hong Kong. "I'll show you the mystery in action," said Duchesne. "If you can figure out anything in depth, let us know."

"There it is, there's the mystery," he exclaimed, pointing to a scrawny man dancing along the road with two filled baskets hanging from a stick across his shoulders. "Fill those baskets with anything, even junk from the scrap heap, and he's in business. Business, from Tiger Balm millions to pennies for used toothpaste tubes. That's our only secret. Forget about the mystery of the east."

*   *   *

In the old illustrated family Bibles there was a picture of a rock rising out of a threatening sea. Clutching at the rock was a pyramid of people, obviously terrified and in danger of losing hold. Not all the people were able to maintain themselves in so perilous a situation. Some men and women at the bottom of the pyramid were pictured sliding hopelessly into the rough waves of the engulfing waters.

The perilous rock, lashed by a devouring sea, was a representation of the Genesis account of the deluge. Hong Kong, a vast granite rock culminating in Victoria Peak, brought to mind the old print.

At its occupation by the British in 1841, the rock was unin-

280

habited, rising bare and uninviting out of the coastal waters. The occupation was not dictated by Hong Kong's charms but simply by its position. It was the way station for the chests of opium which reached China through the British East India Company of Calcutta. It is a footnote to colonial history that the tea company encouraged the cultivation of the poppy in India and promoted the sale of opium to China. So important was the opium revenue to the British colonialists that when the imperial government of China forbade its import, the British fought a war to ensure their right to sell opium to the people of China.

In 1839, the Chinese emperor wrote to Queen Victoria that since opium smoking was forbidden in England, she must be aware of its evil effects. "Let us ask: where is your conscience?" asked the emperor.

Hong Kong became British as part of the victory settlement when Britain won the opium war, referred to in British text-books as the trade war.

A hundred years later, in 1941, another imperialist power, Japan, accepted the surrender of Hong Kong and its million and a half residents.

By the time I first saw Hong Kong, in December 1955, it was as though the biblical print, which had haunted the imagination of so many children, had come to life. Clinging metaphorically to it were hundreds of thousands of refugees, lashed by waves of hunger and fear, blown about by actual typhoons, and threatened by the great ideological sea which surrounded them.

Of the millions of refugees who poured into Hong Kong between 1948 and 1950, when the Nationalist forces of Chiang Kai-shek fell before the communist armies of Mao-Tse-tung, one million could go no further. They clung to life on the rocky island and spilled over into the bay, living by the tens of thousands in tiny fishing boats and all types of frail craft. They also spread out into the peninsula of Kowloon and to an area known as the new territories to which Kowloon was attached. The new territories were leased by the British in 1898 for a ninety-nine year period. While the greenish granite rock of Hong Kong covered only thirty-two square miles, the whole area commonly

called Hong Kong included an area of three hundred and ninety-
one square miles.

Reports about Hong Kong's refugees had been reaching CRS
headquarters for six years. "It's that mystery of survival that has
puzzled us all," I remarked to Duchesne. "Water for a million
newcomers to drink, rice enough for a daily bowlful, clothing of
any kind to cover them, shelter! Where does it come from? I
know the totals of relief supplies that come in, but they don't
explain how all these people maintain their hold on life."

"About a quarter million of the refugees are completely destitute but they have managed to keep alive.

"While you are here, you'll see as many as possible of the 159
distribution centers that we supply and manage. There are many
more run by other people-to-people agencies. You'll see Hong
Kong itself, Kowloon, the new territories and one day you'll go
to the Lo Wu Bridge. That's where the trestle bridge crosses
into the mainland—as close as you can get to the People's
Republic. To Rennie's Mill Camp you'll have to go by boat.

"You'll find that 'distribution center' is just a general term
here. Food is given out, of course, but each one has another
specialty: it is a child care center, a community center, a clinic
or a rehabilitation project. Quite a few of them are refugee
schools. You know that there is no free education system in the
colony. Schooling is very important to our people. The religious
groups who were involved in it in China are all working to give
schooling to as many children as possible—to grown-ups, too.
We do it free if we can, but sometimes we have to charge a few
Hong Kong pennies a week."

By that time we were at my hotel, an incredibly British hostel-
ry with people taking tea in a Persian-carpeted lobby. From the
bay window of my room, I looked out onto a tennis court, and
the Chinese waiter who took my order for breakfast asked me if
I wanted "pollidge."

The hotel faced Repulse Bay on the south of the island,
removed from the crush of people on the north side, opposite
Kowloon. Early the next morning, tennis balls ringing from
racket to racket, and round English tones springing back and
forth over the net, reminded me that I was in one of the last,

classic overseas colonies. Then I caught sight of Repulse Bay poised in front of the hotel like a neat blue bowl with the orange, red-brown and purple sails of junks opening to the sun like flowers. Early December was a not too cold, often spring-like month in Hong Kong. I had expected to be plunged immediately into the misery of a pyramid of agonizing people straining to keep from being submerged by misery. I found myself installed in a quietly opulent Victorian hotel facing a peaceable, incredibly lovely inlet of the South China Sea.

As the car drove down the narrow road into the city of Victoria, trees five and six feet high thrust out poinsettia flowers like loud red stars. I asked the Chinese refugee driver the local name of the flowering tree.

"It is 'Sing Taon Fa.' It is the Christmas flower. We Christians call it the 'God-Come-Down Tree.'"

As we reached the limits of the city, the teeming streets gave out the sing-song of countless voices and the clop-clop of the scurrying wooden sandals of the poor. The sounds merged and heightened until they became a roar. Within the roar I knew that thousands of bargains were being discussed, argued, struck, and thousands of objects, from rice bowls to jade necklaces, were being traded every minute. "Much given to traffic and all the arts of gain," had been Lord Macartney's description of the Chinese in 1794.

The roar became deafening as we drove by the larger streets with open markets. It did not take long to learn that noise bothers Chinese not at all.

Our first stop was to be at Ho Man Tin, a refugee welfare center in Kowloon conducted by Maryknoll Sisters, an American community among whose members were teachers, doctors, nurses, pharmacists, and social workers.

It was early and we had time to make another stop before we got there. The father of a young Chinese woman who had worked in our Hong Kong office, and who had become my friend while she was studying social service in New York City, had died and was buried nearby.

"You know how Chinese families are," said Fr. Duchesne. "No act of friendship would be more important than paying a visit to her father's grave." We paid our ceremonial visit and were photographed at the graveside. I-fan, my friend, was an only child, and had adored her father. It was she who had made vivid for me the closeness of the Chinese familial relationship.

At the welfare center, we saw some of the ruins of China's old social security system, the joint family. Not even the nuclear family, consisting of mother, father and children, was complete. Here were refugee widows, left to bring up their children without the buttress of a familiar community, without the wall against adversity provided in the patriarchal family system.

Among the widows were skilled seamstresses whose earnings were adequate to fill the family rice bowl. The workroom of the Maryknoll Sisters was not only a training center but also a market for finished goods. Some of the women were obviously learners, almost as awkward with the sewing machine as I would have been.

I stopped to talk to one of the women. We will call her Mai. She spoke fluent English. She was a bit shy about her lack of ability and her lack of output as compared with the other women. She had only started to learn sewing two weeks before. Her home, she told me, had been in Kwongso, near Shanghai. After her marriage, she had lived in Nanking where her husband was a journalist and writer. He had been on the staff of a Nanking daily paper. He was the author of two books and had contributed to an anti-communist monthly magazine.

"We fled to Hong Kong in 1949. My husband would not say what the new leaders wanted him to say. He wanted to write truth. We first lived in a wooden hut. But the Kowloon fire came—then we had nothing. We were so lucky to have a house from the sisters. We were happy even if my husband was an earth coolie. We had two children—boys—born in the house the sisters gave us." At mention of her boys, she achieved a faint polite smile.

Sister Moira, a tall outgoing American, came over and gently eased the woman into a chair. As Mai looked away, her delicate face changed suddenly, as though stabbed by pain or grief. I thought that the little woman might be ill, since she was expecting another child. I wanted to ask her a few more questions, but

I was led away to another work table by the firm hand of Sister Moira on my arm.

After a little while Sister Moira said, "I think it was too much of a strain for her. She was polite as only our Chinese people can be."

"Wasn't she feeling well?" I asked.

"She would never tell you by even as much as a hint of sadness on her face—but she is a very recent widow. She came here to the workroom only two weeks ago, right after her husband was killed. He was a keen, fine man. All day long he worked as an earth coolie, carrying earth in those baskets like a beast of burden. When he could, he wrote articles for extra money. He was part of a squad clearing earth for a new building project. A truck backed up and crushed him to death. That is why Mai must learn a skill. Before this, she did odd jobs at home."

I marveled at such composure after so recent a tragedy.

"The Chinese people do not like to lacerate your feelings with their problems. She is a very cultured woman, with great control," said the sister.

I asked Father Duchesne if this had been so with the village people he served in South China.

"Yes, even rough villagers have something of this code of conduct. I saw it during the war in China. The long lines of men from other provinces would march, tired and battered, through our village. They were not complainers, though you could guess what they had been through. It is a form of charity to save someone's feelings!

"Once, when I was speaking to a group of these soldiers," Father Duchesne went on, "I asked one of them how long it was since he had been to his home village."

"Eight years," he told me.

"Have you written to them or heard from your family in that time?" I asked him—out of curiosity mostly.

"No," said the soldier. "I cannot write."

"If there is someone in your village who can read, I will write the letter for you," I offered.

"He said there was, and he went over under a tree to think about what he wanted to say. He put his head in his hands and seemed to be pondering deeply. After half an hour he came over to me.

"Are you ready?" I asked. "Let's go."

"I don't want to send a letter. I have nothing to say," he told me quietly.

"Nothing?" I asked. "You must want to say some few things about what happened to you."

"He was definite. 'Nothing,' he said and went back to sit under the tree.

"I suppose that as he had nothing good to say, he would not send any message at all. But he did not explain any further. I often think of the thousands of men like him who trudged through our village, uprooted, ordered about year after year in a never-ending war. And now so many of them are refugees here and in Taiwan."

The Ho Man Tin Center was open mornings, afternoons and evenings. Besides the workroom serving a hundred women, there were four classrooms continually in use. Young girls were given a basic education as well as vocational training in sewing and embroidery. Private agencies were rewarded for their efforts by the zeal for study of Chinese youngsters. Every space was put to use for classrooms—but even then tens of thousands of eager students had no place where they could learn.

*　　*　　*

Not far from the center was a row of one-room houses for refugees, a pilot project of the Maryknoll Sisters. Little housing was constructed at first for the mainland refugees. The newcomers were expected to proceed to the island of Taiwan. When nearly three million, including masses of Nationalist soldiers, flooded into Hong Kong, it was only as a stepping-stone to Taiwan. They moved out very quickly. The last million would also have continued the journey, except that, in 1952, Taiwan was so glutted that it could take no more refugees unless they could prove that they had means of livelihood. The voluntary agency focus was that last million squatting in Hong Kong, spilling over into downtown streets, building their shacks in every unused corner, covering the coastal area and the "nine dragon" hills of Kowloon with their wood, tin and cardboard shacks. A roof of flattened tin cans was a luxury. Most roofs were of straw matting. One spark from a tin open-topped cook-stove, and a whole hillside would be denuded of the fragile housing. That is what happened in December 1951. Sixteen thousand refugees were milling about in the cold, doubly homeless.

The women of Maryknoll had long been thinking of trying to construct minimal but fireproof housing for the refugees. Now it was urgent to make a start. With a grant of funds from CRS, the first twenty-eight one-room cement brick cottages were put up and given to the neediest families who had lost their shelter in the fire. By the time of my visit, the little housing project had grown to sixty-four homes.

The rooms, about twelve feet by twelve, were dry and clean; an alcove for a kitchen and scullery was at the side. Families of eight somehow managed to live calmly and with order in this limited space. This small settlement has been called the first free housing development in Asia.

The Far East Refugees Program, the title given to the International Cooperation Administration in Asia, began to make funds available to U.S. voluntary agencies to build such homes. Each project was a separate contractual arrangement. When another fire, fed by typhoon winds, made sixty thousand persons homeless on Christmas night, 1953, housing programs were intensified. Government officials of the Crown Colony initiated a crash building program, using the willing labor of unemployed refugees. Seven-story mountains of apartment houses sprang up to house the homeless. Each family had one room; in fact the average occupancy was five persons in a room, with two children under twelve counting as one adult. A hall toilet served a group of families. Soon the crowded tenements had thousands of squatters on their flat roofs. An attempted census of Hong Kong included an inspection and estimate of the numbers of roof-dwellers by low-flying helicopter. The seven-story tenements, topped by nests of the shelterless, garlanded at the sides by myriads of drying garments, and surrounded by endless groups of children, soon came to be known as the "chicken coops."

The privacy of the cottages was a gift of great luxury. What amazed the refugees who received the first cottages was that people far away, united to them by no ties of kinship, should send money to aid them. The fact that the break-up of their joint family system, the only social security system they had ever known, would not leave them totally helpless was a revelation to them. It made their exile a far more bearable thing. One of the first recipients of a free cottage wrote to the sisters at the King's Park Center: "And now to us who had nothing, and no one to help us from our own family, you have given a home. Truly, this is our beautiful life of exile."

The unusual expression "beautiful life of exile" arose out of the enormous surprise and joy at the discovery of a basis for mutual help and charity other than blood ties.

Father Duchesne favored the cottage-type homes and had worked with designers and architects to make them more livable and attractive. Before he left Hong Kong, he had superintended the building of several thousands of the very practical little homes terraced in long curving rows on the solid rock foundation. Painted red, light green and white, they looked like drawings from a child's coloring book. The government of the Crown Colony bore all the costs of utilities, including roads and sewers.

*   *   *

In a nearby colony that was almost completed, we were in time to see the Leung family move in after living for four and a half years as street dwellers.

The father, mother and two little boys managed the moving in one operation. They had, of course, no single piece of furniture. All their possessions were in wicker baskets which were piled up against the wall. Leung, a shock-haired, tired little man was in fine spirits. His wife, dressed in dark blue trousers and padded jacket, smiled through our talk.

"I came from near Canton," Leung told me through Father Duchesne. "I was a soldier in the Nationalist Army from the time I was nineteen. I went to many parts of China and I learned to understand how the farmers speak in other provinces. I was lucky because I got back to my home before we had to come here. That is how I married my wife and we came together."

I asked him what work he did.

"I have done everything. I have been an earth coolie. I have worked in the fireworks factory."

"Ten American cents a day," interjected Duchesne.

"But now I work at home with my wife and children. I work with these." He uncovered two enormous wicker baskets of pink plastic buttons. He took out a button and showed it to Duchesne.

"What he does," Duchesne explained, "is to correct the imperfections on each button."

Leung took out a button and extracted a small nail clipper from his jacket. He went around the button, clipping off small projections that marred the smooth edge.

"I get paid by the pound when I bring the perfect buttons back to the factory."

In the past two days he had earned one Hong Kong dollar, about a sixth of an American dollar.

"In the market," he said, "I can buy two pounds of middle grade rice for a dollar."

I pictured this worn little man, no more than thirty-five years of age, against the cataclysm that engulfed China with the Japanese invasion. He had lived through the Japanese war, when at least twenty million Chinese had moved westward, tearing up the railway lines as they went, to impede the enemy. He must have been present at many deaths, since one battle could cost two hundred thousand lives. He had continued to fight when his gun was turned against other Chinese in the civil war. His peace-time reward was exile, a dawn-to-dark struggle to keep alive, and, until this December day in 1955, homelessness on a city street with only a piece of canvas to protect his shivering family from rain and wind.

We were able to give the family as a house-warming gift a fifty-pound family food package.

* * *

In a shack perched among a warren of shacks on a Kowloon hillside, I saw how one of the most threatened families was aided in the struggle for life. As I drew near, the crush of children made it almost impossible to move forward. The walls of the hut were pressed cardboard mounted on a wooden frame. The door was a flap of heavy burlap. As we stepped on the earth floor I thought that on a rainy day it would be a mud puddle. The tin roof was barely higher than my head, and Paul Duchesne had to stoop during the visit.

A family of six, a husband and wife, two children and the wife's two sisters, all dressed in American relief garments, stood shoulder-to-shoulder to greet us. They stood around the usual large wooden bench, an all-purpose item which was table, sitting stool and bed. This must be one of the households where the family members took turns sleeping. All the family had tuberculosis in some form and were being treated through a mobile clinic. Without more food, in particular protein food, the medical help could accomplish little. Every month, the family received a package of fifty pounds of the most prized local foods, including rice, dried fish, meat, beans, dried vegetables and oil.

The man had a long face with an aquiline nose over which the skin was stretched taut. His long bony fingers looked as though they had never held anything heavier than a pen or a mah-jongg piece.

"The coolies bring the packages up the hill from our truck. They don't take any money because it is for their sick neighbors and because they know that the food is a gift," Duchesne told me.

A regular package of food, a visit to the public clinic on wheels—these were the small alleviations in lives of slow and silent crucifixion.

* * *

The service of the mobile clinics went on every day of the week. On our way to a mobile clinic station, we talked about the lack of water in the cavernous "seven-story mountain" refugee apartment houses. The irony in the situation was that while the colony was lashed by the waters of the bay and by the most devastating of typhoons, the single greatest need of Hong Kong was drinking water. It was only by strict rationing that the most minimal needs of the refugees were met. For long periods, water taps ran only a few hours every fourth day. Around the community faucets, serving as many as forty families, refugees gathered with taut nerves. There was always fear that the supply of water would give out before all the family pails had been filled. When two women fell into a violent quarrel at the community tap, one of them was arrested. Her arrest arose not out of the fact that she struck and pummeled her opponent, but because she threw a bucket of precious water in her face. During the dryest months, tankers went up the Pearl River into the mainland to fill up with water and return to the Crown Colony.

We stationed ourselves alongside one of the "seven-story mountains" at the base of one of the Kowloon hills. Around and above it, thousands of shanty huts crawled like packs of disheveled rats.

Mary Lam, the wife of a Hong Kong doctor, was one of the volunteers with the clinic corps of Chinese doctors and nurses. As the men, women and children disappeared into the body of the ambulance for examination, Mary Lam took down the facts on the waiting patients. The cards had short case histories. Over ninety percent were marked as tubercular—a general condition of the refugees because of overcrowding, exposure and hunger. One third of all the deaths from tuberculosis in the colony were of children under five years old—children who were doomed by the conditions of exile.

The people lining up for treatment were the teachers, the journalists, the small landowners, the petty government officials, the soldiers of China. They were eating the rice of exile, they were wearing the clothing of strangers, they were carrying about on their bodies the scourges of want and privation because they had been caught in a cataclysm of history they could neither mend nor cure—and in some cases not even comprehend.

We spent one whole afternoon at a dead-end street near one of the newest "chicken coops." The street was constantly thronged with people of every Chinese type. There were wiry barefoot coolies, older women in peasant trousers and overblouses, young women with babies sprawling over backs in small cloth slings, a few young girls with dresses slit to show the length of a slender thigh. I thought back to the "human dead sea" of Bengal's refugees, and the crowded streets of Calcutta. But here, movement was purposeful, quick; the voices of a tonal language were overpowering, incisive. As the driver turned the mobile clinic around to leave the outdoor consulting room, the people parted before us like the waves of a sea—a noisy, choppy, unconquerable sea.

* * *

In those Hong Kong days of 1955, filled from morning to night with meetings and visits, I began to feel as though I were on a trapeze, swinging wildly between contrasting scenes. One day it was lunch with a group of British ladies in a modern apartment at the top of Victoria Peak, eighteen hundred feet above sea level. Almost to the last gasp of colonialism, non-Europeans were not allowed to have homes beyond a certain height on the peak. Before us stretched the shining harbor, with its naval anchorage, and the cargo that still represented the great meeting place of the world's goods and produce.

It was a sunny day, and the curving Bund, or waterfront, and the open channel to Kowloon were clear and lovely. The women were concerned as volunteers with various social welfare services for refugees, and talked in well-modulated tones of their plans. What struck me most about the peak was the lack of noise. In its gracious quiet, the horror and want of the destitute quarter of a million seemed to recede before a more reasonable world, invented and believed in by reasonable people. Later, I stood in a refugee workroom in Tsuen Wan on the Kowloon Beach. All types of metal containers, from vegetable cans to oil drums, were being pounded flat and reshaped into frying pans, and small stoves, all by hand. The noise of this was bearable, but nearby was a real factory, a one-room affair with machinery for the making of tin cans. The pounding was enough to make nerve-endings leap in pain, but across the channel toward the silent peak was another world.

* * *

A ferry brought me to Junk Bay, to a sequestered community of five thousand mainland refugees at a place called Rennie's Mill. In a wooden room, seated at a long table, were a former judge, a teacher, a general, and several officers of the Nationalist Army. They had originated in various parts of the mainland. Their livelihood consisted of making flashlight bulbs. Day in and day out, the men, old and diligent, turned out thousands of the tiny bulbs. Their daily pay was four Hong Kong dollars, about sixty-five cents.

As we left, an old man came over to Father Duchesne. He walked with difficulty, but even in his shuffle there was self-respect. There was a short talk and a handshake. The former army official, an advanced diabetic, was thanking Father Duchesne for helping him keep alive with a regular supply of medicine.

These lone men, once men of consequence, had come to Rennie's Mill Camp along with twenty thousand refugees, chiefly Nationalist soldiers and officers. Fifteen thousand of the group had gone on to Taiwan, the others were "remaindered" in Rennie's Mill. Behind them on the great rock face were painted six giant Chinese characters. They stood white and stark: LONG LIVE THE REPUBLIC OF CHINA. The defiant characters remained for long years after the republic itself had become a refugee in Taiwan. The characters loomed over us as our small ferry boat took us back to Hong Kong.

*   *   *

One of the long-term leaders of people-to-people effort in Hong Kong was John Romaniello, a priest of Maryknoll, the same American order to which Paul Duchesne belonged. He noticed one day, after the distribution of flour to a large group of refugees, that many of them went to a local merchant where they had to pay to have the flour turned into noodles. It was before a percentage of the wheat had been turned into bulgur for boiling. Romaniello found a way to turn wheat flour, cornmeal and powdered milk, all supplied from America's multi-billion dollar mountain, into noodles. With a dozen electric-powered noodle machines working in Hong Kong and two in Macau, there was a constant supply of noodles over the leanest years.

"I know what it meant to our poorest families," said Romaniello. "A Cantonese came to me one day after he had taken his five-pound bag of noodles for his family. 'I want to tell you how grateful I am for this food,' he said. 'Each evening when I come to the block where I live, my wife waits for me anxiously. She even has her head out of the window. In the past, if I turned up my palms to show that I had not sold enough to make my five dollars (about eighty-eight cents in American money), she would be sad. She would put the children to bed without supper. But now if I turn up my empty hands, she pulls down the noodles and we all have something to eat.'"

Marco Polo, who first revealed the secret of Genghis Khan's fateful mobility, entered the Hong Kong story.

"For centuries," said Romaniello, "my Italian forebears enjoyed spaghetti, the food brought back from China by Marco Polo. I brought noodles to the Chinese at the rate of millions of pounds a year."

* * *

Lo Wu Bridge, the link between the new territories of the crown colony and Kwangtung Province of the People's Republic, was frequently filmed in the years when Americans or Europeans were freed from mainland prisons. They were escorted to the far end of the bridge by Chinese authorities. On the way to Lo Wu, I stopped briefly at a remnant of Old China, the walled village of the Hakka people, the widely-traveled and seafaring segment of the children of the Han.

The railroad trestle which was part of the bridge carried no trains into the colony. I had seen films of the last trains into Hong Kong, packed with exhausted people, and with others clinging desperately to the roofs of the railroad cars. Many of those who crawled out, or were carried from the cars, were old people, fleeing before unending violence; large numbers were children, too young and too tired to know that in crossing the trestle they were joining the world of the refugees.

I sat down to look over the trestle into the vast expanse of China where "the great leap forward" had changed the lives of hundreds of millions of people.

"No one is crossing Lo Wu today," said Duchesne. "But that does not mean that people haven't been coming into Hong Kong all through 1955. They creep in by land, through Sha Tau Kok over there. They come in curled up in the bottom of fishing boats. 'Twisted snakes' we call them here. Some have even managed to swim across the channel into Macau. And Macau makes me think of the groups that come out of the mainland freely."

"Who are they?" I wanted to know. "Spies?"

"Lots of agents probably move in both directions," Duchesne replied. "No, the ones who came freely were brought to Macau by the mainland police and dumped there. They were blind people, old people, men and women who could barely walk. They couldn't do anything for the new China. Caritas and religious orders are taking care of them.

"Macau is already over-loaded with refugees. Several groups of these helpless people were brought in and literally thrown away. There was no chance of sending them back even if the Macau officials wanted to try. Now the struggle is to keep them alive, to find everything they need.

"Well, that's what we're here for," Duchesne commented, "to help keep our people alive. And we have to think not only of the ones that are here, but of the ones who are coming in. Thousands every month. As many as one hundred thousand a year if there is a poor harvest. We have to find ways to absorb them right here. No country is opening its doors to them."

* * *

It was fifteen years before I set foot in Hong Kong again, and I saw how the refugees had survived. Tsuen Wan was a case in point. All I could recognize from the earlier visit was a long row of shed workshops along the Kowloon shore where used metal containers were still being pounded and noisily reshaped into frying pans and household utensils. Tsuen Wan counted over a million inhabitants in contrast to thirty thousand a decade and a half earlier. Tall tenements for the refugees were everywhere and more were under construction. In the resettlement blocks, as they were called, each family had only one room, but it was larger than the rooms in the old "seven-story mountains," and each family room had its own water tap and toilet.

The "seven-story mountains" were still there, and I walked through the long tunnel-like hall of one of them. Forty-eight families cooked, ate and slept in the forty-eight rooms that opened off each side of the dank, barely-lit passage. There was a washroom and toilet for each twenty-five families and the pervasive smell informed you of that fact before you learned the statistic. But there was something new—the blare of television sets perched on high shelves in almost every crowded room.

"Many of these are rented," said the young Chinese girl who accompanied me. "You can see the young children watching the afternoon program. The mothers are working and the television is the baby sitter."

Other multi-storied buildings had also sprouted in Tsuen Wan. One such building was typical, a six-floor industrial construction with a different factory on each floor. Two floors housed textile factories, one, rubber goods, another, cutlery, another, cooking utensils and still another, a variety of metal products. Each of the factories worked three shifts, right around the clock.

The core of "old China hands," who had initiated the voluntary agency health and feeding programs along with a myriad of small self-help projects, were still in Hong Kong, aided by large number of younger Hong Kong hands. In Tsuen Wan, an international team of religious sisters, including doctors, nurses, social workers and teachers, were committed to putting their combined skills at the service of the neediest in Hong Kong.

I sat in the waiting room of the Star of the Sea Clinic where six days a week between one hundred and fifty and three hundred women and children came daily for help. A mother of five children was examined by Dr. Juliana Bender. She was given medicaments and a supply of vitamins for herself and her children.

"Kwan has had an operation for cancer. We must watch her. Her husband earns so little that we must give her food and vitamins to keep her going and to keep the family together. Most of the mothers work. When she can't, it is hard for the family to get by." Dr. Juliana Bender, a tall, ebullient American, led a team of fourteen sisters of eight nationalities, including Italian, Chinese, German, French, Japanese, Belgian and Irish. They belonged to a Catholic order known as the Society of Helpers.

"When we started here in the 1950s, we called our clinic 'Star of the Sea' because we served the boat people. The clinic was right on the shore and the boat people could look into our window. We are still in the same building, but from this window you can see our changed view. We are six long blocks from the water—all filled-in land."

I looked out on a street whose American name was Texaco

Street. Not only houses, shops and a cinema but the Texaco Company, the Esso Oil Company and a Coca-Cola plant had all established themselves on land stolen from the sea.

I remembered the thousands of frail masts that rose out of the water, each representing a boat that housed a family.

"Where are the tens of thousands of boat people?" I asked.

"There are only two hundred sampans here now. We almost never have to go on the boats anymore. When we first started, we used to have to 'walk the plank' to get from boat to boat to reach a woman who was about to give birth. They were hard days for everyone. Now most of our people live on land and they come to us here. The people have other needs. Now that the mothers have found work in the Tsuen Wan factories as well as the men, they came to us to help them with their children. Around the corner from the clinic, we have a day nursery for three hundred children.

"Our people are desperate to have their children go to school. They want them to get a school certificate. And the children are incredible students. A few years ago we opened a primary school. Our sisters run it in two sessions. Now we have eleven hundred children. They are the boys and girls whose mothers and fathers keep the factories on the three-shift basis. They are here waiting to get in for the session that begins at 7:30 in the morning and for the second session at 1 p.m. You know that there is no free school system in the colony. They hope to have it in a couple of years, but now the children pay fifty cents, in American money, every month. Some parents can't afford even that, especially if three or four children are coming to school. We get funds from other sources for these children. We know the families and they tell us their griefs. If they think they may have to take one of their children out of school, they come and talk with us. Six of our team of sisters are Chinese themselves; two belong to the Hakka people. We are part of this community. Sister Mary Renée is a refugee herself after spending twenty-five years in Shanghai. We'll stay with them while they need us. You know the Society of Helpers has the rule that we move in where a new job has to be done, and when another group can take it over, we move on to some other pioneering project."

It was midday and the members of the team were darting in and out, picking up their supplies for the afternoon shift. Though they were of vastly differing human types, they seemed to blend unassumingly into the Chinese background in their simple, gray work-outfits.

It was with the Irish member of the Society of Helpers that I paid my second visit to the Lo Wu Bridge. Sister Ann Gallegher was a handsome woman of thirty whose eyes in a young face were unutterably tired. She did not complain of the work but mentioned that the sing-song of the hawkers on the street below the convent window until two or three o'clock in the morning made life a bit difficult.

There were many things that had not changed at all in fifteen years, including the Hakka village with its massive, gray stone walls and the Hakka women like walking lampshades with their broad, flopping cloth hats. We drove through the agricultural part of the new territories where every hillock was terraced for the cultivation of vegetables and every inch of free land planted with lettuce, Chinese cabbage, sweet potatoes, string beans and sugar cane. Plantain and palm trees were in every nook, and there were even stretches of paddy land. There were water buffaloes and bulls pulling small plows. There were men carrying dark brown, shining roast pigs on heavy sticks.

Because Sister Ann Gallegher could speak Chinese to the border guard, we were able to enter the section behind a large yellow sign which read: "Frontier—Closed Area." I was again at the gate of the most populous nation of the entire globe. It occurred to me that the revolution that had come to the people within the 2,700,000 square miles of the People's Republic of China was in one sense the same as the one that had come to the people in Hong Kong.

The traditional extended family, with its Confucian ideal of filial piety, its regulation on relationships between family members, its power as conserver and transmitter of values, and its limitation on the individual through its role as social security system, had been weakened by the politicization of the communes as it had been by the agony of flight and exile. The primary loyalty of the ordinary Chinese had to be broadened beyond blood relations.

For the refugees of Hong Kong, army men, teachers, journalists as well as men and women from China's thousands upon thousands of villages, the evolution that had taken place through centuries in developed countries took place in a forced leap forward. In a time of agony, after the mass displacement of war, they had begun as refugees to live as nuclear family units, and had conformed to the harshest demands of industrial life. Simultaneously with their fabled habits of hard and unremitting work, Chinese men and women exercised their equally fabled financial ability.

Year by year, Hong Kong grew in economic strength. It became a jewel mart, attracting the world's pearl and diamond buyers. Here was a calling suitable for a terrain where space was at a minimum. Its garment industry gained international renown. In the 1980s Hong Kong had become a financial giant, a financial nexus, where world currencies were quoted along with London, New York, Zurich, Frankfurt and Tokyo.

Accepting the ineirtable end of its ninety-nine year lease in 1997, Britain signed an agreement with mainland China providing for the relinquishing of its last colonial outpost. In the agreement, Hong Kong would be privileged to continue its free enterprise way of life for fifty years.

From a perilous rock, with refugees clinging to it for their very lives, Hong Kong had become not only a center of unparalleled productivity, but a place where fortunes had been made.

The worst days of the 1940s and 1950s were hardly more than a memory. Yet it was important to remember that people-to-people organizations, through the sacrificial efforts of men and women unheralded in history, had made a crucial contribution. Their contribution englobed countless works of mercy as they stood by their Chinese brothers and sisters in the darkest hour of homelessness and suffering.

3. Korea: Is There Peace with You?

I had never thought that the word "peace" could be the cruelest word in a language until I traveled about Korea. After I had heard the traditional greeting, "Anyung hasimnika," pierce the air thousands of times amid the wreckage of a divided country, and the wreckage of appallingly victimized human beings, I felt that "peace" was the most excruciatingly tragic word of all. "An" means peace, and "anyung hasimnika" is the question Koreans use in place of "How are you?"

The literal meaning is, "Are you in peace?" "Is there peace with you?"

"An" was the word I heard more often than any other, day after day, in the height of the winter of 1955, two years after Korea's three-year war.

Sometimes the salutation was shortened to "Anyung ha?" as Americans say "Hi" in casual greeting without waiting for an answer.

I first heard the greeting outside the battered city of Seoul, the city that had changed hands four times between June 1950 and July 1953. I had just come from the center of the city where I had surveyed the capital from the Han River Bridge. The shattered artery that led to the port of Inchon had been knit together as soon as hostilities stopped and military and civilian traffic rumbled past me.

I knew of the human traffic that had once tried to use this bridge to escape one of the worst air attacks of the war. It was night. It was winter and probably the cold was as bone-chilling as I was experiencing it. Unprepared for the deluge of bombs, the Koreans thought that by fleeing to the opposite side of the city, they could escape death. The only passage to the other side was the Han River Bridge on which I stood.

300

In the midst of the mass flight, the bridge itself received a direct hit. The press of running people continued. The clogged roads continued to disgorge men, women and children into the only river crossing.

Amidst the screams of bombs and the answering human screams of horror, the people in the rear could not know that those ahead were being pushed not to the safety of the other side, but into the waters of the Han. The bridge had been cut in two. Wave after wave of helpless Koreans fell to their deaths. The churning bodies were thick in the swirling waters before the press of people could be halted and their direction turned back to the flaming city.

Not all died in the icy water. Many were pierced by the sharp, broken off girders and, like impaled birds, bled to death. Their transfixed bodies were removed later.

When I asked how many had died in the doomed attempt at escape, no one seemed to know for sure. The most frequently expressed estimate was two hundred thousand.

The Korean greeting of peace came from the mouths of ex-soldiers who were inhabiting a housing and work center set up with voluntary agency funds. The veterans, all men from the army of the Democratic People's Republic of North Korea, were separated from whatever was left of their homes and families. Some were legless, some were without an arm, some were eyeless, and all were pensionless. Their work colony was a chicken farm.

The veterans, squatting legless, or holding a tool in the arm that was left, faced me and recited in deep, sing-song tones, "Is there peace with you?"

My interpreter told me that I was supposed to answer "Neh. Anyung ha simnika," "Yes, is there peace with you?"

As I gazed into the disfigured, war-shattered face of one of the homeless men, I found the words were stillborn in my throat.

Peace, I found, lived on chiefly in a word in this landscape raked by sixteen armies. Fifty-three of its fifty-five cities with their productive plants had been devastated by bombing, and twelve hundred of its villages were nothing but charred ruins.

Roads and bridges had been severed. More than eighty percent
of the war casualties had been civilians, and between 300,000
and 500,000 widows were left to face the future benumbed and
lost without the cocoon of the joint family. Scattered everywhere
were some four million refugees from north of the 38th parallel,
trying to live by scavenging from people already scavengers. The
refugees were among the five million who lacked homes and
had to live in huts thrown together from scraps and debris, or
had to depend on the windbreaks supplied by caves, by the arches of destroyed bridges, or by sections of sewer pipes.

In a few days I had heard "An, An, An," from the lepers, dispersed during war and flight, as they were being herded into
leper villages or makeshift leprosaria. Their disease was advanced
through interrupted care, their bodies wasted and filthy. Fear was
everywhere that during the years of disruption their infection
had been irreparably shared with the community at large.

"An, An, An," I heard from the mouths of three hundred
orphans in the battered port of Inchon.

"Peace, Peace, Peace. It is an eternal, ironic question to which
no one expects an answer," I said to my interpreter, a refugee
from Pyong Yang in the north.

He undertook to explain the greeting in literal terms. "Our
way of greeting is not a question when you visit a Korean house.
You say 'Remain in peace' to the family as you leave. To you, the
Korean would say goodbye with the words, 'Anyung hi
Kasipsio.' This means 'Go in peace.' These are not questions."

There were situations, I thought, where the Hebrew greeting
"Shalom aleichem," "Peace be to you," and "Salaam" of the great
expanse of the Arab world from Egypt to Bengal, sounded
equally ironic. It was just that I was not expecting to find a similar peace greeting as the common coin of social intercourse in
an Oriental nation, gutted by twentieth century total violence.

* * *

What could people-to-people agencies do in the face of massive destruction? They could do nothing toward the mending of
destroyed cities, ruined factories or severed bridges. These were
the tasks of governments and of the United Nations which

promptly organized UNKRA, the UN Korean Reconstruction Agency.

What people-to-people agencies could do was the simple task of mending human lives, and mending them as quickly as possible. Human beings, unlike houses or cities, need aid immediately if they are to be saved. If compassionate hands do not reach them in time, they are no longer there when long-range plans are perfected. The people-to-people groups, chiefly American, sprang to the aid of the Koreans in innumerable ways.

Among their services, the agencies counted the struggle for the right of asylum, such as they had known in western Europe after World War II. This question arose in the case of the North Korean veterans, some of whom were sheltered in the chicken farm near Seoul. They were among twenty-seven thousand soldiers of the North Korean Army captured by the United Nations and Republic of Korea forces. Claiming the right of asylum, this large group of men refused repatriation to their homes north of the 38th parallel. The men were held in stockades while military chiefs and political leaders discussed the matter. There was some discussion of evacuating them to camps in India.

Suddenly, while their fate was being discussed, they took it into their own hands, and burst forth from the stockades. With them, they carried their wounded comrades. All claimed asylum in South Korea.

People-to-people agencies like Catholic Relief Services and Church World Service came to the aid of the most helpless among them. Funds were given out so that the men could set themselves up in chicken farms, in duck farms at lakesides, in small workshops of various types. In these work projects, the men could pool their depleted human resources and save each other. From the multi-billion dollar mountain of U.S. surplus foods came a lifeline of items in danger of spoilage—powdered milk, cheese, and dried eggs. These were combined with rice to provide a simple basic ration.

Church World Service specialized in supplying prosthetic devices, the needed arms and legs for amputee veterans, as well as for civilians. Medical experts were sent from the United States to perform necessary surgery and prescribe the correct devices. Koreans were eventually trained to produce the devices needed throughout South Korea.

*   *   *

Food was the lifeline that kept all other aid programs in motion, whether healing programs or work projects. Besides the work projects which mended lives as well as a broken society, there were large numbers of works of healing. They consisted of hospitals and clinics organized by Americans, by Danes, by Germans, by Swiss, by religious and secular groups. Medical help from the outside was crucial since in Korean cities medical services were woefully inadequate, and in the rural areas a species of witchcraft.

In Pusan, on Korea's southern coast, was a clinic run by American religious sisters. They belonged to the Society of Maryknoll, and had been evacuated from the Pusan clinic after the hostilities of 1950. With the mass flight southward, the perimeter of Pusan contained the concentration of Korea's agony.

In March 1951, at the height of the war, the sisters were brought back. They were the first civilian women permitted to return to Korea. Their insistence on going back was soon justified when the starving, wounded, homeless Korean civilians began lining up before dawn for a little alleviation of their pain. In a few years, the team had treated a million patients and had been called "the largest charity hospital in the world." This team of nineteen American women, all members of the Society of Maryknoll, included three doctors, as well as nurses, pharmacists, and medical technicians. Replacements were sent in as heart attacks and physical exhaustion felled team members.

I had heard of the lines of the two thousand people that daily crowded the main lane and side alleys leading to the clinic—and now I finally saw it. There were mothers with babies in their arms; there were sons carrying their mothers on their backs in the characteristic A-frame, a triangular piece of wood; there were old people squatting against the wall, their heads swathed in rags against God-knows-what pains. They were all clutching the numbered card which meant that the Maryknoll clinic would attend to them that day. They noted our presence among them, and the pain-blurred voices sent up an excruciating anthem of Anyungha simnika, Anyungha, An, An, An, An, An. I felt it was the bleating of lambs over a desert landscape after the lion's roar of pulverizing fighter planes had died away.

These were the people who had survived the long journey south, so many of them on Korea's overworked trains. People clung to the tops of railroad cars and huddled inside. One train was delayed, and those who had escaped the fire of war succumbed to the Arctic blasts of a Korean winter's night. An Englishman who helped to remove the congealed dead bodies, one by one, from the tops of the cars said, "It was a mass descent from the cross in a hundred grotesque positions."

It was from such lines of pain that the news headlines of the day and of many years to come originated—the headlines about family suicide. When things seemed too hopeless, the father and mother would gather their children around them, and leaven their meal with rat poison, easily obtainable in Korea. This was their means of escape from trapped tomorrows; Korean parents with their strong sense of family unity, would not do the cowardly thing and leave their children to face those tomorrows alone.

* * *

It was while I was in Korea that I was shown a cable announcing a new lifeline of food. It was from the New York headquarters of Catholic Relief Services, and was dated December 15, 1955. "Grains in surplus released for vol-agency overseas feeding programs by Presidential proclamation of December fourteen letter follows."

What this meant was that the "moral challenge of American abundance" had at last been accepted by the U.S. government, and that not only foods in danger of spoilage but all available foods, including wheat and cornmeal and even beans, would be included in the meals of the hungry. Food for Peace, the program authorized under Public Law 480 in 1954, could now provide a fuller diet for the hungry overseas. Under Title II of this law, free grants of food were allowed through voluntary agencies. In those days of a cruel peace, the people of South Korea were among the hungriest in the world, and of them, the hungriest were the refugees from the north.

Our agency was already operating emergency feeding stations simply to keep men, women and children from dying. Milk stocks were combined with purchased foods such as rice. I made my way to one of the feeding stations through a street that led out of a chief avenue of Seoul. On one side of the street was a row of silent old people, still as mummies. Each one was guarding a little stand on which were spread out tiny items for sale, rows of blue and white plastic combs, pencils and pens, cigarettes, beans, all manner of small items that they had been able to buy for a pittance.

The temperature was below freezing, and a wind from the Arctic assailed our faces with a thousand icy needles. Some of the old men had tapering stove-pipe hats of white or black material with flat brims. Many of the old people wore an unbleached cotton garment over amorphous layers of clothing. To Koreans, the white outer covering was worn as a sign of mourning. I wondered how many dead each of these still figures would count in their once-large tribal families, so protective of older members. Wrapped around the statue-like figures, whose rheumy eyes stared unblinkingly past us like the eyes of the dead, the white garments seemed like so many shrouds. Their faces, so cruelly clawed by the fingers of time and its dark tragedies, were like the ravaged, gullied hills of their long-occupied land.

I wanted to wave my hands before the glazed eyes, to touch the huddled, bundled forms for any indication of life. But my companions, a Korean refugee from the north and Msgr. George Carroll, the far east director of our agency, had seen the spectacle before, and assured me that the aged men and women could still move; they always took away their wares at night and reappeared the next day.

I was reminded of a description by Alexis de Tocqueville of the homeless poor of Ireland as they waited for their single meal, a bowl of soup in a Dublin poorhouse.

"They sit on wooden benches, crowded close together and all looking in the same direction, as if in the pit of a theater. They do not talk at all; they do not stir; they look at nothing; they do not appear to be thinking. They neither expect, fear, nor hope anything from life."

I heard from many that the Koreans were "the Irish of the east" and had no doubt that the decimation of the Irish by pauperism and hunger in the nineteenth century was being matched by what was happening to the Koreans in the middle of the twentieth century.

The expressionless eyes, expecting not even deliverance, filled my thoughts as we arrived at the shack city. Like an endless colony of rabbit warrens, the hundreds of huts stretched before us. They were put together of oddments of wood, cardboard, tin from pressed-out food and beer cans, and mud from the banks of the Han River. Whole families were crowded into each warren of the benumbed community that seemed like a temporary encampment in an icy desert.

Suddenly we came upon a little oasis of heat and color in the freezing grayed-over capital. An enormous black iron vat was steaming over a crackling coke and twig fire. Protected by a three-sided corrugated iron shed, the fire curled its brilliant orange tongues around the twenty-gallon rice pot, once part of a Korean Army field kitchen.

A Korean woman was stirring the steaming mixture, American powdered milk, with enough rice to make a gruel. At the ringing of a bell, a procession, chiefly of women and children, emerged from the shacks. A few of the women had children strapped on their backs. Many of them were widows; many of them came for the north.

Rations of gruel were ladled into tins and pots of all sizes. When they saw us behind the feeding station, there were thin smiles and murmurs of the traditional greeting "Anyungha simnika." Young and old bowed politely with their filled vessels and trooped down the alleyways into the shacks. The winds swept after them, and followed them inside their frail shelters like savage intruders.

I wondered how life could be maintained in the mud-floored heatless little huts so open to the pitiless blasts. In peacetime, even the poorest Korean family in the northern provinces would have an ondol floor, or heated floor, for its one-room house. The cooking of the evening meal over the iron bucket stove of the tiny dropped kitchen would have sent streams of hot air through

conduits under the living-sleeping room floor. Ingeniously constructed of layers of rammed earth, flat stones, and a cement-like
mixture, the ondol floor was the Korean equivalent of the
American electric blanket. Wrapped in their heavy quilts, the
Koreans stretched out on the warm smooth floor without need
of beds. Without the ondol floor, the Seoul winter was death,
and that is what I had glimpsed in the heatless warrens of the
shack city. The milk stations set up by our agency supplied hot
gruel in hundreds of centers of burning misery. Clinics, schools,
hospitals, improvised shacks and tents were used as distribution
points. The hot meal served as buttress to the health of a million
and a half of the very poorest Koreans. Other agencies, notably
Church World Service, operated a similar network.

What seemed to me a dread sight was still far better than the
real famine of war and post-war days when our reports from
Mok-Po had read, "Our people have eaten the bark off the
trees. The guerrillas have scorched the earth and there is nothing else." From Cheju-do, one of the desperately poor islands
off the southwest coast, had come a cry for help: "I've been
through the houses here. There is not only no food left at all.
There is no moss left on the rocks. That has all been eaten."

* * *

Work projects, from the tiny rehabilitation schemes for individual widows, to the workrooms for groups of war widows, and
later to the "Assimilation Projects" for whole communities of
the homeless, absorbed the poorest of the poor. All were fueled
by regular supplies of food stuffs.

Some of the widows were given their individual kit of bar-
ber's tools, and a quick course in barbering. As this was a time-
honored trade for women, there was little problem in getting a
whole new crew of barbers operating in the cities. The new barbers were given food rations for their families, and often a
small money subsidy.

Other war widows, especially those from refugee families,
were set up in hundreds of workrooms where they were taught
the intricacies of the sewing machine. Through funds from our
agency, large wooden workrooms were constructed and stocked
with sewing machines and materials.

*   *   *

The most ambitious and taxing of the projects using American foods were known as "assimilation projects."

When the promised wheat, often in the form of bulgur for boiling over the tiny fires, and other grains began to arrive in Korea, the voluntary agencies were able to parallel the larger aid programs by helping resettle homeless families on the land. The lines of men, women and children moving pathetically over the face of the peninsula did not end with the ending of the war. Thin lines of hopeful or glumly determined people trekked out from the glutted cities, from the shacks, from the shelters of bridges and sewer pipes, to the open country. With them went supplies of foodstuffs and the promise of a regular lifeline of food while they drained marshland for new villages or worked over the charred remains of communities emptied by war.

A typical voluntary agency "assimilation project" was started by fifty families in the rocky, yellow-earthed hills north of Seoul. It was not far from the 38th parallel where the rocket known as Honest John glared into the part of Korea north of the Yalu River. As part of the cold war games practiced in 1958, Honest John would periodically spit out missiles which leapt screaming into the air like scalded cats. Of course there were no warheads.

In the shadow of the continuing war game, fifty refugee families initiated a work of peace on marginal land. Each person was to receive every month twenty pounds of American food while the new village was being built up.

The transplantation of the families in the open country took place in stages. In early summer, ragged, second-hand tents were pitched, and huts were thrown together. The primitive shelters looked like summer playhouses for youngsters, but here the families lived for their first few weeks in the mountains. All meals were cookouts, and all washing of clothes was done as usual by beating them on stones in a nearby stream. Oil drums were used to boil the garments.

Five projects were entered into with driving zeal: the digging of a well; the building of a large central shelter in the valley to house the families in mass quarters during the winter months; the damming, deepening and widening of the stream for a fish hatchery; the raising of fish in a temporary pool; the preparation and planting of rice paddies in the small plots of arable land nestled among the hills.

Men foraged in the hills for saplings and came back with great loads on their backs perched on wooden A-frame triangles. Other men took time out to hunt game in the hills to add an occasional grouse or pheasant to the common diet. A team of men worked over a small brickmaking machine turning out mud bricks strengthened by a minimum of cement. As soon as the bricks were properly dried, the large central house was carefully constructed. Wood, glass, cement and roof tiles were a contribution of the American aid program. The central large hall was intended for use as a community center and workshop following its use as a winter shelter for the villagers. A part of it was planned as a sort of motel for the hunters and fishermen who were expected to visit the mountain area once they could count on a center of habitation. It was clear that additional income would be necessary above that from the land.

By August of the same year, the community center was well on its way to completion. The paddy land showed by its thin green shoots that patches of land were already reclaimed. Forty thousand tiny fish were growing in the pool feeding bed, ready for transfer to the nearly completed reservoir. To frighten away the birds that hovered over the richly stocked pool, one project member was on constant guard. His straw hut was hardly larger than a bulky overcoat. After periodic inspection, he returned to his hut, from which he regularly pulled a string. Coca-Cola bottles then jangled together and marauding birds were frightened away.

On the ledges on the barren hillsides, simple but solid Korean homes slowly rose, the men, women and children giving to home-building the time left over after attending to the most urgent tasks of the community. The village was being born out of dawn-to-dark labor, with an American voluntary agency and U.S. aid serving as midwives.

Each American voluntary agency served hundreds of thousands of Koreans in "assimilation projects." It was American food abundance, the multi-billion dollar mountain, which provided the basic tool for self-sufficiency in the new communities that sprang up like pale green shoots of spring rice in the war-ravaged Korean landscape.

It was only then, when the works of peace had begun to take root and the specter of hunger had been routed, that the question "Is there peace with you?" ceased to sound pitilessly ironic.

* * *

Through such small beginnings, the Koreans displaced from the north were able to put down roots south of the 38th parallel. It was not long before the greater number of four million displaced had somehow been integrated, putting an unstoppable energy into new rural communities or into raising up flattened villages, towns and cities. Somewhere, South Korea passed a "take-off point" into a recovery that could hardly have been imagined in the decade of the 1950s. It was this recovery that Americans could note in their own daily lives, in the presence of Korean-made cookware, radios and, in time, automobiles.

4. Food for Peace

From 1954 onward, the food shared with refugees and the needy overseas was described as "Food for Peace" rather than "surplus." Its distribution was formalized under U.S. Public Law 480. The new name was a happy one for the whole overseas program but particularly for Korea. There, the word SURPLUS stamped on every grain sack or case of milk powder was rendered by the recipients into its nearest equivalent, "trash." This nomenclature came as a surprise to American voluntary agency workers. It helped us realize that in marginal economies, ordinary people do not have the concept that basic resources such as wheat, rice and milk can exist in such huge surpluses that they can be given away.

Voluntary agencies had fought for the sharing of their country's abundance on the basis of need. They had fought a second fight to have wheat processed into bulgur and noodles to meet the cooking and eating habits of the people served. They shared a sense of achievement when Public Law 480 went into action, utilizing as its symbol a stalk of wheat over a globe. It was proof that their voice of conscience had been effective. There are few more difficult achievements, even in a democratic society, than translating specific moral concerns of citizens into public programs. "Food for Peace" was an outstanding example.

What was surprising to many was that the resulting program, at least the food grants handled by people-to-people agencies, did not become a simple arm of government. The feeding programs did not express simply the concerns of the cold war, for example. A well-known historian of American social history, Merle Curti, addressed himself to the "remarkable partnership" of government and voluntary agencies in his study, *American*

312

Philanthropy Abroad. He conducted extensive interviews with the personnel of all the major voluntary agencies and studied the development of the overseas feeding programs which by 1960 had attained enormous proportions in eighty overseas countries and areas. Against his own pre-judgement, he decided that the people-to-people agencies had managed to maintain their independence and thus fulfill humanitarian rather than political aims.

"It seems to me," he wrote to the author, "that government support of a voluntary enterprise would lessen its freedom of action and infuse it with an official national policy as opposed to, let me say, a religious, ethical or humanitarian aim. Yet there seems to be a considerable opinion for holding that 'the remarkable partnership' of voluntary agencies and government in the surplus commodities distribution was somehow an exception to he supposition."

Curti was of course referring only to Title II of the "Food for Peace" program, under which voluntary agencies distributed outright grants of food to refugees, the needy and to those affected by disasters. The greater part of "Food for Peace" stocks was distributed under Title I in government-to-government transfers. In governmental transfers, goods, not unexpectedly, served national security interests as well as need. Foods also helped to buttress friendly governments when they were used to meet emergency needs, either in give-away programs, or sold at controlled prices through government outlets. The funds built up from these sales were known as counterpart funds and were utilized in development projects.

As for the mountain of food drawn upon by people-to-people organizations, its diminishment resulted in an increase of compassion in the world. It carried out for the nationless, those who could call on no government, as well as those whose governments were powerless to stem famine, what Senator Hubert H. Humphrey had described as the moral duty of government. "The moral test of government," said Humphrey, the champion of feeding the hungry overseas through people-to-people agencies, "is how it treats those who are in dawn of life—the children, those who are in the twilight of life—the aged; and those who are in the shadow of life—the sick, the needy and the hand-icapped." Fortunately, there were many in decision-making positions in the U.S. government who continued to carry out policy in the same spirit. Millions of hapless people overseas, in particular the uprooted, were the beneficiaries.

Chapter Eight

NATIONAL GOLGOTHA— VIETNAM

1. Three Hundred Days—
The First Exodus

The 1975 exodus of the Vietnamese people, when hostilities actually ceased in their land, saw uncounted numbers commit themselves to the sea in every type of craft from frail raft to sampans to fishing boats to barges to coastal junks. Some Vietnamese moved west and reached Thailand, others braved the South China Sea and reached Malaysia or Hong Kong, while still others reached the far coast of Australia. Many reached only a watery grave.

The compassion of the world was aroused at scenes of men, women and children being snatched from certain death on the high seas by passing ships. At first doors were opened for Vietnamese refugees by many receiving countries, above all the United States. Doors began to be slammed shut when the escapes by sea persisted year after year.

* * *

The exodus which began in 1975 was in fact a second exodus. The first exodus had occurred two decades earlier, when Vietnamese had in similar fashion taken off from shore points into the sea. Nearly a million of them had taken off from North Vietnam, chiefly from the Gulf of Tonkin. Their destination was South Vietnam. The first exodus helps in many ways to explain the second exodus when so many people preferred a perilous journey by sea to an unknown destination over life in their own country.

In 1955 I traveled throughout South Vietnam as part of a CRS program to resettle hundreds of thousands who chose life south of Vietnam's 17th parallel. The movement southward had been termed "the swiftest migration of people in history." It may well have been since those who started their escape from northern shore points in tiny fishing craft were picked up by ships of the French navy—as well as by some U.S. naval vessels. There resulted what was surely the swiftest resettlement on record since Vietnam was a well-watered landscape, richly productive and mild in climate. Help was available from governmental sources and from many people-to-people organizations. There was hope that a nation emerging from colonialism would give its gifted people the chance to create a peaceful future. Instead, between the first exodus in 1954 and the second exodus beginning in 1975, the people of Vietnam became a crucified people and their homeland a national Golgotha.

Hanoi in the early fall of 1954 was packed with newcomers. Masses of people found temporary shelter in schools, public buildings and church temple compounds. As more men, women and children poured into the city, their refuge became the open street. The director of Catholic Relief Services, Joseph Harnett, deluged the New York office with reports of the emergency along with appeals for staff and future aid. The agency, the only American voluntary agency serving at that time in Vietnam, had been active in the country since 1950, when it started relief operations in Hanoi. With an occasional visit from agency headquarters, the relief effort was conducted by local church people, who soon opened branches in Hue for central Vietnam and in Saigon for the south.

The newcomers had come from all parts of North Vietnam, in particular from the rich, crowded Red River delta of North Vietnam, from communities marked by the criss-crossing of canals and dykes. Some had come from more remote regions, trudging through insect-clouded jungles and wading through paddy-land to avoid detection by those who might hinder their passage. Among the great flow of people were thousands of Nung and other tribespeople, strong, hardy villagers who had made their way from areas near the Chinese border.

Hanoi was not their final destination. It was their first step in an escape route that they hoped would take them to the port of Haiphong, and then by sea to the south.

The south meant south of the 17th parallel, the demarcation

line decided upon at the Geneva truce agreement signed by the Viet Minh and the French Union in July 1954. This ended the French Indo-China war. It had begun in 1946, when the French, attempting to reassert their authority over a colony, took the fateful step of shelling Haiphong, killing some six thousand inhabitants.

The truce agreement specified that three hundred days would be allowed for the regrouping of the Viet Minh, the Communist forces under the leadership Ho Chi Minh, and the non-Communist forces under the French-backed government of Emperor Bao Dai. Article 14D stated: "From the date of entry into force of the present agreement, until the movement of troops is completed, any civilian residing in a district controlled by one party who wishes to go and live in the zone assigned to the other party shall be permitted to do so by the authorities in that district."

A certain number, estimated at ten thousand, hastened northward. Many key followers of Ho Chi Minh, the cadres, remained in South Vietnam. In the main, those who rushed to take advantage of the freedom of movement were northern Vietnamese villagers who were ready to suffer every form of deprivation to escape from their home places.

The freedom to exercise the three hundred day option was to be guaranteed by an International Control Commission composed of representatives from India, Poland and Canada. The commission was to have access to villages to interview the inhabitants so that those who wished to leave could do so, or obtain local permission if this were necessary.

In 1946, after surviving the Japanese occupation, the Vietnamese rallied around the charismatic Ho Chi Minh, "He who shines." His opposition to French colonialism had earned him a death sentence from the French. His long years of exile had given him the opportunity for active service with the communist parties of France, Russia and China. In the declaration of war against the French in December 1946, he vowed "everlasting resistance," and in this he was supported by Vietnamese nationalists of various groups.

Among Ho Chi Minh's supporters were hundreds of thousands of Catholics. They might have been expected to favor the French, but in point of fact they were fervent nationalists, tired of French hegemony, of being impressed into tea and rubber plantations, and of all the humiliations, big and small, of the colonial condition. Ho asserted that he wanted a democratic society based on the principles of the American constitution. One of the chief promises was complete religious freedom. He chose as one of his supreme counselors an austere Catholic bishop, Le Huu Tu, the bishop of Phat Diem. He dispatched an invitation to a fellow nationalist Ngo Dinh Diem, to join his government. In his reply, Diem specified certain conditions, including full representation of all the nationalist groups, even in the army. These were not accepted, and Diem chose exile in the United States so as not to be involved with the other side, the French. Le Huu Tu remained in the coalition, the National Front, even as he saw how the communist faction was gradually taking all power to itself.

After October 1949, the Viet Minh dispensed with protestations of democratic rights and freedom of religion. A great purge of non-communists began in 1950. Joseph Buttinger, whose expertise on Vietnam was exhibited in many published works, wrote: "The Communists' policy of killing all true nationalists who opposed the Viet Minh had profound and lasting consequences on the future of Vietnam." He pointed out that Vietnam was thus deprived of nationalist leaders who could have played important roles in the rebuilding of a nation gutted by Japanese occupation and by the war against the French.

An implacable Marxist regime followed the example of China in the remaking of society by forced indoctrination, imprisonment, executions, and attacks on religion. Buddhist pagodas and monasteries were closed, and bonzes were arrested, some sentenced to forced labor. The Catholic population suffered varying degrees of humiliation and persecution. Ho Chi Minh's photograph had to be hung inside the church itself. Every Catholic village had a school and soon the schools were politicized with teachers given Marxist tracts to teach.

In one matter, the Catholic villagers won their point. Political meetings were ordered for Sundays in the Catholic villages, so that indoctrination could take place in front of the church before the congregation could disperse. This was often an invitation for the French to strafe the village. The villagers then absolutely refused to gather for politicization on church grounds. They explained that church precincts were "papal land" and therefore neutral. The Sunday mass meetings were discontinued, but the struggle continued. Priests disappeared and were presumed dead. Some were placed in house arrest and others in forced labor. During the period when the Geneva truce agreement was being discussed, priests were being held in the prisons of North Vietnam. As in China, people's tribunals were held in the villages, and persons against whom accusations were made were often executed on the spot. The chief targets were "landlords," and this included those who owned plots of three acres. One estimation of the number liquidated between 1946 and 1954 was two hundred thousand.

By 1954, when the siege of Dien Bien Phu marked the doom of French hegemony over Vietnam and the cessation of what the Vietnamese had come to call the "everlasting war," the villagers of the north, in particular the Catholics among them, wanted the chance to live beyond the terrors of an oppressive regime. They thought that there was hope of this in the south. The attachment of Vietnamese to their home places, and in particular to the burial places of their ancestors, is deeply ingrained in their hearts and minds. To make the decision to part from their homes and honored graves was a wrenching one, one that left painful wounds, but the people who flocked to Hanoi had made that decision. The decision to move southward was a mass, nonviolent expression of dissent in a land already divided, polarized and poisoned by violence.

*   *   *

Patrolling the coastal waters around Haiphong were French naval vessels ready to evacuate army men and their families within the allotted period of three hundred days. The ships had to remain beyond the three-mile limit by order of the Viet Minh. When the magnitude of the exodus became clear, the French asked for American help. Five troopships made their way from the Philippines to Haiphong.

The crews of these vessels found that their passengers were villagers who had learned of their right to move southward. Word had filtered through, even to the furthest villages in the Tonkinese mountains or to points near the Chinese border, not only that northerners had the right to move, but that there might be a ship that would take them aboard. The group that played a crucial role in informing the Vietnamese of their freedom to leave the north was, I was told, the "petits còmmercants," the hawkers of vegetables and other staples and the laundresses of Hanoi. This group composed chiefly of peasant women had free access to the city, and were the carriers of the word to their native villages.

In the heavily Catholic sections, the network of the church, the catechists, pastors and bishops, played a role in getting the word through, but the women and hawkers were more effective since they were not under the same surveillance. Viet Minh troops threatened and even fired on groups of villagers who got the news and packed up to leave for Hanoi. Circumventing every obstacle, the villagers managed to reach coastal communities and with their last piastres purchased flimsy bamboo rafts from the fishermen. Sometimes the fishermen were willing, for pay, to take them beyond the three-mile limit where they could be rescued. Some stole away by night and stacked piles of bamboo at secret meeting places. On a given night, they gathered, tied the wood into makeshift rafts and took off.

On the fishing rafts which usually carried a half dozen fishermen, the two or three dozen escapees would lash themselves together and stand upright like sardines as they set out to sea. The troop ships began to ply their giant searchlights shoreward after a few sea rescues. As the circular beams lit up the dark waters of the Gulf of Tonkin, they revealed hundreds of tiny craft bobbing helplessly about. The people, often standing on rafts that were partly submerged as water entered through the bamboo slats, were waving pieces of clothing in efforts to attract help. Some waved flags.

Sailors, as they drew close enough to fish the exhausted people out of the choppy waters, were surprised to find that the flags were of gold and yellow. Some were of finely woven silk, others of white and yellow patches of rough cotton. They were in fact papal banners, denoting the religious identity of the villagers. Some of the banners had been brought from village sanctuaries; others were hastily put together for flight. The madness of putting out to sea with no more certainty of rescue than being spotted by a roving searchlight was discussed with those who were rescued. They explained that they had done it deliberately. If they had not been rescued, they would have lost their lives. But if they had remained behind, they were convinced that they would have risked losing their souls and the souls of their children.

Some of the escapees from the province of Thai Binh who reached the coastal point of Tray-Ly could go no farther. They could neither buy nor fashion rafts, nor could they pay fishermen to take them beyond the three-mile limit. A large group of Christians decided on a desperate measure. Not far from the shore was a sandbank island. At high tide, the island was completely inundated. They would wade out to the sandbank and pray for rescue by the patrolling ships. If they were not sighted, they would be in danger of being carried off by the next high tide.

Fortunately, the navy ships came close enough to the sandbank to focus their searchlights on it. Navy men saw hundreds upon hundreds of people clinging to the sandbank, waiting for rescue or for death. The ship put down launches and snatched everyone from the perilous perch. Night after night, ships came back and found the sandbank crowded with clinging refugees. Launches were dispatched until every last person was taken off. All in all, over five thousand persons were saved from the Tra-Ly sandbank.

U.S. naval vessels were assigned to help with the evacuation. Soon there was need of planes for the Hanoi-Saigon shuttle. In ten months, nine hundred thousand men, women and children were brought south by sea, a third of them on American ships.

American sailors began to see that the Vietnamese people who came aboard dirty and smelly possessed a certain indefinable dignity. The scene was described in a moving dispatch from

Patrick O'Connor, correspondent of the National Catholic News Service.

By the time the two hundred thousandth Vietnamese refugee had boarded an American ship, it was decided to have a special luncheon of celebration in the officers' wardroom. The refugee who happened to be number 200,000 came aboard the *General Howze*, a ship which made nearly a score of trips and carried over fifty thousand from Tonkin into southern exile. The refugee's name was Tran Duc Hoa, a sixty-two year old man accompanied by his wife, two daughters and a little grandson. The whole family had spent a month at a shore point hoping to be able to escape by sea. By that time, the Viet Minh had such heavy guards on the coast that they could not obtain a craft to get away. Finally they found an inland route to the port of Haiphong.

The family of Tran Duc Hoa were honored guests for the voyage. The festive luncheon was scheduled for 11:10 A.M., the ship's chaplain reported later. The family came politely and sat down but would not eat anything at all. When the officers asked what was wrong, the father explained that they had heard that the chaplain was celebrating mass at noon on deck, and they were fasting in preparation for taking communion.

The ship's chaplain told the news correspondent of the National Catholic News Service: "I remember how thrilled I was the first time I offered mass for the refugees. We had more than two thousand aboard, and no single area on deck was large enough for the crowd. Before mass, the refugees recited the rosary. You could hear them throughout the ship. Then during mass, they sang hymns in Vietnamese and afterward the Salve Regina. The crew watched them, fascinated, from mastheads, cross-beams and even the crow's nest. In that sea of faces beneath them they saw genuine faith. Night after night, the ship resounded with the refugees' prayers."

As the refugee service was regularized, a Vietnamese team of priest, bonze, Buddhist priest, nurse and social worker traveled on each voyage to interpret between the crew and the Vietnamese. At the end of the exodus, figures revealed that two-thirds of the refugees from the north were of the Catholic faith.

*   *   *

Large numbers of people, especially those from central Vietnam, came south on their own. Fishermen packed their boats with family members and relatives and hugged the coastline until they were south of the 17th parallel. Others made their way across the demarcation line which soon became a six-mile-wide slash to form a buffer zone between North and South Vietnam.

Saigon readied itself as well as it could for the influx from the north. Forty-two reception centers were hastily set up, some simply army tents to provide a sheltering roof if nothing more. The cavernous rice milling warehouses on the banks of a canal at Binh Dong housed more than a thousand persons each. The opera house in the very center of Saigon was filled with fifteen hundred refugees. Shelters were found for evacuated orphanages, including the An Lac Orphanage conducted by Madame Ngai Van Vuy. The Bui Chu Hospital of the Canadian Brothers of St. John of God came with staff, supplies and patients.

The neediest among the refugees were reached by the network of feeding stations set up under the direction of Joseph Harnett. Army field kitchens were put in place by the French. At first the food was a gruel of rice and powdered milk. It was hot; it could be fed to all, even children and the aged; it was easily prepared. Vietnamese sisters, some of whom were nurses, joined with volunteers to make the feeding scheme a success. In a few weeks, close to one hundred thousand of the neediest refugees in all parts of the city were receiving the hot food. Soon wheat flour, butter and oil were added to the available foods. In ovens built by the refugees, bread was baked with U.S. surplus flour—crusty long poles of French bread. A new product, provided for mass feeding from U.S. government stocks, proved to be immensely popular. It was cotton seed oil and reminded the Vietnamese of the taste of a prized food—pork.

By plane and ship, from the United States and Europe, food, clothing, medical supplies, even hospital beds, reached Saigon. A half million dollars from CRS funds were put at Harnett's disposal. Other voluntary agencies, including CARE, Church World Service and the Mennonite Central Committee, sent staff and supplies.

With financial aid from the United States, a daily dole of seven piastres was given to each refugee in the first days after arrival. With this minimal amount, the refugees were to scrounge on the market until they found a kilo of rice for five piastres, with two piastres left over for a piece of dried fish. Somehow, the provisioning of Saigon from the lush well-watered hinterland and from overseas sources allowed the refugees to keep alive. No one died of starvation and there was no epidemic.

*   *   *

When I reached Saigon in 1955, Joseph Harnett, the CRS director, arranged for me to have guides to places he didn't have time to visit. I soon discovered that French was truly a "lingua franca" in Vietnam. I was able to converse with teachers in village schools throughout the countryside. The great rice bowl of the Mekong River Delta yawned emptily, and the rice milling sheds were swarming with South Vietnam's first bumper crop— displaced people. In order to reach the sheds, we had to pass through Cholon, the vibrant, noisy Chinese city of half a million souls that abuts Saigon.

A camp spokesman for Binh Dong One took me through the earth-floored shed, every foot of which was allotted to living space for families. "We have two hundred and seventy-eight families. We are one thousand and twenty-five people—all from Vinh." He was a big-boned man, tall for a Vietnamese, with deep-set eyes and a strong, jutting jaw. He was measured and heavy in his speech. He led us into the center of the shed where a paraffin lamp gave out yellow gleams over people squatting on low slatted wooden beds or on coconut matting. Here he had some stools for us. The briny smell of *nuoc nam*, the ever-present fish sauce, seemed to rise from every family nook.

"How did you escape. Were you brought south by ship?" I wanted to know. Anh, a Vietnamese social worker who had studied in Chicago, was translating for me.

"No, he says he came on foot. And he wants to know if you understand about the Quatrième Zone?"

"This is the first time I have heard it mentioned. To what does it refer?"

"In our tongue it is the Chien Khu Tu, the CK4. He says to tell you it was the part of Vietnam where Ho Chi Minh carried out all the plans he had in his head. That is why most of these families left behind their homes and walked through the jungle land to come here. Many were hurt in the jungle, and some were shot at by Viet Minh soldiers."

I was to hear the Quatrième Zone of north central Vietnam referred to many times after that—especially by the last arrivals among the refugees. Even in Vietnamese, I noticed, the French phrase was sometimes used. The numbers were given to the zones by the Viet Minh military command. Battle Zone 4 fell in the province of Vinh.

"What was so bad about the Quatrième Zone?" I asked.

"People from Vinh are stubborn," translated Anh. He waited to see if I showed any reaction. Then he went on to explain in short pithy sentences the changes that had occurred since the people of Vinh had first thrown in their forces with the armies that promised liberation from the French. The Viet Minh assumed all the leading posts, in the military as well as the political life.

"It was supposed to be liberation, but men had to work in forced labor battalions. Outsiders moved in and made themselves members of our village councils. We could not talk about things like free men." Anh translated each sentence.

Then there was a pause and what seemed to be a long sigh. "It was our own people who did this to us, not the French. It was our own people who sent some of the farmers from our village to the prison. They were beaten and tortured. When they came back they would not talk out loud, but only in whispers out in the fields. Our own people were spies."

"What about their crops?"

"Of course, every village had its quotas. But we are hard workers. We would even have done that if we were free. But then they spied on our *cha* (priest). The outsiders would make him come and answer questions. He was our *cha*, the man of God for our village. But they wanted him to be their servant. It was secret, but we knew.

"We are a stubborn people. We could not give in to this. We could not fight guns with *coup-coups* (small hatchets). So we walked through the jungle. They wanted us to stay. Who will work in their battalions? They want workers for their battalions. They want good crops. Not from us."

A group of men and women had gathered around us. He turned to them. Anh explained that he was asking if anyone would want to leave these dark rice sheds to go back to the Quatrième Zone.

"They said 'no,' of course," said Anh. She gave her quick little laugh. "These are strong stubborn heroes—not like us lazy Saigonese."

The refugee glowered at her. It was my first experience of the North-South clash of temperaments in Vietnam. He knew no English, but he clearly felt that the levity was somehow insulting.

Binh Dong Two was also filled with refugees from central Vietnam, the area occupied so long under the Viet Minh that a new pattern of life had been imposed on the villagers. Under an altar complete with the colorful ikon of Duc Me, Our Lady of Perpetual Succor and a small red vigil light burning in a glass, a middle-aged fisherman told us that he had escaped along with several hundred villagers from the coastal area around Ha Tinh.

"Our two boats were shot at from the shore. We were without weapons. Twenty-four of our people were killed. They are with God. Forty of us were wounded. But we reached Saigon."

"Do you regret leaving now that you have suffered so much and you are living like this?"

Despite the more than a thousand people who were sleeping, cooking, eating, trying to keep clean in the vast shed, there did not seem to be an atmosphere of unhappiness.

The fisherman fingered a silver religious medal hanging from a chain around his neck.

"We did the right thing. In a week we will go to Baria. A hundred and fifty of us. We have no nets, no boats, no fishing tackle. But the sea is filled with fish. We will not die."

* * *

"Gia Dinh," said Joseph Harnett, "has seventy thousand refugees. It is one of the most crowded areas around Saigon."

All the refugees were from Phat Diem, and they maintained

their community identity in exile. Schools, vocational training, workshops and even a religious seminary were all in full activity.

They were packed into a small space, living and working in old buildings, sheds which must have been warehouses, and quonset huts. This corner of Gia Dinh seemed to be in a constant subdued roar, not only from the press of people who had tumbled in to fill every available space, but from the sound of many workshops and small factories in continuous operation.

In one shed, a large group of girls were apprentices in the making of women's tunics, the *ao dao*, and trousers, on a row of sewing machines. Their teachers were the members of a Vietnamese congregation of nuns, the Amantes de la Croix, Lovers of the Cross. A group of nuns had their own sewing machines, turning out pillow cases, bed sheets and church vestments. Others were embroidering the word PAX on the pillow cases. The colors were yellow, pink or blue, each enclosed in a gold circle. To their delight, I purchased a dozen.

In one house, the room partitions on the lower floor had been removed to accommodate the machinery of a silk loom one of one hundred and twenty-five such looms supplied by Vietnam's ministry for refugees. The loom was clattering deafeningly. Some of the silk carried the Fu Chu, the Chinese character for happiness.

In other flimsy, overcrowded homes, mosquito netting and sleeping mats were being fashioned. I was ready to come away with an unforgettable picture of transplanted Vietnamese clinging to work in the midst of noise and wild overcrowding, when Harnett mentioned that there was an opportunity to see a sight perhaps more unforgettable, a legendary transplanted bishop. Bishop Le Huu Tu, the bishop of Phat Diem, lived in the midst of his flock. He received us clad in a long white cassock. On his head was a white skull cap. He was skeletally thin, which made him seem unusually tall, and his face was as elongated as a Byzantine icon. His eyes shone as he told us of his pride in his people, their hard work, and the fidelity of the young people to their faith and to school work. Exile in the south had not interrupted their progress in school, nor the seminary training for future priests.

Bishop Le Huu Tu was a member of the Cistercian order, one of the most austere orders of the Catholic Church. I asked him about his acquaintance with Ho Chi Minh which had been mentioned to me. In the early days of the break with France, he had welcomed Ho's leadership.

"Ho, I thought, was a reasonable man. I heard him quote the wisdom of the sage since he was a Confucian scholar."

The long brilliant eyes shone with a steel-cold merriment.

"Ho made me a supreme counselor in his government. During that time, he asked me to meet him in a remote country dwelling. After the midday meal, we shared a mat for the afternoon siesta. 'This makes us brothers,' Ho told me. 'We can never oppose each other from this time forward. Brothers,' Ho repeated to me." The bishop made it clear to Ho that as long as Ho was fighting for the independence of Vietnam, he would always be at his side. If, however, Ho wanted the country to become communist, he would fight against him.

Le Huu Tu became sad as he explained that the time of "la main étendue," "the extended hand," came to an end. Councils of elders in the villages found that they had to accept political infiltrees from the outside, Marxist indoctrination became obligatory. Bands of militia entered the villages to carry off supplies, and sometimes drafted young men of military age. The people of Phat Diem organized their own village militia as protection.

I learned that the French command eventually assigned some of the Phat Diem village militia to man part of the defense line against the Viet Minh.

From other northern villagers, I learned two Vietnamese words, "trum chan," whose meaning they revealed when they trusted me. The meaning was those who "hid under a blanket," those who simply wanted to get on with their own lives. The people were tired of famine, of occupation by French or Japanese, of renewed violence and of a new system of harshness from their own people. They longed for the rhythm of village life, of planting and harvesting, of caring for the irrigation dykes and canals on which their survival depended. Their only wish was to hide until the violence was past. It might have seemed selfish, but as I thought of what the past sixteen years had brought them in intrusions from the outside, I could see the reasonableness of the choice of the "trum chan." They were an unheard third force rejecting the hammer of Ho Chi Minh's iron discipline and the anvil of French colonialism.

I followed the progress of the Phat Diem refugees in Gia Dinh. In five years, the one hundred and twenty-five looms that I had seen in operation had grown to five thousand. The fledgling industry had increased to such a size that Gia Dinh's army of weavers were turning out over twenty-five million yards of cloth a year.

2. New Villages That Died Young

On the main road leading north out of Saigon toward Bien Hoa, I was in time to see the remaining examples of what had been called "roadside resettlement." On the same road I saw also the remains of colonialism—the last of the French Foreign Legion, forty thousand of whom had fought with the French Army in the Indo-Chinese wars. Dark-skinned Senegalese or fair-haired Germans, they wore the white kepi with the same nonchalance as they guarded leftover military installations. The small American presence was hardly visible—a military assistance training group and a team of aid personnel from the U.S. operations mission.

On both sides of the road, new villages squatted, agglomerations of mud-brick and palm-thatched homes. In their first painful months of homelessness the refugees, camping out along the roadside, had been offered jobs in nearby rubber plantations. "Plantation" was a terror word to Vietnamese who remembered how members of their families had been virtually impressed into the rubber and tea plantations of Tonkin. Despite their need, and the offer of improved working conditions and regular pay, the northerners were adamant in their refusal to work the plantations. We used to see the great rubber plantations looming still and idle as we drove through the countryside around Saigon.

But though they scorned plantation labor, and no other jobs were offered them, the newcomers did not remain idle. They went in teams to the nearest jungle and with their *coup-coups* cut down small trees. These they bound into neat piles of firewood. Saigon was glutted with firewood in those days, and the piles of neatly cut wood rose high at both sides of the main exit road from Saigon. Meanwhile, the underbrush was growing in the despised plantations, giving them an untidy look.

Once after a long drive we stopped off and entered a grove of rubber trees. The high foliage imprisoned the long straight trunks in a sea of deep green gloom. Unexpectedly finding a brick open-air fireplace, we built a fire and heated cans of hamburgers and beans. Seated on the floor of the rubber forest I looked down the long lanes of trunks on all sides. There was a neglected air about the whole scene, and I felt as if I were in the great pillared reception hall of some deposed potentate.

* * *

No one could forget the barefoot men and women jogging in dance-like steps along the road leading north out of Saigon. They carried two huge bundles, often of palm leaves as tall as themselves, slung on a pole across their shoulders. These would be the palm-thatch roofs for refugee huts.

The villagers wanted to work, and voluntary agencies like CRS were ready to help them. Grants of funds, seemingly insignificant but crucially important, allowed the people to resume the activities of their life in the north.

In these roadside villages, the cooperatives founded almost overnight included charcoal-making and carpentry shops—especially for making slatted beds. There were busy cooperatives for the fabrication of mosquito netting, silk, and sleeping mats.

The charcoal makers of the north were operating their kilns as we paid a visit to the roadside villages on November 1, 1955. It happened to be a religious feast of the Catholic Church, the feast of All Saints. We could tell which of these villages were Christian because over the schools and thatched houses flew thousands of papal yellow and white banners.

The feast of All Saints was important in itself, but the day that followed it was of special significance to Vietnamese—the feast of All Souls. On the latter day, there are special prayers for the "faithful departed." Given the special Vietnamese homage tendered to ancestors, the feast of All Souls was celebrated with unusual devotion. It had been hard for the Christians as well as the Buddhists to desert the tombs of their ancestors.

It was not long before most of the crowded roadside villages seemed to fade away. The Vietnamese Ministry for Refugees allowed the northerners to settle in various parts of the fertile land. Often carrying their burdens in the traditional twin baskets slung over their shoulders, they moved in droves into plots where new villages could be founded. Some, like the hamlet of New Hanoi, a hundred miles north of Saigon, blossomed with amazing speed. New Hanoi counted over five hundred families. From Hanoi itself had come a nucleus of new settlers; united with them were settlers from Phat Diem, Bui Chu, Thai Binh and Bac Ninh. New Hanoi was nestled among tiny hills and shaded with mangrove trees. In the little paradise of green shade, a deputation of elders met us. On their white heads were the black mandarin hats; on their bent old bodies were long black coats. Clasping their hands before them, they bowed in unison. The pastor welcomed us.

"I speak for the elders and people of New Hanoi in thanking you and all those who have helped us put down roots. We have more than five hundred families in Tan Hoa. You see around you fields filled with new roots—half a million new tea plants, forty thousand pepper plants. These are crops for our future. We hope they will yield. Also for future harvest, but in another realm, are our schools. Next to our primary school, we have our village high school with nearly a hundred pupils. We thank you again and hope that the future will prove that your trust was well placed in us, our people, who represent every part of North Vietnam."

When I saw the kitchen gardens bursting with potatoes, manioc, a type of tapioca, and su su, a green leafy vegetable, I could see in my mind's eye the work of those thousands of patient hands, the hands of men, women and children, who without tools had separated and softened the bulldozed earth for the new plants. Every inch of soil was weeded and cultivated.

"Each garden," explained the pastor, "is of the same size, eight hundred square meters. In the forest each family has been given a plot ten times as large. They are already spending every spare minute clearing their space in the woods."

We saw the school children playing in the open yard in front of the cement school building. Their clothes were clearly of

American origin, but were in the Vietnamese mode. I asked about the matter.

"These clothes are from your stocks," we were told. "But they have all passed through our atelier."

In a secluded corner of the village was a workshop for several seamstresses and a couple of tailors. All garments were ripped apart and expertly put together again. Next to the workshop was the atelier of a sculptor. His output consisted of workmanlike statues of the mother of Christ and of the twelve apostles. He must have been a busy man judging by the numbers of statues awaiting delivery to the new churches of the area.

* * *

In the midst of the new villages was the transplanted hospital already mentioned. At Honai, twenty miles out of Saigon, the Canadian Brothers of St. John who had to abandon their hospital in Bui Chu were already giving medical service to the poorest of the poor. Refugees and the inhabitants of the whole area were flocking for care. We saw the lines of people in the waiting shed—obviously victims of trachoma, of open pus-exuding sores, of wasting diseases and of other maladies that left them bloated and misshapen. Nearby, the pavilions of the new hospital, financed by a grant from American aid funds, were nearing completion. The new medical center, to which our agency made available doctors, nurses and eye specialists from the United States, became a health resource for an area lacking any medical facilities.

* * *

Myths grew up around the refugees from the north. Since so many of them were of the Catholic faith, and often carried statues of the Virgin Mary from their churches, a persistent myth asserted that they believed that the Virgin Mary had migrated to the south. The northerners then left everything to follow her. The origin of this myth is not known, but for anyone with knowledge of the refugees, it amounted to an attack on their character and intelligence. Such superstitions were never once raised in any of our visits to refugee groups.

A peculiarly Vietnamese institution was, however, repeatedly discussed as leading to the decision to leave their home places, namely the councils of elders.

In the daily lives of the villagers, of whatever belief, even among the animist mountain tribespeople, an ancient system of local government was preserved. The deep Oriental respect for age and its wisdom helped keep alive the balance and continuity of Vietnamese life throughout the vicissitudes of invasion and occupation. One could not share Vietnamese life without hearing impressive stretches of the Hue Van, the epic commemorating the victory over Mongol invaders. We learned the story of how Kublai Khan, the grandson of Genghis Khan, invaded the Red River Valley with, according to the Vietnamese, an army of half a million men. The Vietnamese side, we were told, had scarcely two hundred thousand men to throw into the field. The year was 1584. The decision to offer resistance or to submit to superior force was put to the elders of villages of the area. Ten thousand of them were gathered together and the fateful question of surrender or war was in their hands.

"War," chorused the elders in united fervor. And war it was. The Vietnamese, one of the few peoples able to boast of such a feat, repelled the Mongols on the field of battle.

When the news of the Geneva truce agreement and the option of three hundred days reached the Red River Valley four hundred years later, the dilemma was submitted to the council of elders in each village. Not all of the elders counseled flight; some counseled flight for only part of the village population.

A description of how a Christian village arrived at its course of action came from Georges de Rochcau, representative of Secours Catholique, a French welfare organization.

"The elders, after taking into account the probable future for those who stayed on in the north, and for those who quit their northern homes, gave it as their opinion that some, if not all, of the older inhabitants might stay on. Younger people, and especially those families with children, would depart for Haiphong for evacuation to the south. One council of elders phrased their decision as follows in informing their spiritual leader, the bishop of Bac Ninh, of their own resolve to remain on in the north: 'We want to remain here where we are because in these grave moments, we want to be a testimony of the Christian faith in a land where Christians have lived for so long. Our sons and grandsons will continue our traditions when they have founded new villages. With your permission, we will remain here and with the help of God we are going to defend our faith.'"

The people who addressed their bishop in this way were the descendants of the martyrs of North Vietnam who had laid down their lives for Christianity not too many generations earlier.

During the nineteenth century in what was then called Indochina, there had existed for nearly fifty years a steady persecution of Christians. Any northern Vietnamese suspected of being a Christian was ordered to step on a crucifix. To refuse meant torture and possible death. No accurate count was ever possible of the number of men and women who were put to death for their Christian beliefs in towns and remote hamlets of the "approximate country." The lowest estimate was a hundred thousand martyrs. Many died by the savage "death of a thousand wounds," a systematic hacking away at the flesh of the victim with short knives.

Whether they left for self-imposed exile, tearing themselves away from everything they held most dear, or whether they remained to face continued anti-religious pressures and outright persecution, the villagers were bearing witness to their beliefs.

Commenting that poor villagers could not lose much under the Viet Minh, de Rochcau observed: "They are leaving the North because they know by personal experience that the Viet Minh will not permit them to practice their Christian faith. . . . The non-Christians from nearby villages looked at them with amazement and kept saying, 'What kind of madness makes these Christians leave their home places and go to face an unknown life? How are they going to live? Where can they go?'

"My work in helping refugees and migrants," he wrote, "gave me the possibility to come in contact with different groups of people all around the world, but before I came to this area, I never had the opportunity to meet Christians with such deep faith, with such resignation in facing problems, and finally with such unlimited confidence in divine providence."

*   *   *

During the fall of 1955, I was able to see evidence of the massive and speedy transplanting of whole villages. By American jeep, by French Deux Chevaux, the tiny car which was literally two horsepower, by flashy green convertible once the chariot of Emperor Bao Dai, by British land rover, the finest opponent of rutted roads, by French-built railroad, by dugout canoe, and by American cargo planes, we were able to visit scores of refugee villages. The only invitation I reluctantly refused was an invitation to traverse the central highlands by elephant. What we saw in the tropical countryside, with its wet green flatlands, its tiger-infested jungles and boar-rich highlands, its coastal area jumping with marine life, was an astounding saga of collective courage and unremitting work. Once we accepted the offer of a taxi driver to drive from Pleiku in the central highlands to Saigon, when a plane broke down. With very few stops for repairs, he brought us to our destination.

Crucial to the speed of the resettlement was the high motivation of the move southward. The fact that villages moved and resettled as living social organisms was a key factor in the quick reprise of economic life. Only in such natural communities of work would it have been possible to hack living space out of the jungle, utilizing everything at hand from a U.S.-loaned bulldozer to a *coup-coup* hatchet held in the hand. In fact, despite the hurried import of such immense juggernauts as the earth-moving bulldozer, it was the oldest tool of all, the human hand, that was basic to the rapid return to self-sufficiency by the refugees in South Vietnam. It was the human hand that I saw hovering over hundreds of new vegetable gardens, turning the earth and transplanting tiny plants and seedlings.

The newcomers were certainly fortunate in finding themselves in a land that for Asia was incredibly fertile and well-watered. But unless significant aid had come from the outside, they could hardly have succeeded in dotting the landscape with so many new villages in little more than a year. The aid came from half a world away, not solely from the U.S. government, but from a growing number of people-to-people agencies like our own.

One of our forays was to begin at the old capital Hue, the tomb-filled relic of the Nguyen dynasty. This was the dynasty which ended with the removal of Bao Dai from the Vietnamese scene. We circled nine times over the city in a tropic downpour that made our small plane shake like a cat with wet fur. What brought the image of a cat to mind was our CAT (Civilian Air Transport) plane, trim and purposeful. Below us, ringing the city, were flat round stones. These were ancient tomb markers. In the rain-battered earth, they looked like giant waterlily pads. Finally, the plane landed in the midst of the lashing hurricane, and we made several efforts to step out into a landing field that was under a foot of water. The CAT plane, piloted by an American who had made hundreds of flights before and during the fifty-five day siege to the Dien Bien Phu fortress, took off again.

The pilot asked us for our second choice of destination. He left his scheduled course and took us to Nha Trang. This gave us the opportunity to drive around the immense and protected bay of Cam Ranh. This, a proud Vietnamese asserted, was one of the finest, if not the finest, harbor in all Asia. It was almost deserted except for a few fishing boats. I could not have imagined that Cam Ranh Bay would, by the expenditure of billions of dollars, be turned into the busiest war port of the world and that hundreds of thousands of men in battle gear would be debarking on this isolated shore.

At Nha Trang, a field worker for the U.S. operations mission, Richard Evans, was experimenting with simple ways to preserve the bumper catches of fish against lean seasons and also for shipping inland. He had developed an ingenious, home-made oven for the speedy smoking of fish, a good example of appropriate technology. When I saw the Vietnamese method of preserving fish—allowing it to dry in the sun, the target of thousands of crawling flies—I understood Evans' zeal for the project.

* * *

There were many times when attempts to reach isolated villages were difficult or even dangerous. Early in November 1955, a party of four people, including three from our agency and a member of the U.S. operations mission, found ourselves on the bank of a swollen, grayblack river near the town of Kontum in the central highlands. We were not far from the 17th parallel.

Our landrover was halted at the river's edge because the pontoon-type bridge had disappeared under the rising flood waters. We knew that the bridge, a rustic plank-covered trestle, still held secure since a row of little eddies and ripples marked its hidden presence. A probe showed that it was little more than a foot below the surface of the water. The Vietnamese driver insisted that he could negotiate the crossing. I demurred.

A government engineer from Kontum came to discuss our problems. When he learned that we were working with refugees, he offered his help. I accepted his offer to take me across the river in a peasant's canoe in preference to taking the landrover. We were soon zig-zagging across the swirling river in a dugout canoe. He guided the dizzying ride with a practiced hand. After a while, I had to close my eyes and kept them closed till we reached the far side.

The engineer, a spare Vietnamese with brilliant black eyes behind oversized glasses, wore a dark business suit. His exquisite French matched his smooth professional appearance.

"I myself am a refugee," he told me. "I chose to come south after the news of the agreement. My home was in the north, in the vicinity of Hanoi." He paused. "I had to sacrifice all," he went on. "I had to leave my home, my possessions, even the tombs of my ancestors." By the tone of his voice, I knew that the listing was in an ascending order of importance. The heaviest sacrifice was that of deserting, perhaps forever, the graves of his fathers.

"Vous êtes Américaine. You know the importance of freedom—that it is necessary for the correct life, for any life at all."

He was a Buddhist, he told me, and by that I understood Vietnam's tolerant, loose-structured Buddhism, overlaid with Confucian and Taoist influence. Despite his modern scientific education, the proper regard for the role of his ancestors was central to his life. But one thing above all was necessary for him, after freedom from colonial oppression—freedom from political oppression.

The engineer stood for one group of northerners, educated,

aware, and determined nationalists. They were townspeople, but they shared with the villagers a devotion to hard, unremitting work. Whenever I saw the newcomers leaning over paddyland with passionate care, or patiently tending wooden logs to bend them by fire, one of the oldest methods known to man, I thought of the place of origin of so many of them, the Red River Delta. They told me about the maze of dams, dykes, canals and locks, six hundred miles of dams athwart the red-silted river, fifteen hundred miles of great dykes, the earth-moving and water-watching system fashioned and maintained by villagers throughout the ages. This was not only irrigation but flood control. I longed to see it all, but had to depend on their description, and I was moved by the proud tone of their voices as they talked. I came to the conclusion that the irrigation system was one of the Orient's monuments to the immemorial patience and industry of Asian man, and was the surest clue to the diamond-hard caliber of the Delta's inhabitants.

Every delay or side-trip revealed another fascinating or hidden aspect of the life of Vietnam. Not far from Kontum, we visited an orphanage conducted by the Daughters of Charity of St. Vincent de Paul. French and Vietnamese sisters worked together for the children of the Sodang tribespeople of the neighborhood, referred to as montagnards by the Vietnamese. One of the Sodang customs, a sister told me, accounted for many of the children under their care. If a mother died giving birth, the child, though alive, was buried with her. "The mountain people think it is more cruel to let a child live without a mother's love," the sister explained.

Farther on in the central plateau, we saw the little leprosarium run by the sisters. Men or women with signs of the disease are put out of their village. They then gather into a separate village. The sisters brought them food and the latest anti-leprosy medicaments from France. The people were happy with our visit, and within minutes they were playing a noisy serenade on their gong orchestra. Our response to the music resulted in another invitation to view a hidden jungle organ.

Two breech-clothed Sodangs led us into a lonely corner of the forest. As we made our way through the jungle, we heard an unearthly four-note melody, endlessly repeated and echoing from tree to tree.

As we neared an open space, a mountain rice field, we finally came upon the source of the sounds, the jungle organ. It was a maze of bamboo pipes, strung in rows, and situated in a protecting glade. It seemed to play by itself as sticks struck bamboo pipes of different lengths. The striking sticks were operated by strings which came together in a master string at the far side of the organ. I asked who tugged at the master string which then operated the smaller strings. All the strings were made from twisted bamboo tendrils.

Our guides smiled delightedly when they heard the question and led us down a steep slope.

The master string, balanced on slots carved in tree branches, was stretched across a stream five hundred feet down. The stream was dammed to form a tiny waterfall. From the cable was hung a scoop, which filled every three seconds. When filled, it dipped and emptied the water, then swung back into position to be filled again. Each time it dipped, it tugged at the master string. The motion was carried by the master string which controlled the melody made by the striking of the sticks against the bamboo pipes.

There was no human puller of the strings. Our breech-clothed guides turned to us and made a gesture with head and hand as though to say, "Here is the secret power we have in our jungle." Our words of admiration were translated to the men who stood proud and smiling next to their masterpiece which seemed to us the primitive jungle ancestor of all the organs in the world.

The bewitching view of the jungle organ protecting fields of glutenous rice was only one of the detours that took us far from the more familiar rice paddy landscape with massive water buffalos wet and shining in the sun.

In a lonely landscape we came upon the Chams, living vestiges of the once powerful Champa kingdom, undone by its unsuccessful wars. The men still wore turbans and their poverty-stricken villages were marked by half-ruined towers of once great temples. There were still bas-relief sculptures of what looked like the gods of Hinduism, but the attrition of time had worn away the rounded arms and busts.

"Even the names of these villages are strange to us," our Vietnamese guide told us. "This is Batap. There is also Ponap. The speech of the Chams is different from ours."

* * *

All along the coastline we saw the Vietnamese in the act of building a future through exploiting the riches of a tropic sea. At Baria, we stood in a cove of an extended sandy beach as fishermen docked a large wooden boat. They were proud of a large tuna fish that was part of the day's catch. Many other boats were soon to dock, all fashioned in less than a year with help from CRS. Credit was established with local sawmills which provided the wood not only for furious boat-building but the slats for the flat beds which served during the day as chairs and tables. I remembered what I had heard from the fishermen in Binh Dong One, the crowded rice milling shed in Saigon. They were the tough-minded refugees from the Quatrième Zone.

They had in fact arrived in Baria, and were now working in the boats with the fishermen who had arrived earlier. All in all, there were over twenty-five hundred refugees in the hundreds of palm-thatched dwellings a few hundred yards from the sandy shore. Many of the men and women were wearing the clothes in which they reached the south, black tunics and trousers, now faded, or a similar outfit of a strange red-brown. The northern peasant women wore short tunics rather than the long ao dao of the cities. The red-brown color was a dye the women made from a local root. The children were barefoot.

The daily catch, unfailingly abundant, provided the village with something they pointed out to us, casks of *nuoc mam* sauce. In the bamboo-bound wooden casks were layers of fish and brine. The women and children had prepared the sea salt. Heavy stones were placed on the fish, and the pressed-out fish liquid would seep into vessels underneath. This was the sauce that enlivened the meals whose main ingredient was rice.

The pride of Baria was the school, a large tent-like structure with a board floor which stood a foot above the sand. The roof was palm-thatched and sloping. The sides were open, and class-room partitions ran across the width of the structure.

We stood at the back of one of the classrooms, and watched the boys and girls crouched over the long board which served as a common desk. The unhampered warm breeze troubled ever so lightly the sheets of paper on which the children were writing. Each child had a bottle of ink and pen and was scratching labori-ously with steel nibs a lesson written on the blackboard.

The teacher, an earnest young man in neat white shirt and dark trousers, explained in French, accented but understand-able: "You know, Mademoiselle, that we use the Quoc Ngu. When the Portuguese missioners came, they adapted our speech to the Roman alphabet. This is unique in this part of the world. That may be one reason why so many of our people are literate today.

"Our school has three sets of pupils. It is used all day and in the evening until sunset. All morning, the littlest ones. In the afternoon, these that you see, beginning at nine years. In the evening, we have a class of older people, men and women, near-ly a hundred men and about fifty women. They did learn to read at one time, but they need practice in writing."

The tropical, orange-pink sun was plummeting into the China Sea with startling rapidity as we made our way across the expanse of sand to where we had left our car. At the end of the gray-brown sandy beach stood a lone figure. He was dressed in white from head to foot, and on his head he had a white beret with a loose pancake crown. Suddenly, a thin white arm was waved toward our party.

We stopped in our tracks and stared at the lone figure. He waved again, and pointed to a wooden hut at some distance behind him.

"It is Bishop Le Huu Tu," said Joseph Harnett unbelievingly. "What is he doing on this beach?"

As we came near the bishop, we saw that he had a white cas-sock buttoned tightly from his neck to his feet. His incredibly long, high-cheekboned face was ascetic in an almost aggressive way.

"You have found me in my retreat," he said in French. He led us into a hut made of plain wooden boards. Floor, walls, ceiling were of the same brown wood. The impression was of emptiness. "Here I come to meditate," said the emaciated white-clad figure. "There are some villagers from Phat Diem nearby. They built me this retreat so that I can sometimes be alone."

After experiencing the almost unbearable din of Gia Dinh, one could realize why he needed a place for meditation. His presence was like none other. The floppy beret, careening over his left eyebrow, added a touch of strange metaphysical dash to his appearance.

As we left, he stood still and erect on the gray-brown sands like a slender white tree trunk that one sometimes sees rising stripped and sere out of a sandy swamp.

*   *   *

At Xom Dom, we stood on a pale morning-lit beach. It was deserted but for two teams of men. They were placed at the ends of the beach and were pulling on an enormous net hidden by the waves. At what must have been the center of the net a man in a small boat was giving signals. We left and came back at midmorning. They were still working like teams of horses maneuvering and pulling the great catch, and at noon when we went back to see the developments, the net, jumping with fish, was still a distance from shore. By afternoon, the catch was in, and the villagers were sorting it.

At Tan Binh, we saw more people from the Quatrième Zone. A leathery-faced young man fixed his eyes on our interpreter and gave us his tale: "We are nationalists, but we began our resistance to the Viet Minh when they made us forced laborers. We had to carry rice and weapons for the soldiers. From 1952 we had a communist as the chief of our village. We would be doing forced labor still, but the international commission came to us in 1954. They had to give us the permit to leave. We had to wait until May 15 of this year. But I was fortunate. I was not put in prison.

"I am twenty-two years old," the man continued. The pastor of the village translated into French. "We asked for the permit to leave our village, myself and all my family and many others. Thirty-one of us they took away from our own homes and brought us to Vinh. The Franciscan convent there has been made into a prison. Finally, nine of us were set free.

"We went back to our own village. When the international commission came to talk to us, the Vietminh soldiers answered the questions. They took off their uniforms and became like the other villagers. They could not keep us quiet. We told our story. We got the permit to leave, but the twenty-two men of our village we know nothing about. We think they are still in the Vinh prison.

* * *

The Trung Duc village, which came south as a unit with its twenty-five fishing boats, was a mixed Buddhist and Catholic village. They were saving money from the heavy catches to buy two large junks. "We have one school for our village," a teacher told us. "All the children attend the same school."

The Christians were building a church. "As we are fishermen," they explained to us, "we will dedicate it to our patron, St. Peter the Fisherman."

At Binh Hung, a village of nearly two thousand souls, we saw another group of people who had survived the experiences of the Quatrième Zone. They had arrived in Haiphong in February 1955.

Binh Hung village was in a bad way. The villagers who knew nothing but fishing did not have a single boat. Like the villagers of Xom Dom they fished by wading out into the sea, but unlike them they lacked a large net. They cast a number of small nets. The line of waders were stationed along the shore when we walked out on the beach one morning. The pastor of the fishermen's church accompanied us. He had taken us around the poor barrack-like structures put together from flat unpainted board.

Right in the center of the pale sandy beach a group of older men were toiling over two large unfinished boats.

As we came near them, we noticed that they were working with a sort of desperate earnestness on two large wooden beams. The beams were as thick as railroad ties, but about three times as long. When they knew that we had stopped to study their work, the men stole quick glances at us out of the corners of their eyes. Work went on uninterruptedly. Two older men were directing the heating of the beams which were suspended on stands over fires built in cast-off oil barrels. I could see other beams of the same size already fitted into the hulls of the half-finished boats. The fine curved sweep of the sides of the boats were dark from the application of fire.

"It is an age-old way they have of making their boats," the pastor, Father Tran Huu Thanh, explained to us in French. "The heavy wood is trained by fire to bend as much as needed. It is slow but sure. These men from Nghé An have always had this skill."

He introduced us to the two older men who were the leaders of the boat-building team.

They bowed and stood before their handiwork with the composure of men who had stature in their village. Their frames were heavier than those of many Vietnamese men. Their hands were large and gnarled.

"Where did you get the beams of wood?" I asked. "Were you able to hew them out of some forest yourselves?"

"No, Mademoiselle," said the elder of the two gravely. "We have no machinery and no animals to pull them. We had to buy our wood and other materials."

"Were you able to bring any money out of the village you left?"

"Bring money out? We were lucky to bring ourselves out. We left everything behind—our boats and nets. They wanted to keep us, too. The Quatrième Zone was all theirs."

"Theirs? Who are they?"

The old man looked out over the gray-blue sea with its line of surf-fishers in domed hats of straw. Perhaps he was trying to sort his memories for the most correct answer: perhaps he was trying to control his feelings.

"They were the Vietcong—the men of Ho Chi Minh. They owned our zone, and they thought they owned us."

"What did you feel about them?"

He looked at me with an implacable expression. "We could have no love for them. We hated everything they did. But we had to obey their orders."

"Is life better since the General Howze brought you to South Vietnam?"

The old man looked grave. "We could only start to make our new boats by borrowing money. We are poor. We catch fish every day to sell. It is enough to keep paying the moneylenders. But here on this new shore we are free. When our boats are finished, then life will be better."

I turned to the pastor.

"How much do you pay the moneylender?" I knew about the murderous interest rates of the Orient.

"We pay three percent interest."

I looked at the pastor. "This is unusually low. Is there a credit cooperative here?"

"He means three percent per month," interjected the pastor. "That is not bad for this type of loan. Only, the best of the catch must go for payment. Everybody fishes, even the boys and girls. And everybody is poor and hungry."

I looked again at the coastline dotted with busy fishers, tall and small.

"Thirty-six percent per year. That is what they are working for," I remarked.

We said goodbye to the boat builders and returned to the meeting room alongside the church. Joseph Harnett sat down with the priest and some elders and younger fishermen of the Binh Hung village. Emergency action was needed to break open the trap of usury in which the villagers found themselves. They were actually suffering hunger to ensure the possession of boats in the future. For the rest of the morning, there was a long discussion in French. Charts were produced and columns of figures were added up.

The result was a prototype of what had happened in scores of villages following a visit by Harnett. The loan was refinanced out of the funds of our agency. The catch of the surf-fishers could, from then on, go into the purchase of daily food and the other necessities of the people of Binh Hung. Enough money was granted to ensure the completion of the big junks and the acquiring of nets, tackle and other needs of a newly founded fishing community. The grant would not enrich any members of the community but rather be the seed of a producers' cooperative for present and future inhabitants of Binh Hung. We toasted the new cooperative with warm Saigon beer.

Children must have carried the word down to the surf-fishers. A crowd quickly assembled outside the meeting room. The grant of half a million piastres was announced to them.

First there came a cheer. Then a religious anthem was sung by the ragged, wet people facing us. Their black garments were grayed with brine, their coned hats slung over their backs. High spirits and confidence were in their voices and expressions. We left to the gliding tune of the Vietnamese hymn.

The only people still working on the beach were the men busy with the unfinished fishing junks. They undoubtedly knew the good news, but could not interrupt the unremitting testing of the huge beams with fire.

* * *

Hunger was the companion of many refugee communities during their first months or years in the south. Once we paid a surprise visit to the village of Lac Lam, in the valley of the River Dran. The people looked completely dispirited and seemed leaderless. Finally a spokesman came forward.

"This is a hungry valley for us all," he told us. He held out knotted brown hands. "What can you do with these when the earth is hard and dry as 'bois de fer'?" The wood he referred to comes from an almost indestructible tree grown in the Vietnamese highlands.

There was hardly enough water to drink. Vegetable plants died in the earth. We looked down the rather narrow valley where over five thousand newcomers from Haiduong and Bac Ninh had been deposited during the mass resettlement scheme.

"What do you eat, if even rice and su su will not grow?"

"We are coming to the end of the rice that was given to us through the government. It is many weeks now that all of us, children and all, eat one meal a day. Only rice and *nuoc mam*. Every day, only that."

We realized that the people were close to starvation.

"We have been here nearly a year. We still get a little money from the commissariat in Saigon, otherwise we would be lost."

There was no whining tone in the recital, merely plain statements of fact. Then his voice became spirited.

"It is time to build our village somewhere else. A few people
left here for Dalat. Perhaps the commissariat will give us hectares
of land up there."

We promised we would take the whole story back to Saigon,
and we did. Harnett left behind emergency help for the purchase of rice.

The people of Lac Lam were right about Dalat. In the pine
and fir covered hills, the French had built their summer retreat.
Vietnam was left behind in Dalat. It was a town that could have
been put down in the French Alps without any incongruity.
Solidly built, gabled houses lined the streets. The cool dry winds
were revivifying after the somnolent heat of low-lying Saigon,
stretched between a river and a canal.

Around Dalat were several flourishing settlements, each with
a cooperative based on the skills of its people. Canadian missionary priests and brothers had trained the people in managing
credit cooperatives. One village group founded a cooperative of
transport which ran two buses on a regular schedule between
the new villages. Another group purchased wild rice, polished it
and sold it at a profit. The cooperatives were already working
with local craftsmen to make the articles of furniture and clothing needed by many Vietnamese families, in particular the
refugees.

*   *   *

Among the visits to refugee settlements, the one to Gia Kiem
was especially memorable. Gia Kiem was the name given to
four villages, comprising four parishes and fourteen thousand
six hundred people. The settlements were ensconced in rich
land newly cleared from the jungle. The homes were straw
thatched and fashioned from bricks baked in the sun, chiefly
mud with a minimal admixture of cement.

In one of the tiny "cottages" lived a family who arrived in the
south just before Christmas 1954. They had fled through the
thick jungle and muddy paddyland pursued by Vietminh soldiery. The father and mother had shepherded four small children, and had carried as well a few poor belongings.

An American reporter interviewed the family immediately after the midnight mass of Christmas in the newly built church.

First he talked with the father, Toan, who for thirty miles of the trip had carried two of his children. The destitute refugee was asked what Christmas could mean to him. "It means," said Toan, "that Christ came upon earth to help the poor."

"And has he helped?" asked the American. There was a long pause.

"He gave me the strength to carry my children," said Toan finally.

The same questions were put to the wife of Toan, who had been wounded and was lame from an ulcerated leg. One of the children, a little girl, had been blinded by the mortar shell which had injured the mother.

"Has he helped?"

The woman considered the question.

"He gave me the strength to walk with pain." she replied.

Up to the doors of the new homes manioc and papaya were flourishing. Wells had been dug for sweet water. The light green plant with a feathery white bower called in French "lisseron d'eau" flourished everywhere. It crept around the wells, and surrounded the man-made ponds where talapia fish were flourishing. It made much of Gia Kiem look like a rustic flower.

I remarked that "lisseron d'eau" would justify its existence as decoration alone.

"Lisseron d'eau is more than a decoration," said a teacher.

"'Su su' we call it. It is our watercress and spinach combined." I picked a branch that was lying near my feet. It was a large-leafed watercress. The stalk was hollow.

"We can eat everything but the flower," I was told, "leaves, stalk and all."

We went into one of the wood and sheet-iron churches. It was after five o'clock of a weekday afternoon. A group of old men and women were kneeling down, reciting in unison their evening prayers. It could have been a song. They intoned the sounds in a pattern of pitch that showed us the loveliness of a tonal language. We knelt behind them and wondered at their total absorption in worship.

"You have heard of the pastor asked us.

We told him we knew the story of the people who had braved the peril of drowning on the sandbank off Tra-Ly in order to escape from the north.

"These are the refugees of Tra-Ly. They were settled with us in Gia Kiem."

We looked at their strong, composed faces as they filed out of their church and climbed up into their thatched cottage poised on stilts above the earth. They would soon be asleep. Many was the time we drove by a Vietnamese village after sundown and experienced the palpable silence of a community at rest. There would not be a single kerosene lamp burning.

"They will be up with the sun," I said as they disappeared under the palm-thatched roofs.

"Yes, even earlier," replied the priest. "I call them at fifteen minutes after four in the morning by beating this drum. This is our alarm clock. Most of the villagers start the day with the holy liturgy."

The wooden drum outside the church was in the shape of a long fish. The fish drum is not rare in Asia, but in Gia Kiem it had a special significance. The fish was an ancient, secret sign employed by catacomb Christians during the Roman persecution. The five Greek letters spelled the word "fish" formed an acronym describing the mission of Jesus, namely Jesus Christ, Son of God, Savior. It did not seem strange that these eastern Christians, descendants of Vietnam's one hundred thousand martyrs, should start their day under the fish sign. The same sign had been used at the start of an era by similarly persecuted and homeless people—the progenitors of all the Christians living in the world.

Gia Kiem, like New Hanoi, Baria, Lac Lam, Xom Dom, Tan Binh, Trung Duc and Binh Hung, was a prototype of three hundred and twenty resettlement villages added to the landscape of South Vietnam. Two hundred and eighty-eight of these new villages were farming communities, twenty-six were fishing communities, and half a dozen were for artisans. By the middle of 1957, the special South Vietnamese Ministry for Refugees had been disbanded and all new villages were grafted into the local administrative structure.

All aid from overseas, like that of CRS, was shared without distinction with the needy of South Vietnam. The antipathy between Vietnamese of the north and those of the south, always not far from the surface, seemed to subside, as did the aversion to Christians held by some Vietnamese. An important addition to village life in areas of paddyland was the introduction of fish farming. Tilapia fish were stocked in paddyland so that the meals of the villagers could be enriched. The tilapia fish was first popularized by a group of volunteers from the Philippines who came to help the refugees. Vietnamese villagers owed this innovation to the presence of their refugee brothers and sisters among them.

The members of American people-to-people agencies like the International Rescue Committee, Church World Service, the Mennonite Central Committee, CARE and Catholic Relief Services who had aided the victims of a mass exodus came away with the conviction that they had played a part in one of the swiftest resettlements in recorded history. We came away also with admiration for the small, lithe Vietnamese, for their powers of resilience and unremitting work, and for their dignity and unexampled endurance.

* * *

The one thing I brought with me from Vietnam was a replica made by a refugee of the frail craft in which numbers of North Vietnamese had taken off into the Gulf of Tonkin in the South China Sea. It was fashioned of slats of bamboo and was equipped with a bright-red sail, the color of dried blood. This was the earth dye applied by northern women to their heavy cotton garments and seemed to recall their link with that earth. It seemed to me an epiphany of the migration from the north. I valued it as a memento of time when, with some cooperation, the Vietnamese had built new shelters for themselves and in three years had formed three hundred and twenty new hamlets which melded into their surroundings.

Those of us concerned with works of peace could not know how many of the newly-born hamlets were marked for an early death. The resettlement had coincided with an interregnum in Vietnam's "everlasting war," when one could travel anywhere in the south with safety.

The Vietnamese, and those of us who had no faith in violence, hoped that the interregnum in the "everlasting war" would be a healing peace.

It was not to be.

There were revolts in the provinces north of the 17th parallel. They were put down by the army with a loss, according to reports, of over fifty thousand lives. A new social system was being imposed from above. Landlords, even owners of small parcels of land, were executed.

Everything changed after August 7, 1964. The U.S. Senate passed the Tonkin Gulf Resolution. It was based on reports of an attack by North Vietnamese torpedo boats on U.S. destroyers in the Tonkin Gulf, an arm of the North China Sea between Vietnam and China. The resolution was used to justify U.S. military action in Vietnam. The "everlasting war" was resumed Technological warfare, along with the spraying of poisonous defoliants, assaulting the people and the very face of an ancient land, also caused a savage wound on American society.

The war did not abate even after the Paris cease-fire of January 2, 1973. Between January 1973 and the definitive end of hostilities in April 1975, an additional 1,400,000 people were thrust from their home places. Vietnam became a nation of internal refugees.

The replica of the escape raft became an augury of the future. A symbol of the first exodus, it turned out to be an even more tragic symbol of the second exodus.

3. The Second Exodus

The second exodus from Vietnam took place in blood and tragedy.

Before the inexorable advance of the army from the north, the South Vietnamese moved farther south into places they considered zones of safety. They put out to sea in a flotilla of rafts and fishing boats of all sizes. As the coastal cities were occupied, the South Vietnamese moved still farther southward.

One destination was Vung Tau, a port southeast of Saigon. A group boarded a barge which was drawn by a Korean tugboat. This took nine days to reach Vung Tau, during which time food and water had given out. After the survivors had crawled ashore, some fifty dead bodies, bloated and blackened by the sun, were carried off. In the first weeks of April 1975, four hundred thousand arrived in Vung Tau. Every day, naval barges from the coastal cities disgorged living and dead Vietnamese on the beach.

The surrender of Saigon took place with stunning suddenness on April 30, 1975. Evacuation had been proceeding throughout the preceding weeks. Finally, Option IV, providing for the emergency helicopter evacuation of Americans and high risk Vietnamese, was put into operation shortly before the surrender.

Panic seized the refugee-swollen city. Scenes of would-be refugees attempting to scale the ten-foot wall of the American embassy tore at the heart. Their bleeding fingers clawed at the crown of barbed wire while guards dislodged the shredded hands with pistol and rifle butts. A middle-aged man and woman who had tried to lift themselves over the wall were impaled and lay bleeding on the wire. Other Vietnamese stood weeping, holding up their children in the vain effort to have Americans and Vietnamese inside the wall take them.

The Vietnamese associated with the Americans and those who feared reprisals from the Viet Minh (counting family members) were thought to number hundreds of thousands.

The final perilous helicopter lifts were made from the embassy compound and the embassy roof. The Vietnamese were deposited on the landing pads of the carrier ships of the U.S. Seventh Fleet, waiting in the South China Sea.

Father John McVeigh, then directing the Catholic Relief Services program in Saigon, refused to take advantage of evacuation without his immediate staff members. These would surely be marked for persecution. He waited with some staff members until one day before the surrender of Saigon. One of the staff members was John Cullen, who told of escaping on the very last day of Option IV.

"I was lifted from the American embassy roof by helicopter on April 29," he told me. "The next stop was the helipad of the SS *Vancouver*. We were there for a few hours when an LST came over and the marines led us into it. The LST took us to a large freighter, and nearly six thousand of us walked up the gangplank of the *Pioneer Commander*."

We were talking in an office in Fort Indiantown Gap in the Blue Mountains of Pennsylvania. It was one of four military installations that received the evacuated and fleeing Vietnamese who were arriving by planeloads.

It was September 1975, just five months after his escape. His wife, Huynh Ngoc Thanh, had been evacuated earlier by sea, and had taken with her the members of her joint family.

Cullen continued: "It took us a full week to reach Guam. There was not much food aboard, so our ration was two bowls of rice a day. At first there were traces of tuna fish in the rice. Later we noticed there were pieces of canned beets. On the last days, we found a few slivers of canned peaches in the ration. There were no complaints, even though we left the ship lighter than we got on. There was enough water for drinking and washing. On some of the ships, people had to line up twice a day for a cup of drinking water. We were all looking forward to Guam, to being with our families again. I identified with the pain of the Vietnamese because I was in the same situation as they were."

"How large is your family?" I asked.

"There is my wife, and my two daughters, three years and one year old." He went on to explain that, along with his wife and daughters, came his father-in-law, mother-in-law, six sisters-in-law, two brothers-in-law, three nieces, one nephew and two cousins. At thirty-two, he was the head of a family of twenty. Another brother-in-law, in the Vietnamese military, had not been heard from after Da Nang changed hands. Two nieces and a nephew were fatherless. Their father, a Vietnamese Air Force pilot, had been listed as missing in action since March 1974.

For the first weeks of his return, Cullen chose to live the life of the Vietnamese in Fort Chaffee, one of the military installations used for receiving stations. In a barracks building, Cullen, his wife, two children and two young relatives shared a space about twelve by twenty feet, each being assigned to a bunk bed. In a barracks space of similar size the eleven remaining members of the family had their allotted bunk beds.

At Fort Indiantown Gap, referred to as the "Gap," Cullen had private accommodations as a staff member of migration services of the U.S. Catholic Conference.

Though Catholic Relief Services was no longer part of the program for the Vietnamese, I was interested to see how their fate was determined in resettlement.

The Gap was a solidly built military reservation set in a rich but sparsely peopled expanse of farmland. To meet the refugees, I had to enter the fort through two squat fieldstone pillars near which a slender mounted missile pointed harmlessly to the sky. This marked it as the base of an armored unit, later utilized as the headquarters of the Pennsylvania National Guard. Probably no one mentioned to the Vietnamese residents that the "Gap" had also served as a prison stockade for American soldiers, including many who objected to service in Vietnam.

Out of the original camp population of nineteen thousand Vietnamese, there remained forty-five hundred still awaiting homes and jobs in American communities.

Someone had mentioned that the remaining refugees in Indiantown Gap would be there a long time because so many of them were "illiterate fishermen." I objected to the designation.

The technicians and doctors and those with marketable skills in office work, mechanics and language had left the camp first. Those with skills less marketable in the context of American living, like rice culture and fishing in tropical waters, took longer to place.

One large white frame building opposite a helicopter launching pad with rows of standing helicopters housed American people-to-people agencies.

It was the agencies, with the help of government funds, which had to reach into American communities to find work and shelter for the Vietnamese.

Desks, telephones and file cabinets had been hurriedly installed to allow voluntary agency staff members totaling more than a hundred persons to carry out the tasks of interviewing and matching refugees with the requests of sponsors. I sensed the organized confusion in the large partitioned offices of the voluntary agencies (including International Rescue Committee, Church World Service and Lutheran World Relief) on my way to a large corner office with the sign HOI-DOAN CONG-GIAO HOA-KY. HOA-KY is United States and the rest spelled out Catholic Conference. A branch of the conference, the migration service, had a staff of thirty, along with double that number of interpreters and refugee assistants. The insistent hum of many conversations was punctuated by the ringing of dozens of telephones.

*   *   *

Soon I was talking with a refugee, who represented, I was told, the most difficult type to resettle, the extended family. His name, he told me, was Nguyen Van Huong, and he had operated his own fishing boat out of Phan Thiet, about a hundred miles up the coast from Saigon. I felt as if I were back in Vietnam as I talked with the small, wiry man in a U.S. Army work jacket, whose sleeves were too long. His skin was walnut brown, much darker than that of other Vietnamese, and rough from exposure to sun and rain and the salt water spray of the China Sea. It was the second time he had become a refugee; the first time had been in 1954 after the Geneva truce accords.

Through an interpreter, the fisherman told me the story, not unfamiliar in Vietnam's recent history.

"I was born in the village of Tien Lang, not far from Haiphong. I am thirty-five years old. My father was a fisherman and also his father. All my relatives in our village were fishermen. We are Catholic Vietnamese and our church was the church of St. Peter who was a fisherman like us.

"I was a boy when my father left Tien Lang. The communists came to our villages and took whatever they wanted. They wanted us to work, and then they ordered us to give to them what we had earned. In some of the villages the people refused. A group of people would be made judges. People came in from outside the village to tell some of the villagers that they had to be judges."

There was an exchange between Mr. Nguyen and the translator. I was asked if I knew what he meant when he said that some of the villagers had to become judges.

"Don't you mean 'people's tribunals'?" I asked.

There was another rapid exchange. The fisherman nodded his head several times.

"Yes, 'people's tribunals.' In the villages near us people who refused to give up food and money, or fought against the new government men, had to confess to the 'people's tribunals.' Many were condemned to death. It was mostly by shooting. My father decided he would leave. He heard that if we went to the sea, we would be picked up by big ships. So he brought my grandmother with us in our boat because my grandfather was dead. There were eight in our closest family, my mother and five children, three sons and two daughters. I am the eldest son.

"The ship filled with American sailors brought us to Saigon, and we stayed all together with many refugees until we went to Phan Thiet in 1955."

From this coastal city, his father went out to fish in the South China Sea. I remembered standing on a beach looking out at those warm waters in 1955 and remarking that any hardworking fishermen would do well in a sea literally jumping with fish. When Nguyen Van Huong finished his education he joined his father in a fishing schedule that started on Sunday evening at 10 P.M. and ended only on the following Saturday. That meant that the whole family would go to church on Sunday. Those who stayed at home often took part in the Catholic liturgy every day.

"We went up and down our shore from Nha Trang to Vung Tao. We would come back with twenty thousand kilos of fish on Saturday," he said proudly.

I asked how large his fishing boat had been. There was another conference with the translator. It was twenty-seven yards long, I was informed. When I showed my surprise at this, they showed me how they had worked it out from the measurement in meters.

"We owned the boat," said the little man.

"We did not make our own boat," he replied in answer to my query. "We earned enough money to buy it. I paid fifteen million piastres for it. I told the men what I wanted and they built it especially for me." I was told that it was motor-powered.

He laughed with delight when I told him how much I admired the way that Vietnamese fishermen hand-fashioned their boats, bending the wooden beams by the slow application of fire. A couple of upper front teeth were missing, as well as one of the lower front teeth. This somehow added to the toughness of his appearance.

Nguyen Van Huong was the perfect example of the energetic, aggressive northerner, the type who often enraged the more easy-going South Vietnamese.

Then he smiled, as many Vietnamese do when they impart sad news. It is only after a long time that one realizes it is a special smile, a sort of controlled grimace.

"And now it is all gone. No boat. No piastres. Nothing."

"But you have your family," I interjected, knowing that he had brought out all of his children.

"Yes," he said, and the smile was now a genuine one. "I have six sons. My youngest son was two months when we left Vietnam. My father is here with me, Nguyen Van Gian, and my wife, Nguyen Thi Mong and my two youngest brothers Hoang and Giang. They are all with me at the Gap."

I learned that the word "gap" was also a Vietnamese word meaning "to meet" or "hurry," depending on the tone. I was then introduced to a much taller man, with the same brown, rough skin, who had been sitting quietly next to Nguyen Van Huong.

"This is my brother-in-law. His wife is with him and his mother-in-law and four sons and one daughter."

I began to write down the brother-in-law's name and found Mr. Nguyen looking over my shoulder, ready to correct me when I made a mistake in spelling his first name Khan as Khanh. I wished that those who had the image of "illiterate Vietnamese fishermen" had been there to see the reality.

I asked about the circumstances of his leaving Vietnam. "At first we had no plan to leave our country. That changed when we heard that cities were being occupied," explained Mr. Nguyen. "We all escaped because forty people could fit into my boat. Before Phan Thiet was occupied we went down the coast in the boat. We did not want to live again under those people who came into our villages in the north. Also, I had been a soldier. I was afraid of what they might do.

"Fifteen of the people in the boat were of my own family and we had enough rice for many weeks. We tried to land at Vung Tau but it was being bombed. From Vung Tau we went to the island of Con Son.

"An American ship came there. That was when we left our fishing boat in the sea. The American sailors took us to the Philippines and then we all got on the plane for America. Now we are waiting at the Gap.

"I want to be a fisherman again," Mr. Nguyen announced. "I am not working here and I want to work again."

"It is going to be very different as you know," I said. "You will probably have to work on a big boat—a boat that is not your own. Will you mind that?"

He replied that he was ready for that. He could work with others. All he wanted was to get back to work. Another man might have been slow to leave the cocoon of the "Gap." The two-story World War II barracks had been partitioned into practical sections according to family size. The rice-based meals, for which the refugees lined up army style in the mess hall, were adequate. There were even schools in the camp, and teachers from nearby Lebanon Valley College were giving courses in practical English.

There was a newspaper in Vietnamese, as well as television programs and movies.

It was clear that this small assertive man saw his dignity as head of this family group as of utmost importance, and his support of them as necessary to his dignity. In talking with John Cullen, assistant director of the Catholic Conference office, I learned that just that day Nguyen had realized that his file was separate from the file of the brother-in-law to whom he had introduced me. If the families were listed in separate files, they could be separately relocated. Nguyen demanded, as head of the entire family group, that the files be joined, so that all would resettle in one place.

Cullen's voice was rueful. "We were having a hard enough time settling Nguyen's family, a total of twelve people. We had been thinking of New Orleans where we have settled a number of Vietnamese fishermen and their families. Now we have to find an opportunity for twenty-one people.

"Did you agree to his demand?" I asked.

"Yes, I did," said Cullen, as he carefully placed the two files under one folder. "Our policy is not to violate the integrity of the family, if it is at all possible. This policy makes it harder for us and it makes resettlement slower—but we always find a way. I think we will find some way with Nguyen.

"And that wasn't all," he added, referring to the request to have the dossiers united. "Nguyen made another stipulation. New Orleans is out of the question for him. The whole group, he tells me, should be resettled on the Florida coast with another brother-in-law. He escaped separately, and found sponsorship there. That gives us an extended family of thirty-three persons."

The primary loyalty of Vietnamese to the family could not have been better dramatized.

* * *

In all the refugee installations and in American communities the extraordinary value that the Vietnamese gave to the family was both a revelation and a practical problem. A society already living by the nuclear family of two parents, often only one parent, with children, found it hard to accept the insistence of Vietnamese families in finding sponsors who would take all of them. Having lost everything else, the immemorial and mystic tie of the family was the only value to which they could cling.

Vietnamese, who tend to restrain their emotions in public, actually groaned when they learned how American families have been so split that children rarely see their grandparents.

The Pennsylvania Commission on Women sponsored a series of lectures at Fort Indiantown Gap on "The American Family." The speaker explained through an interpreter that in America there was no real extended family system like that of Vietnam. Families often have to live far apart from each other. That means children rarely see their aunts and uncles and parents. As an example she said that her youngest child had only seen his grandparents once. Her audience groaned. When she went on to explain that old people do not get much respect in America and it is youth which is valued much more, the audience groaned again.

Reverence for ancestors made its presence known in camp life. On the anniversaries of dead fathers, the altar with candles, food, articles of clothing and money would be set up and the incense burned. The eldest son would call out to the spirit who had given him life.

That Confucian ceremony, ending with the burning of the money and clothing, in paper representation, seems to be a way of calling forth the strength and blessing of those who have gone before. There were bonzes, Buddhist monks, in most camps. Anniversaries are of the utmost importance to Vietnamese. Margaret Mead, the anthropologist, considered one of humanity's great discoveries "the discovery of anniversaries by which, throughout time, human beings have kept their sorrows and their joys, their victories, their revelations and their obligations alive."

The Catholics among the refugees, who numbered about thirty-nine percent of the total, remembered the anniversaries of their dead parents in prayers in the course of the liturgy. Masses were held daily in most camps by refugee or local priests. Those who had been convinced that thirty years of war and displacement had meant the end of the extended family only had to visit Fort Indiantown Gap, Camp Pendleton or Fort Chaffee to know how tenaciously the Vietnamese preserved it.

Before I left Fort Indiantown Gap, I was taken into a small room, the quietest, most orderly room in the entire building housing the voluntary agencies.

Three television screens were flashing what I thought were news releases in bright green letters. The machines were utterly silent. Three persons sat intently before the television screens transcribing on noiseless typewriter-like machines the messages being flashed on the screen. I studied one screen. It flashed one name "Tran Van Truong" twelve times. After each listing of the name were numbers and other information which I could not interpret. A young woman who had noted the information on the screen explained that a search was on for Tran Van Truong, a not too uncommon name. His age, alien registration number and other available information had been fed into the computer.

This was relayed to the computer center in Wheaton, near Washington, D.C., which was in instant communication with Fort Chaffee and Fort Pendleton. Every Vietnamese refugee was already registered in the computer system. Twelve men of the same name had been located and flashed on the screen. When the other information was compared, the right Tran Van Truong would be put in contact with the other members of his family.

All day the terminal, as the operator referred to the combination of television screen and transcribing machine, was sending out or receiving news of the location of Vietnamese fathers, mothers, sons, daughters, sons-in-law, daughters-in-law, and cousins, as well as information regarding where, in the great expanse of America, sponsorships would allow them to resettle. Already Vietnamese had found new homes in fifty states and in Puerto Rico. The utmost in technology, which had been used during hostilities in Vietnam to fragment homes, workplaces and whole villages, was now part of the search for work and shelter.

It was through computer technology that the fisherman Nguyen Van Huong learned that a brother-in-law, who had escaped by a different route, was in Florida.

Through the computer I learned that Nguyen Van Huong was one of the 24,522 heads of families among the Vietnamese refugees in the United States immediately after the April 1975 exodus. The same technology that could serve to kill, wound and scatter the human family could also bring the human family together.

*   *   *

The computers that sped the resettlement of the refugees of April 1975 from U.S. military forts continued to be used in the United States. With enormous help from voluntary agencies, including church-related agencies, who combed local communities for homes and jobs, over eight hundred thousand Vietnamese put down roots all over the United States in fifteen years. Vietnamese were soon to be found in fishing communities from Louisiana to Florida, and in urban communities from San Francisco to Boston. Among the immigrants were the peoples of Laos and a number of Kampucheans who had come through Bangkok, but large numbers had arrived by the perilous journey on the sea.

*   *   *

The refugees of April 1975 were only a foreshadowing of one of the longest lasting and most wide-ranging of the diasporas of the twentieth century. The odyssey of the Vietnamese "boat people" had begun.

From the long coastline of South Vietnam, from secluded coves and beaches, came a flotilla stranger than the world had ever seen. There were frail rafts, sampans, fishing boats of every type including those whose beams were hand-turned by fire, coastal junks and an occasional barge. In whatever perilous craft, the Vietnamese dared the sea to lead them to a point of safety and dared the world to take cognizance of their plight. They themselves were accepting the dare of a watery grave rather than the certainty of persecution.

Sometimes they were rescued just in time. An Israeli ship captain picked up thirteen people from a disintegrating raft and took them back to Israel. There their sea diaspora ended. They were granted asylum and a new home. A moving report on one small group of boat people came from a young seminarian who escaped with fellow seminarians and a priest.

"As we drifted helplessly, we had mass. Like Jesus coming to his disciples, walking on the water, Jesus came to us in our little boat. We thought we might become food for the sharks, but instead God became food for us. From that moment on, our spirit became strong and we were able to trust in God's love more than we trusted in our boat."

After a week of drifting, the little boat containing seminarian (later a priest) Nhuan Nguyen was rescued by a U.S. military ship.

Boat people told of signaling passing ships by waving clothing on sticks only to see the ships ignore their plight. Shipmasters admitted to a breach of the law of the sea. They explained that the delay in picking up refugees, feeding them and taking them to a destination would nullify the profit of a voyage. There was no reimbursement for such outlays until the Office of the United Nations High Commissioner for Refugees set up a fund for this purpose.

The South China Sea saw the flotilla increase in the late 1970s and throughout the 1980s. Ports in Malaysia and Indonesia began to turn away the would-be arrivals. Hong Kong, one of the great refugee havens of Asia, reluctantly accepted more and more Vietnamese, especially those refused at other points.

Relentlessly, the fleeing Vietnamese took to the sea even when Thai pirates found them to be the easiest of prey. The refugees were relieved of what little possessions they could bring with them.

By the 1990s the situation in Vietnam had improved as far as the guarantee of the rights of dissidents was concerned. The Vietnamese government went on record that it would not persecute refugees, but would, in fact, help them in finding homes and work.

Over 50,000 Vietnamese were housed in detention centers in Hong Kong. All hoped for overseas migration, but hope dwindled to nil when they were screened by refugee officials. Only a minuscule number conformed to the definition of a refugee eligible for asylum and resettlement. This definition states that a refugee is a person fleeing "a well-founded fear of being persecuted for reasons of race, religion nationality, membership in a particular social group or political opinion." The vast majority of the Vietnamese were economic refugees escaping hardship at home. The United Nations High Commissioner for refugees declared early in 1994 that fleeing Vietnamese would no longer be automatically eligible for consideration as political refugees. The Vietnamese in Hong Kong detention centers and in camps in other parts of Asia, over 60,000 in all, would, after screening, be legally repatriated.

This decision closed the chapter of the "boat people"—but only after nearly a million of them had set sail from a war-ravaged nation.

AFTERWORD

Many of the wounds depicted in these pages have been stanched, but not all. The odyssey of thousands of Vietnam's "boat people" ended not in new lives and new places of resettlement, but in a tragic existence in camps in Hong Kong. From there, many had no choice but to return to their country of origin, hoping that the promises of just treatment would be honored.

As some wounds were stanched, however, others appeared, and new wanderers needed rescue, shelter and the putting down of new roots. The link between violence and homeless wandering was from the beginning. The book of Genesis tells us that after Cain, Abel's killer, was rebuked with the words, "The voice of your brother's blood cries to me from the earth," he was made a homeless wanderer.

In our century, with its massive violence of global wars, and the local outbreaks of violence, the blood of millions cries out from the earth. The uprooted, the refugees, were not those who inflicted the violence, but rather the innocent victims of a cruel history.

Their plight brings to mind the whole mystery of suffering, in particular that of innocent suffering which is linked to the mystery of evil. We cannot but recall the drama of righteous Job upon whom agony after agony was visited. Job insisted on his innocence even when his friends were urging him to confess that he was a wrongdoer. His own wife told him, "Curse God and die." Job's response was that as he came forth naked from his mother's womb, so he would return. In words of faith that ring down the ages, he asserted, "The Lord gives and the Lord takes away. Blessed be the name of the Lord."

Millions of the uprooted might have been tempted to curse God for their fate at cruel human hands. The marvel is that so many retained their faith in God and in their fellow human beings. Those who accepted the suffering which descended upon them could be seen with the eyes of faith as joining in the redemptive suffering of the Lord. People who choose to accept suffering rather than inflict it in return are not only a part of the redemption but are a reminder that no innocent suffering is lost or wasted. Innocent people driven across borders to hunger and want can be signs of that redemptive suffering; they are a counterpoise to something at its polar opposite, and perhaps more acceptable to people in general, namely, redemptive violence. Redemptive violence is a term in recent use to describe the unleashing of every kind of force, every weaponry, to drive out evil and right wrong. Some of us have lost faith in so-called redemptive violence, since history proves that the outcome of violence is more of the same.

What can be achieved by learning of the suffering of those who have been driven over borders, castaways, reduced to living by the compassion of others?

First of all, there can be an increase in compassion. The heart-stopping stories of victims of violence and homelessness can break into our lives as a warning that we cannot live our lives as though these other lives are not being destroyed.

The accounts, though harrowing, can serve a spiritual purpose in helping us to identify with the enforced pilgrimages of the refugees and the displaced. Life is often likened to a pilgrimage, and it is well to remember the need to reach out in understanding and love to those embarked on pilgrimages not of their choosing.

As a world-girdling agency of mercy, CRS stands for the unfailing concern of those who give of their substance year after year for members of the human family they will never see. Yet, despite the fact that the recipients of their generosity may be across borders and seas, they have an identification with those people "who have not whereon to lay their heads," people who belong to every race and country under heaven. Without reference to any other criterion than need, CRS aimed to put the strengths of the American Catholic community at the service of countless members of the human family whose lives and human rights were at risk. To the driven, the rejected, the humiliated, the help of CRS, and even its presence, brings a message—the message of their inviolable dignity as children of God. "God's temple is holy," says St. Paul, "and you are that temple" (1 Cor 3:17). In *Confessions of a Guilty Bystander* Thomas Merton reinforces the gospel message in pointing out that "God has one indestructible temple; which is man himself."

Many CRS programs of mercy not described here deserve recounting. Examples include help to the people of Africa, victims of mass displacement due to civil strife and revolution; to the people of Afghanistan, who took refuge by the millions in Pakistan; and to the refugees of the western hemisphere—in Guatemala, Nicaragua, El Salvador, Cuba and Haiti.

The link between violence and homeless wandering was seen once more when Bosnia in flames sent close to three million men, women and children from their home places. The former Yugoslavia was again a crucible of violence—violence fueled by ethnic and religious differences. Ethnic strife in Rwanda gave rise to the uprooting of hundreds of thousands of persons, and before the eyes of a horrified world, the brutal massacre of as many more.

Thomas Merton recalls to us that we will find Christ in the rejected, the refugee "for whom there is no room." We will only find Christ if we first find room for the forsaken ones in our heart.

Catholic Relief Services has gone out and goes out without respite to meet Christ in his chosen identity. He tells us in Matthew 25:31-45: I am the hungry one; I am the thirsty one; I am the naked, homeless one; I am the suffering one.

When we meet Christ with works of mercy, we are carrying out his central teaching and command, since mercy is only love responding to need, love consoling, feeding, sheltering, relieving the suffering of the Person Loved.

And for those who have endured "the world at its worst," the help that comes to them with a recognition of their common humanity and holy dignity gives them a glimpse of the world at its best, even a sign of the reign of God.

INDEX

OTHER WORKS BY EILEEN EGAN

The Works of Peace
1965

Transfigured Night, with Elizabeth C. Reiss
1965

The War That Is Forbidden, Egan editor and contributor
1968

Dorothy Day and the Permanent Revolution
1984

Such a Vision of the Street
Mother Teresa: The Spirit and the Work
1985

For the Life of the World
Catholic Relief Services: The Beginning Years
1988

Blessed Are You: Mother Teresa and the Beatitudes,
with Kathleen Egan, OSB
1992

Chapters in:
War or Peace? The Search for New Answers,
ed. Thomas A. Shannon
1980
The Causes of World Hunger, ed. Willian Byron
1982
Famine, ed. Kevin Cahill, MD
1982
A Revolution of the Heart, ed. Patrick G. Coy
1992